Henry Huth, Joseph Lilly, George Daniel

A Collection of Seventy-Nine Black-Letter Ballads And Broadsides

Henry Huth, Joseph Lilly, George Daniel

A Collection of Seventy-Nine Black-Letter Ballads And Broadsides

ISBN/EAN: 9783744724913

Printed in Europe, USA, Canada, Australia, Japan

Cover: Foto ©Thomas Meinert / pixelio.de

More available books at **www.hansebooks.com**

A

COLLECTION OF SEVENTY-NINE

𝕭𝕷𝕒𝕔𝕶 = 𝕷𝕖𝕥𝕥𝕖𝕣 𝕭𝕒𝕷𝕷𝕒𝕕𝖘 𝕒𝕟𝕕

𝕭𝕣𝕠𝕒𝕕𝕗𝕚𝕕𝕖𝖘,

PRINTED IN THE REIGN OF QUEEN ELIZABETH,

BETWEEN THE YEARS 1559

AND 1597.

ACCOMPANIED WITH AN INTRODUCTION AND

ILLUSTRATIVE NOTES.

LONDON:

JOSEPH LILLY, 17 AND 18, NEW STREET,

AND 5a, GARRICK STREET, COVENT GARDEN.

1867.

PREFACE.

LOVE a ballad in print," are the words put by Shakefpeare into the mouth of one of his characters, and from his evident fondnefs for them we muft infer that he is conveying his own feelings through the mouth of the fpeaker. Another great writer of our own days, Sir Walter Scott, had an equal predilection for this fpecies of literature, and has availed himfelf of them in the fafcinating productions of his pen.

The Collections of Phillips, Percy, Evans, Ritfon, Pinkerton, Jamiefon and others, are a convincing proof of the favour with which they have been received by the public.

It may be confidently afferted that the prefent collection is not lefs interefting, and is certainly much more curious, than any that have preceded it, illuftrating as it does the language, opinions, manners, ufages, the feelings and pafling events of the greater part of the reign of Queen Elizabeth.

Thefe ballads, all of the higheft intereft and curiofity, hitherto unknown and prefumed to be unique, are reprinted without the flighteft alteration from the celebrated Collection formerly in the library of Mr. George Daniel, of Canonbury Square, at the fale of whofe library it was purchafed by the publifher for Henry Huth, Efq., to whom his beft thanks are due for his kindnefs and liberality in permitting the prefent publication.

The Introduction and Notes are fupplied by two gentlemen profoundly verfed in early Englifh literature.

JOSEPH LILLY.

INTRODUCTION.

IT is remarkable how foon after its invention the art of printing became an inftrument of popular amufement and inftruction,—an active agent in the development of the mind of the people. This character, however, arofe in fome degree out of the neceffity which called the art itfelf into exiftence, and which would naturally extend itfelf rapidly in proportion as it was indulged. The works which the firft experimenters in printing fought to produce were prints and fmall books intended for religious teaching, which had been previoufly drawn and written by the hand, and which were thus neceffarily fold at higher prices than the majority of the clafs for whom they were intended could afford to pay. The great want, therefore, to be fupplied, was the means of producing an indefinite number of copies of a book in the fame time and at the fame coft which had formerly been employed in producing one, and thus reducing the coft of each individual copy to a very fmall fraction of the whole. In moft countries, for fome length of time after the introduction of printing, the full advantage of the art was imperfectly appreciated, perhaps for want of an agency by which a great number of copies of a

b

book could be rapidly and widely circulated ; and
the firſt books were bulky, no doubt expenſive,
and calculated for anything but what we ſhould
call popular reading.   It was in France that the
art of printing firſt aſſumed a more popular character.   There already exiſted in that country
during the laſt twenty years of the fifteenth century, which muſt, therefore, have originated
within very few years of the invention of the art,
an extenſive literature of a very popular character,
conſiſting chiefly of farces and drolleries in a
dramatic ſhape, poetical tracts on various ſub-
jects, tales in verſe and proſe, ſatires on contemporary manners and ſentiments, almanacks and
facetiæ, many of the later degenerating into
ſimple coarſe obſcenities, ſo early did the objec-
tionable uſes of printing accompany this more
than uſeful art.   All theſe appeared in the form
of ſmall pamphlets, of a few, often not more
than three or four, leaves each.   They appear to
have been ſold by itinerant bookſellers, who
hawked them about the country, and were called
technically *biſouarts*, and who ſtill preſerve in
France another of their old names, that of
colporteurs.

   This literature ſpread from France into Italy
and Spain at an early period.   It was introduced
into England at the beginning of the ſixteenth
century, no doubt from France, becauſe nearly
all the Engliſh ſamples of it we know are tranſ-
lations or adaptations from the language of that
country.   Our literary antiquaries call them *chap-
books.*   They were a claſs of books expoſed by
their nature to ſpeedy deſtruction, but a ſufficient
number of them are preſerved, though in unique

or very rare copies, to leave no doubt that they were very numerous, even at an early period.

There was another clafs of literature, we may perhaps fay ftill more popular, which appears to have flourifhed moft in England, and which we ufually call *broadfides*. The Germans call them *fliegende Blätter*, and the French *feuilles volantes*, both comparatively modern terms, and the laft perhaps tranflated from the other. Thefe broadfides became far more popular in England than in other countries, and during a long period they have been the ufual mode of publifhing popular ballads. They were the form employed with us for royal proclamations and fimilar documents from a very early period in the hiftory of printing. Setting thefe afide, the broadfide appears to have been employed firft for printing papal indulgences, feveral examples of which, dating from 1513 to 1527, will be found in the collection of broadfides preferved in the library of the Society of Antiquaries, of which a valuable catalogue, compiled by Mr. Robert Lemon, has been recently publifhed. In this collection, which is, for the earlieft period, the richeft and moft valuable in exiftence, we find no example before the middle of the fixteenth century of what we now underftand more fpecially by the name of ballad,—of that peculiar clafs of popular literature which belonged to the long period of tranfition in our country between mediæval fociety and the fociety of our own times. We foon find the printed broadfide employed in the various circumftances of temporary agitation, whether political or focial. In fact, the prefs was deftined very foon to become the

moſt powerful agent in all ſocial agitation. On
the 11th of June, 1540, late in the reign of
Henry VIII., Thomas Lord Cromwell, that
king's miniſter and counſellor in all his aćts of
hoſtility againſt the Church of Rome, fell into
diſgrace, and was committed to the Tower. To
the papal party it was of courſe a ſubjećt of
exultation, which was diſplayed in a ballad, publiſhed no doubt ſoon after his impriſonment, at
all events before his execution on the 28th of
July following. The Proteſtant party took up
the cauſe of their protećtor, and the reſult was a
rather bitter warfare carried on by means of
poetical broadſides, eight of which are contained
in the collećtion of the Society of Antiquaries.
The original ballad againſt Cromwell is printed
in Percy's "Reliques." Cromwell's aſſailants
offended the king, who was perſonally identified
with the ačts for which they cenſured Cromwell,
and it is curious that the writer of moſt of the
ballads in defence of the fallen miniſter was
Thomas Smith, who deſcribes himſelf as "ſer-
vaunt to the kynges royall majeſtye ; and clerke
of the queenes graces counſell, though moſt un-
worthy." Three or four known broadſides of a
ſimilar charaćter belong to the cloſing years of
the reign of Henry VIII. When we enter the
reign of his ſon and ſucceſſor, Edward VI., we
find rhyming broadſides of the ſame charaćter.
Firſt in date of thoſe preſerved in the collećtion
of the Society of Antiquaries are two ballads for
and againſt Biſhop Gardner, printed probably in
1548, when that prelate was committed to the
Tower. We now fall in with the names of
printers who were ſubſequently remarkable for

the number of ballads which iffued from their preffes. John Waley, who lived in Fofter Lane in London, printed " A Newe Balade made by Nicholas Balthorp, which fuffered in Calys the 20 daie of Marche, M.D.L.," which means March, 1551. In the year following, another of the great printers of ballad literature, Richard Lant, introduces us to a new controverfy in thefe poetical broadfides. It was provoked by a young man in literature who afterwards rofe to confiderable celebrity, Thomas Churchyard, who wrote a fhort metrical fatire on contemporary fociety entitled " Davy Dycars Dreame." Churchyard found an opponent in a man who figned himfelf T. Camel, and whofe printer was Henry Sutton, another well-known printer of ballads, who dwelt in St. Paul's Churchyard. In the collection of the Society of Antiquaries there are no lefs than thirteen broadfide poems belonging to this controverfy, thofe by Churchyard and his friends printed by Lant, and thofe of his affailant by Sutton, and all within the year 1552. The number of broadfides of this defcription belonging to Edward's reign is very fmall, but among them is the earlieft example of which we have any knowledge of the true ballad literature, though it is not written in what was afterwards confidered as fpecially ballad verfe. John Waley printed, as it is prefumed, in the reign of Edward VI., a broadfide in verfe, entitled, " A new mery balad of a maid that wold mary wyth a fervyng man," the author of which informs us that his name was Thomas Emley. Two or three poetical broadfides printed in the reign of Queen Mary are all more or lefs of a political character.

One only, which is afcribed by conjecture to
Mary's reign, and which is entitled, "A new
ballet entituled howe to wyve well," is a veritable
ballad, and is written in ballad metre. The author was Lewis Evans, and it was printed by Owen
Rogers, " at the Spread Egle, betwyxte both the
Saynct Bartholomews." It is probable, however,
that it belongs to the beginning of the reign of
Elizabeth, rather than to that of her predeceffor.
We are thus only able to point out one literary ballad printed in England previous to the
middle of the fixteenth century, and that belonging to fo late a period as the reign of the Sixth
Edward, and we can hardly imagine that this
clafs of literature was very common at that
period. We know that it was circulated in a
very perifhable form, and we fhould not expect
to find now any very large remains of it from fo
early a date, yet ftill we ought to find more frequent allufions to it. We are unable to fay
exactly when the literature of the ballad firft
came into exiftence, but it appears to have
become fuddenly very popular. It was a new
branch of commerce, and which, as is often
the cafe, created a new want. The Stationers'
Company was incorporated in the year 1556,
and its regifters begin in the following year.
When we look at thefe, we are aftonifhed at the
great number of ballads which, from the firft
opening, were licenfed for publication, and yet,
of them all, there is only a rare example here and
there of which we have any trace beyond the
entry of the title in thefe regifters. But it would
feem that this multiplicity of broadfide ballads
was then only beginning, for at the commence-

ment of the Stationers' Regifters we find only
one or two printers of ballads, and it is a year or
two later when they become more numerous.
During the firft ten years of the reign of Queen
Elizabeth, the names of about forty printers
from whofe preffes ballads were iffued appear in
the regifters of the Stationers' Company, and
other names of ballad-printers are met with which
are not to be found in the regifters.

It is chiefly to this moft interefting period of
the hiftory of our ballad literature that we owe
the ballads printed in the prefent volume. The
greater number of them range from 1560 to
1570, and only a very fmall number pafs the
year 1572. They have no doubt been originally
collected by fome man of pofition who lived at
that time and took a lively intereft in all that
was paffing around him, and were moft likely
preferved among his family papers. Mr. Payne
Collier, in 1840, edited for the Percy Society
twenty-five ballads of the fame character, and
belonging to the fame period, which are known
to have belonged to the fame collection. Altogether they form, no doubt, the moft extraordinary and valuable collection of early Englifh
ballads now known to exift. They are the more
interefting, becaufe they have not been collected
by one whofe tafte ran upon any particular clafs
of fuch productions, but they prefent a variety
which embraces the whole field of broadfide literature ; and it will be worth our while, in our prefent confideration of them, to treat them in detail
in this point of view. In the firft place, they
naturally feparate into two great divifions, thofe
of a purely literary character, and thofe which

are more or lefs political or relate to contemporary events or feelings.

To the former of thefe divifions belong fentimental and love poetry, romances and ftories,
and facetiæ. A part of the latter clafs was taken
or imitated from the French popular literature ;
they were the fabliaux of an earlier period.
Many of them were fatires upon the failings of
the other fex, which then formed a favourite
theme. Of thefe we have examples in the prefent volume, in the ballad of " The Pinnyng of
the Bafket," (p. 105), in " A mery Balade, how
a wife entreated her hufband to haue her owne
wyll," (p. 129), and in " A very proper dittie, to
the tune of Lightie Loue," (p. 113). Some are
loofe and indelicate ftories, fuch as that of the
Brewer and Cooper, (p. 60), a true reprefen-
tative of the ancient fabliaux, which appears to
have been very popular, as two or three editions
of it have been traced. Others, again, are more
or lefs openly obfcene, of which there is one example only in the prefent volume, the ballad of
" Mother Watkins Ale," (p. 251). This, alfo,
appears to have been extremely popular, for it is
not unfrequently alluded to in the lighter literature of the Elizabethan age, though no traces of
its exiftence had been difcovered until the prefent
collection came to light. Perhaps we may confider as belonging to this clafs the dittie "Shewing what vnkindnes befell by a kiffe," (p. 214),
and the verfes entitled, " Adewe, Sweete Harte,"
(p. 222). This defcription of literature appears
to have been fufficiently abundant in Elizabeth's,
as it was indeed in the ages which followed.
Among the " Old Ballads" is one by a preacher

named Thomas Brice, who is known as the
author of fome other publications, and died before
1570, " Againft filthy writing, and fuch like de-
lighting." This ballad appears to have been
directed againft two of the licentious writers of
the day, who had written ballads in defence of
their productions, and it commences with the
lines,—

> What meane the rimes that run thus large in every fhop
> to fell,
> With wanton found and filthie fenfe ?   Me thinke it grees
> not well.
> We are not Ethnickes, we forfoth at leaft profeffe not fo;
> Why range we then to Ethnickes trade ?   Come back,
> where will ye go ?
> Tel me, is Chrift or Cupide lord ?   Doth God or Venus
> reigne ?

In the prefent collection, we have another
fatirical ballad on the contemporary literature, or
at leaft on the poets, which has for its title the
following rather clumfy lines (p. 205),—

> To fuch as write in metres, I write
> Of fmall matters an exhortation,
> By readyng of which men may delite
> In fuch as be worthy commendation.
> My verfe alfo it hath relation
> To fuch as print, that they dee it well,—
> The better they fhall their metres fell.

The writer of this ballad, who feems to think
that it was the duty of the printer to look to
the goodnefs of what came from his prefs, pro-
feffes to imitate the example of Horace, who
protefts againft the inferior poets among the
Romans, fuch as Lucilius for example, and there
were plenty of fuch wretched rhymefters in the
days of Elizabeth,—

> Wherfore let vs not open a gate,
>   Eyther the printer, or they which write
> To fuch as they be, knowyng their ftate.

And he fingles out efpecially for his criticifm
the writers on love,—

> Your balades of loue, not worth a beane,
>   A number there be, although not all;
> Some be pithie, fome weake, fome leane,
>   Some doe runne as round as a ball ;—
> Some verfes haue fuch a pleafant fall,
>   That pleafure it is for any man,
>   Whether his knowledge be great or fmall,
> So that of a verfe fome fkyll he can.

Of thefe love ballads there is no great number
in our collection, and many of them to which
we can give a date, as well, indeed, as of all the
purely literary divifion, belong to rather a later
period than moft of the hiftorical and political
ballads, fo that they were perhaps collected by
another and younger member of the family,
who afterwards mixed them with the others.
To this clafs of amorous and fentimental ballads
belong, "A Newe Ballade of a Louer extollinge
his Ladye," (p. 24), a fheet of poems of this defcription preferved in manufcript (pp. 190-194),
and "A prettie newe Ballad, intytuled,—

> "The Crowe fits vpon the wall,
>   Pleafe one and pleafe all."

The writer of the latter, who is unufually
large and liberal in his fentiments, recommends
his reader to pay his homage to the whole fex
and not to confine himfelf to an individual.

There are three ballads in this collection
which belong to the clafs of novels and romance.
One has for its fubject the well-known ftory of

Patient Griffel (Grifeldis), which has been a favourite with Englifh poets fince the days of Chaucer, and appears here in its earlieft ballad form, under the title of "A moft pleafant Ballad of Patient Griffell," (p. 17). The other two are, the ballad of "The Marchants Daughter of Briftow," (p. 66), which was no lefs popular than Patient Griffel, and that of "The Faire Widow of Watling-Street, and her 3 daughters," both of them in two parts. Thefe are both the earlieft editions known, belonging to a period approaching near to the clofe of the fixteenth century, when this clafs of ballad hiftories was coming into great popularity.

The political and hiftorical ballads in the prefent collection poffefs an extraordinary intereft, for they belong to one of the moft momentous periods of our national hiftory. Little more than a generation had paffed fince the overthrow of feudalifm. Henry VIII. had broken the power of the papacy in England, and his fon, Edward VI., feemed to have eftablifhed Proteftantifm ; but, on the death of the latter, the older religion, in the perfon of Mary, refumed its fway during more than five years, under its leaft pleafing attribute, that of perfecution. Mary alfo was juft dead, and her fifter Elizabeth had ftepped into her place with a cautioufnefs which, although the proteftant party looked upon her as their friend, almoft left room to doubt which party fhe intended to efpoufe. The cloud, which was already burfting over Weftern Europe, added greatly to people's doubts and fears, and they were filled with anxiety, not only to be made acquainted with the prefent, but to get even a flight glimpfe into the probabilities of the future. The publication of news, whether true or falfe,—and the latter was, perhaps, the moft faleable, becaufe it was the moft extraordinary,—became thus a profitable trade. For thefe reafons the political ballads and broadfide literature are now very important evidence not only of the popular feelings of the time, but of the means employed to influence thofe feelings. In the fuperftition of thofe days, every unknown or unufual natural phenomenon was looked upon as a warning from heaven of focial and political difafter, and was, therefore, watched with the moft intenfe intereft.

Among thefe figns, none created greater apprehenfion than monftrous births, which we find continually recorded even by the hiftorians and more ferious writers of the day. The year 1562, the fourth of Elizabeth's reign, is recorded by the Englifh chroniclers, fuch as Hollinfhed and Stowe, as efpecially fertile in monfters. The prefent collection contains nearly a dozen broadfides defcriptive of thefe prodigies, generally accompanied with a picture. No lefs than five of them belong to the year juft mentioned, 1562. The firft (p. 27) is a "true reporte" of a child born at Great Horkefley, near Colchefter, having neither legs nor arms; the defcription of the child is prefaced by verfes fetting forth the myfterious defign of thefe monfters. The next (p. 45) is an account of a monftrous pig with a dolphin's head, born at Charing Crofs a few days fubfequently, fimilarly accompanied with verfes moralizing upon the phenomenon. Another pig, farrowed at Hampftead, near London, in

the October of that year, is defcribed in a third
broadfide, "imprinted" by Alexander Lacy
(p. 112). A fourth broadfide (p. 186), alfo
belonging to the year 1562, as we learn
from the entry in the Stationers' Regifters,
defcribes another monftrous pig, and is accompanied with a poetical "exhortacion or warnynge
to all men, for amendment of lyfe." And
another of the fame year (p. 201), entirely in
ballad verfe, reprefents a monftrous child born
at Chichefter. Another monftrous child, born
at Frefhwater, in the Ifle of Wight, in 1564, is
defcribed and explained in a moral or religious
light, in a ballad by John Barker (p. 63). The
year 1566 produced twins joined together at the
ftomach, defcribed in a ballad by one John Mellys
of Norwich (p. 217), and a child with ruffs round
the neck, born at Mitcham in Surrey (p. 243).
In 1568, we have a monftrous child born at Maidftone, in Kent (p. 194), having "firft the mouth
flitted on the right fide, like a libarde's (leopard's)
mouth, terrible to beholde," which the author of
the ballad explains as a rebuke to the kingdom
for its wickednefs, and as a fign of God's difpleafure,—

> This monftrous fhape to thee, England,
>   Playn fhewes thy monftrous vice,
> If thou ech part wylt vnderftand,
>   And take thereby aduice.

And finally we have a defcription of a "marueilous ftraunge fifhe," caught between Calais
and Dover, in June, 1569 (p. 145).
 People lived in that condition which naturally
arifes out of the breaking up of one great focial
fyftem, and the tranfition towards another, the

character of which is as yet unknown. Men were
confcious that the whole frame of fociety was
disjointed and corrupt, and looked forward
anxioufly to the coming reform. Latterly the
revolution had taken a ftrongly religious character, and the feeling of difcontent partook alfo of
a religious fhade, and one clafs of the popular
ballads, of which there are fome good examples
in the prefent collection, formed a powerful
agent in fowing and cherifhing the feeds of that
puritanifm which was to exercife fo great an
influence on the deftinies of our country in the
next generation. None of thefe ballads, indeed,
are more curious than thofe which attempt to
picture the vices and corruptions of the times
during the earlier, and, perhaps we may fay, lefs
fettled part of the reign of Queen Elizabeth.
One of the earlieft of thefe, belonging to the
year 1561 is entitled, "A balade declaryng how
neybourhed (neighbourlinefs), loue, and trew
dealyng, is gone" (p. 134). The author, John
Barker, complains of the illcondition of the
world generally,—

> How ftraunge it is to men of age,
>   The which they fe before their face,
> This world to be in fuch outrage,
>   It was neuer fene in fo bad cafe.
> Neibourhed nor loue is none,
> Trew dealyng now is fled and gone.

Thefe two lines form the burthen of the fong,
if one can call it a fong. John Barker complains
that flattery and deceit were then the means of
fuccefs; that wickednefs prevailed everywhere;
that covetoufnefs was the great principle of
men's actions; that the landlords acted unjuftly

towards their tenants; and that every man was
the enemy of his neighbour. Another ballad,
publifhed in the fame year, bearing the name of
a better known writer, John Heywood, is
entitled, "A Ballad againft Slander and Detraction" (p. 9). Another ballad of this clafs,
which appears from the Stationers' Regifters to
have been publifhed in 1566 or 1567, is directed
againft the crime of bribery, and, the text being
taken from Scripture, is entitled, "A proper
new Balad of the bryber Gehefie" (p. 42).
Another ballad, printed in November, 1566
(p. 101), is directed againft the licentioufnefs of
the age; as is alfo one publifhed a few years
later, under the title, "Of the horrible and
wofull deftruction of Sodome and Gomorra"
(p. 125). With thefe may be claffed "A new
Ballad againft Unthrifts" (p. 153), which is aimed
againft the then numerous clafs of fpendthrifts
and rioters, who, the writer tells us, fpent their
money in the tavern, or threw it away at dice,
until they fell into ftill worfe practices, and
finifhed with Tyburn and the gallows,—

> Then fome at Newgate doo take fhip,
> Sailing ful faft vp Holborne Hil;
> And at Tiborn their anckers piche,
> Ful fore indeed againft their wil.

Another ballad, "The xxv. orders of Fooles"
(p. 88), which, according to the Stationers'
Regifters, belongs to the year 1569, is more
playfully fatirical. It had long been the fafhion
to reprefent mankind, as then exifting, in the
garb of fools, and claffifying thefe according to
their various weakneffes and peculiarities. The
Ship of Fools, of Sebaftian Brandt, is well

known, and it was popular here in an Englifh verfion as well as in its original form in Germany; and our own Sir Thomas More wrote in praife of Folly. The writer of the ballad divides the fools of this world into twenty-five orders. Some fools, according to his view, look upon wifdom with difdain; fome preach to others virtues which they do not practife themfelves; others fpend all in their youth, and make no provifion for their old age; others again delight in difcord and ftrife; and fo on to the end of the lift. One of the moft curious broadfides in the whole collection is the ballad which pictures the various orders in the ftate, arranged under the heads of the prieft, the king, the harlot, the lawyer, and the clown, each boafting of the power he holds over the others (p. 98). The prieft alleges that he prays for the other four; the king that he defends and protects them; the harlot, introduced in a manner which would feem to fhow a low ftate of morals at that period, fays, "I vanquefh you fower;" the lawyer, "I helpe yov iiij. to yovr right;" the clown, "I feede yov fower;" and death comes in and proclaims his errand, "I kill yov all." This fubject is found, treated a little differently, in the French popular literature of that age, from which the idea was taken by the Englifh ballad-writer, who has, no doubt, modified it a little to make it accord with the difference of Englifh fentiments. It is to be remarked that we have here alfo (p. 173) one of the moft curious and earlieft of the Englifh reprefentations of that well-known allegory, the Dance of Death, a very popular fubject during Elizabeth's reign.

The earlieft dated ballad in this collection is of the year 1559 (the firft of the reign of Queen Elizabeth), and is entitled, "The Wonders of England" (p. 94). It is a brief retrofpective review of Englifh hiftory fince 1553, when God, as a punifhment for the fins with which the land abounded, took away from us the good King Edward. The people had fince fuffered from mental darknefs and perfecution, until God relented and fent us Elizabeth, and,—

> Straightway the pebple out dyd cry—
> Prayfed be God, and God faue thee,
> Quene of England !

It may be remarked that this ballad is one of the poetical productions of the printer from whofe prefs it iffued, John Awdeley, who feems to have fought frequently to exhibit his talents as a ballad-writer. There is another ballad of a fatirical character, which belongs apparently to the earlier part of the reign of Queen Elizabeth, which defcribes the defects of contemporary fociety by their contraries. It has for title, "Other (i. e. *either*) thus it is, or thus it fhoulde bee" (p. 247), and ends with a prayer that Elizabeth might rule her fubjects well, and that they might prove true in their obedience. We have a ballad breathing a fimilar vein of fatire (p. 208), which unfortunately bears no direct evidence of date, though it is believed to be very early. This ballad declares that the gofpel was then read in its original purity throughout Chriftendom ; that all people led their lives "after Chrifte's rule ;" all neighbours lived lovingly together as though they were kinsfolk ; the earth had become like heaven, and the people

c

in it like angels; the prifons were empty; and all things went on fo flourifhingly, that it was believed that doomfday was near at hand; but the writer adds, rather waggifhly, "O wounders good tydynges, yf al fayinges be tru!"

The religious and moral poems are hardly fo numerous in the following collection as might be expected. A poet named Chriftopher Wilfon is the author of a ballad written in 1566 (p. 166), in which an acroftic, containing his name, runs through the initial letters of the lines from beginning to end. In another ballad, printed in 1568 (p. 138), the well-known writer Elderton has expounded the fayings of the ancient philofophers in verfe. A third poet, John Symon, has given a metrical commemoration of Scripture worthies, under the title of "A pleafant pofie, or fweete nofegay of fragrant fmellyng flowers, gathered in the garden of heauenly pleafure" (p. 5). This belongs to the year 1572. The ballads againft popery are more numerous, and every incident which could be made the ground of an attack upon the Romifh party appears to have been feized upon with eagernefs. We have here "A Balade of a Preift that lofte his nofe" (p. 141), to which the writer adds, as a rhyme, "for fayinge of maffe, as I fuppofe." It is a very fatirical defcription of the mifhap of a prieft, ftated to have been the vicar of Lee, who had been waylaid, it would appear, on his return from mafs, robbed, and his nofe cut off. A broadfide, probably of a later date than the laft, gives an engraving, accompanied with verfes, of two friars of the order of Capuchins (p. 156). The pope's bull, hung againft the

Bifhop of London's palace-gate, in 1571, is the fubject of two ballads in this collection (pp. 33, 224). We have alfo a rather earneft proteft againft the mafs, in a ballad printed in 1566 (p. 171); and a rather good ballad, belonging apparently to a rather early period of the queen's reign, and publifhed under the fimple title of a "A newe Ballade" (p. 30), was intended to warn her againft the hoftile defigns of the fpiritualty, meaning thereby the Romifh party, by the examples of fuch of her predeceffors as had fallen victims to the unfcrupulous ambition of the clergy. The ftrong feelings of the proteftant party in England at this time led to a fpirit of exaggerated loyalty and devotion which not unfrequently difplays itfelf in thefe ballads. A curious ballad by Elderton, entitled, "Prepare ye to the Plowe" (p. 174), and to be fung to the rather fingular tune of "Pepper is blacke," reprefents the queen as holding the plough, and exhorts her fubjects to be always ready to help her,—

> The queene holdes the plowe, to continew good feede;
> Truftie fubiectes, be readie to helpe, if fhe neede.

This loyalty, which led Elizabeth's fubjects to employ the extreme of flattery, is fhown in a ballad by a not unknown writer of that age, named Bernard Garter, entitled, "A ftrife betwene Appelles and Pigmalion" (p. 151), who feigns a conteft between thofe two artifts for fuperiority, the refult of which was a ftatue, by· the latter, of a woman of fuch furpaffing beauty as had never been feen before, and dame nature took it away, gave life to it, and reftored it to

earth in the perfon of Queen Elizabeth. The
pious Englifhman of that day imagined, in his
devotion, that no beauty could furpafs that of
the great champion of Proteftantifm.

Thefe earlier years of the reign of Elizabeth
formed, indeed, a period of anxiety and uncer-
tainty among all claffes. Elizabeth and her
minifters knew that the catholic party, not only
at home but on the Continent, were confpiring
againft her, and that not only her religion, but
her throne, and even her life, were in danger.
People's doubts were not leffened by occafional
difplays of exultation on the part of fome of the
lefs difcreet of the catholic party, who could not
conceal their hopes of fuccefs; and by the knowledge that a very great part of the population
of the country was ready to join to whichever
fortune fhould feem to promife fuccefs. People
were, by no means, affured of the fate of Proteftantifm, until the rebellion of the Dukes of
Northumberland and Weftmoreland, in the au-
tumn of 1569, which difplayed the real weaknefs
of the other party. The alarm which this
rifing created, not only among the people, but
in Elizabeth and her court, was very great; but
it did not laft long: before the end of the year
the rebellion was crufhed, and the two earls were
fugitives. This fuccefs evidently drew forth a
great number of broadfide ballads, the titles, of
many of which are entered in the Stationers'
Regifters, and a few of which are preferved.
No lefs than five of thefe are in the prefent collection, the earlieft of which is a metrical prayer
for divine protection againft the rebels (p. 121);
the others all relate to the period which followed

' See Ballads referring to this in Percy's

the fuppreffion of the rebellion. The firft ballad in the prefent volume commemorates the execution of a prieft named Plumtree, who had taken poffeffion of the church of St. Nicholas, in Durham, and of the flight of the leaders of the rebellion. Another, entitled "The Plagues of Northomberland" (p. 56), is alfo fomething like a fong of triumph over the defeat of the rebels; and a third (p. 231), having for its title the diftich,—

Joyfull Newes for true Subiectes to God and the Crowne,
The Rebelles are cooled, their Bragges be put downe,—

is written in the fame fpirit, but in a more fcornful tone. Laftly, we have "A Newe Ballade, intituled, Agaynft Rebellious and falfe rumours" (p. 239), bearing the date 1570, and publifhed no doubt early in the year. Before thefe curious pieces were made known by the difcovery of the collection now printed, only two or three contemporary ballads on the northern rebellion of 1569 were known to exift. Two, publifhed by Bifhop Percy in his Reliques, from his folio manufcript, are border ballads, compofed by minftrels who feem to have fympathized more or lefs with the two Earls and their followers, and they are of an entirely different character from thofe here printed. Among the "Old Ballads" printed by Mr. Payne Collier, which had originally formed part of the prefent collection, there is alfo a ballad on this rebellion, written by Thomas Prefton, and entitled,—

A lamentation from Rome how the Pope doth bewayle,
That rebelles in England can not prevayle.

And there is one in the collection of broadfides

in the library of the Society of Antiquaries, alfo exulting over the defeat of the rebellion, and entitled, " Newes from Northumberland." Thefe are, we believe, all the popular ballads now known to exift relating to this important event; and they are very curious as illuftrating the popular feelings which it excited.

The other hiftorical ballads in this collection are chiefly of a lefs degree of importance, becaufe they relate generally to events of no great intereft at the prefent day, with two efpecial exceptions. Thefe are two Scottifh ballads, both by Sempill, a known Scottifh poet. The fubject of the firft is the maffacre of the Proteftants in Paris on St. Bartholomew's Day, 1572, and it is entitled, " Ane new Ballet fet out be ane fugitiue Scottifman that fled out of Paris at this lait murther" (p. 37). The Scots, who were of courfe by their form of religion more clofely allied in feeling with the French Proteftants than the Englifh, were greatly affected by thefe fanguinary perfecutions in France, and, under the terror they created, the Scottifh government then in power fought to draw ftill clofer its relations with Queen Elizabeth. Such is the fpirit of the prefent ballad. It preffes upon Elizabeth the prudence of united and vigorous meafures of defence,—

> Now, wyfe Quene Elizabeth, luik to yourfelf,
>   Difpite them, and wryte thame ane bill of defyance,
> The Papiftis and Spanjards hes partit jour pelf,
>   As newly and trewly was tald me thir tythance.
> Beleue thay to land heir, and get vs for nocht;
> Will je do as we do, it fal be deir bocht.

The other of thefe Scottifh ballads (p. 49) is en-

titled, " Ane Complaint vpon Fortoun," and was
publifhed early in 1581, on Morton's fall, but
before he was brought to trial and executed.

Of the Englifh hiftorical ballads, or broadfides,
which remain to be mentioned, one (p. 236) is a
poem by " Ber. Gar." (Bernard Garter), entitled
" A dittie in the worthie praife of an high and
mightie Prince," who appears from the context
to have been Thomas Howard Earl of Norfolk,
but the occafion on which it was written is not
explained. There are three ballads on the deaths
of eminent perfons, who were, firft, " my Ladie
Marques" (p. 14), (perhaps the Marchionefs of
Southampton), which was entered in the Stationers' Regifters in 1569; fecond, " the Ladie
Maiorefle" of London (p. 178) ; the third, " the
Earl of Huntingdon," which bears the date of
1596. A ballad named " Saparton's Alarum"
(p. 118), bears the name of John Saparton as its
author, and appears, from another ballad on the
fame individual entered in the Stationers' books,
to belong to about the year 1569; its meaning
is not very clear. We have " A famous dittie"
on a fomewhat memorable vifit of the queen to
the city on the 12th of November, 1584 (p.
182) ; and " A mournfull dittie" (p. 197) on a
fudden mortality which took place among the
judges and others at the Lincoln Affizes of 1590.
There are two ballads on another accident which
happened in the provinces, the burning of the
town of Beccles, in Suffolk, in 1586 (pp. 78,
81); they were both printed by Robert Robinfon in London for Nicholas Colman of Norwich, fo that even at this time ballad-printers
appear to have been only to be found in London.

Laftly, we have a ballad entitled "Franklin's Farewell to the World" (p. 85). James Franklin was the apothecary who fupplied the poifons ufed in the Overbury murders, and was condemned and executed on the 9th of December, 1615. Another ballad, on the fame fubject, is preferved in the collection of the Society of Antiquaries. This ballad muft have been added to our collection long after the original collector had departed from the fcene of his labours.

With the mafs of ballad literature here revealed to us, we may naturally be curious to learn fomething of the ballad-writers, but we can collect little beyond a few obfcure names, and others which are merely hinted to us by their initials. Among them, however, are the names of one or two writers who are better known in the fmaller literature of the Elizabethan period. Such is Thomas Churchyard, whofe name is found attached to one of the ballads feparated from the prefent collection, and printed by Mr. Collier. Such alfo are William Elderton, and Thomas Deloney. The firft of thefe was celebrated for his tippling propenfities, as well as for his rhymes, and is faid to have drunk himfelf to death, fome time before 1592. His fpecial characteriftic is commemorated in a contemporary epitaph, recorded by Camden, and tranflated by Oldys, as follows:—

Hic fitus eft fitiens, atque ebrius Eldertonus,
  Quid dico hic fitus eft? hic potius fitis eft.

Dead drunk here Elderton doth lie;
Dead as he is, he ftill is dry;
So of him it may well be faid,
Here he, but not his thirft, is laid.

He was the author of three ballads in the prefent volume (pp. 16, 140, 178), and of two of
thofe edited by Mr. Collier. One of the latter
was printed on the 22nd of March, 1559, which,
in our reckoning, means 1560. Deloney was a ⟩
profeffed ballad-writer on all paffing events.
His only produ&ion in the prefent volume is
one of the poems on the burning of the town of
Beccles, in 1586 (p. 84); one in Mr. Collier's
volume, printed in the fame year, has for its fub-
je& the execution of the confpirators in the celebrated Babington Confpiracy. Deloney ufually
figns only with his initials, T. D. John Heywood, who alfo is a well-known writer of the
middle of the fixteenth century, was a firm
Roman Catholic, and went into voluntary exile
on the death of Mary, dying at Mechlin, in Bra-
bant, in 1565. If he be the author of the
"Ballad againft Slander and Detra&ion" (p. 9),
to which the name of Haywood is attached, it
muft have been intended as a proteft againft per-
fonal abufe to which fome of the Catholics,
perhaps himfelf, had been fubje&ed. Richard
Tarlton, another well-known minor Elizabethan
writer, is the author of one of the moft fprightly
ballads in the prefent colle&ion (p. 259); as well
as of one in Mr. Collier's colle&ion, to which
his name is given in full. John Awdeley, the
printer, appears not unfrequently to have written
his own ballads. Two of them occur in our prefent volume, the firft (p. 97) printed in 1559,
the fecond (p. 123) in 1569; and there is a third
in Collier's volume, fuppofed to belong to about
the fame date as the former. A few alfo of the
other names of authors attached to thefe ballads

See his performances set out in

are known by fome other contributions to the
literature of the age. John Barker, who wrote
three of our ballads (pp. 59, 66, and 138), one
of them printed in 1564, and another entered in
the Stationers' Regifters in 1569-70, is alfo
known as the author of a ballad " Of the horrible and wofull deftruction of Jerufalem," printed
by Colwell about 1568. The initials " T. Gr."
attached to one of our ballads (p. 94) probably
ftand for Thomas Greepe, who was the author of
a poem on the exploits of Sir Francis Drake,
printed in 1587. Leonard Gibfon, whofe name
occurs here as the writer of a ballad on the light-
nefs of the ladies (p. 117), was the author of a
little book called " The Tower of Truftinefie,"
in verfe and profe, printed in 1555 ; and there is
a fong called "L. Gibfon's Tantara" in the
"Handefull of Pleafant Delites," 1584. The
individual defigned under the abbreviated form
Ber. Gar. (pp. 153, 239), and in one cafe merely
by the initials, B. G. (p. 150), was Bernard
Garter, who wrote the "Tragical Hiftory of Two
Englifh Lovers," printed in a fmall volume in
1565, and " A New Yeares Gifte," printed in
quarto in 1579, and fome of whofe verfes are
prefixed to " Pafquine in a Traunce," 1584.
John Philip, whofe name is attached to one of
our ballads printed in 1570 (p. 182), and to
whom probably belong the initials I. P. attached
to the lines added to the account of the Wonderful Swine (p. 190), is known by feveral poetical
works ftill extant, of which perhaps the moft
curious is " A rare and ftrange hiftoricall Novell
of Cleomenes and Sophonifba," printed in 1577.
John Mellys, of Norwich, the author of a

ballad on two monftrous children, printed in
1566 (p. 220), was perhaps the fame perfon, for
he bears the fame name, as the compiler of " A
briefe Inftruction how to keepe Bookes of Ac-
compts," which bears the date 1588. The other
names and initials found in our collection of
ballads appear to be entirely unknown. When
we compare them with the few other ballads of
this period now known, which prefent us with
many new names, we cannot but be furprifed at
the great number of individuals who muft have
found employment in writing ballads at this very
early period in the hiftory of ballad literature.

·CONTENTS.

Page

ANCIENT BALLADS AND
BROADSIDES.

A Ballad intituled, A newe Well a daye,
As playne, maifter papift, as Donftable waye.

Well a daye, well a daye, well a daye, woe is mee,
Syr Thomas Plomtrie is hanged on a tree.

MONGE manye newes reported of late
   As touchinge the rebelles their
     wicked eftate,
   Yet Syr Thomas Plomtrie their
     preacher, they faie,
Hath made the North countrie to crie well a
   daye.
Well a daye, well a daye, well a daye, woe is me,
Syr Thomas Plomtrie is hanged on a tree.

And now manie fathers and mothers be theare,
  Are put to their trialles with terrible feare,
Not all the gaye croffes nor goddes they adore.
  Will make them as merie as they haue ben
    before ;
Well a daye, well a daye, &c.

B

The widowes be woful whofe hufbandes be taken,
The childerne lament them that are fo forfaken,
The church men thei chaunted the morowe maffe
bell,
Their pardons be graunted, they hang verie wel.
Well a daye, well a daye, &c.

It is knowne they bee fled that were the beginers,
It is time they were ded, poore forofull finners ;
For all there great hafte they are hedged at a ftaye,
With weeping and waylinge to fing well a daye ;
Well a daye, well a daye, &c.

Yet fome hold opynion, all is well with the higheft ;
They are in good faftie wher freedome is niefte ;
ᐱ Northumberland need not be doutefull, fome faye,
And Weftmorlande is not yet brought to the
bay ;
Well a daye, well a daye, &c.

No more is not Norton, nor a nomber befide,
But all in good feafon they maye hap to be fpide ;
It is well they be wandred whether no man can fay,
But it will be remembered, they crie well a daie ;
Well a daye, well a daye, &c.

Where be the fyne fellowes that caried the croffes ?
Where be the deuifers of idoles and affes ?
Wher be the gaie banners were wont to be borne ?
Where is the deuocion of gentyll John Shorne ?
Well a daye, well a daye, &c.

Saint Pall and Saint Peter haue laid them a-bord,
And faie it is feetter to cleaue to Gods worde,

Their beades and their bables are beſt to be burnd,
 And Moiſes tables towardes them to be turnde ;
 Well a daye, well a daye, &c.

And well a daye wandreth ſtill to and froe,
 Bewailinge the wonders of rumors that goe ;
Yet ſaie the ſtiffe-necked, let be as be maye,
 Though ſome be ſore checked, yet ſome ſkape
 awaie ;
 Well a daye, well a daye, &c.

And ſuch ſome be ſowers of ſeedes of ſedicion,
 And ſaie the Popes pardon ſhall giue them re-
 miſſion,
That kepe themſelues ſecrete, and preeuilie ſaie,
 It is no greate matter for this, well a daye ;
 Well a daye, well a daye, &c.

You ſhall haue more newes er Candelmas come,
 Their be matters diffuſe, yet lookte for of ſome ;
Looke on, and looke ſtill, as ye longe to here newes,
 I thinke Tower Hill will make ye all muſe ;
 Well a daye, well a daye, &c.

If they that leaue tumblynge begin to wax climing,
 For all your momblinge and merie paſtimeing
Ye will then beleeue, I am ſure as I ſaie,
 That matter will meeue a newe well a daye ;
 Well a daye, well a daye, &c.

But as ye be faithleſſe of God and his lawe,
 So till ye ſee hedles the traitors in ſtrawe,
You wil be ſtill whiſperinge of this and of that,
 Well a daye, woe is me, you remember it not ;
 Well a daie, well a daie, &c

Leaue of your lyinge, and fall to trewe reafon,
　Leaue of your fonde fpieng, and marke euery
　　feafon ;
Againft God and your countrie to taulke of
　rebelling
　Not Syr Thomas Plumtrie can bide by the
　　telling ;
　　Well a daye, well a daye, &c.

And fuch as feduce the people with blyndnes,
　And byd them to truft the Pope and his
　　kyndnes,
Make worke for the tynker, as prouerbes doth
　faie,
　By fuch popifhe patching ftill comes well a
　　daye ;
　　Well a daye, well a daie, &c.

And fhe that is rightfull your Queene to fubdue
　ye,
　Althoughe you be fpitfull, hath gyuen no caufe
　　to ye ;
But if ye will vexe her, to trie her hole force,
　Let him that comes next her take heed of her
　　horfe ;
　　Well a daie, well a daie, &c.

Shee is the lieftennante of him that is ftowteft,
　Shee is defender of all the deuowteft ;
It is not the Pope, nor all the Pope may,
　Can make her aftonyed, or finge well a daie ;
　　Well a daie, well a daie, &c.

God profper her highnes, and fend her his peace
　To gouerne good people with grace and increafe ;

And fend the deferuers, that feeke the wronge
  way,
At Tyborne fome caruers, to finge well a daie;
Well a daie, well a daie, &c.

Finis.   W. E.

¶ Imprinted at London in Fleeftrete beneath the
  Conduit, at the figne of S. John Euangelift, by Thomas Colwell.

*A pleafant Poefie, or fweete Nofegay of frag-
rant fmellyng Flowers gathered in the Garden
of heauenly Pleafure, the holy and bleffed Bible ;
to the tune of the Black Almayne.*

STOCK of flowers, bedewed with
     fhowers,
   In a garden now there fprings ;
   With mirth and glee, vpon a tree,
A byrd there fits and fings ;
So pleafant is her voyce,
It doth my hart reioyce :
   She fets her tunes and noates fo meete,
   That vnto me it feemes fo fweete,
That all the flowers, that euer could be,
Was neuer fo fwete as this to me ;
   The lyke before I dyd neuer fe.

❡ The Bible it is, that garden i-wys,
   Which God preferue alwayes :
Lykewyfe Gods worde it is that byrde,
   That now fo much I prayfe.
Alfo thofe goodly flowers,
So well bedewed with fhowers,
   I wyll now go about to gather,
   And put them in a pofy together ;
I wyll not put them in no cheft,
But bynd them vp as I thinke beft,
   And kepe them alway next my breft.

❡ The fyrft I fynd, to pleafe my mind,
   Abell be had to name ;
Enoch alwayes is worthy of prayfe,
   Likewyfe of worthy fame.
Looke you what Mofes wrytes,
And in Genefis there refites,
   How God tooke hym the ftory fayth,
   That he fhould neuer taft of death :
And alfo Noe, that righteous man,
A curious worke dyd take in hand,
   To make the arke we vnderftand.

❡ Good Abraham, that faithfull man,
   In God dyd truft alway :
He dyd not feare, nor once difpayre
   His onely fon to flay ;
Ifacke was no weede,
Nor Jacob in very deede :
   Jofeph was a flower of price,
   God dyd hym faue from cruell deuice ;
Alfo Mofes eke we fynd,
And Aaron lykewyfe vp we bynd,
   Jofua is not out of mynd.

❡ The Judges alſo, both leſſe and mo,
    They were of worthy fame :
To ſpeake of all, my tyme is ſmal,
    To rehearce them all by name.
The prophet Samuell,
Our God dyd loue him well :
    Dauid was a flower ſo ſweete,
    To make hym kyng God thought it meete,
For great Golias he hath ſlayne ;
And Sallomon after him dyd raygne,
    Which vnto wyſedome dyd attayne.

❡ When Achab dyd floryſh, the rauens did
        noriſh
    Elia, a man of God ;
Kynge Joſias and Eſdras
    We finde, and pacient Job.
They feared our God of might,
And ſerued him day and night :
    No ioy nor payne could them procure,
    But alwayes by hym to endure :
Eſay lykewyſe and Jeremy,
They preached alway earneſtly,
    And dyd their duty faithfully.

❡ And Daniell deſtroyed Bell,
    The Babilonians God :
The dragon alſo he brought to wo,
    Without either ſword or rod.
To rehearce the Prophets all,
By their names them for to call,
    Although they be of worthy fame,
    It is to long them for to name :
We may not Tobyas leaue behynd,
Yet was he almoſt out of mind,
    But few ſuch flowers now can we fynd.

℀ Full wel we know, no flowers can blow,
　　But boyſterous ſtormes muſt fynd :
For that is no flower, that euery ſhowre
　　Doth driue away with wynd.
For all theſe goodly flowers
Had many ſtormy ſhowers,
　　Before that they could blow or bud,
　　Or bring forth ſeede to doe any good :
They dyd abyde both cold and blaſt,
Yet allwayes dyd they ſtand ſtedfaſt,
　　Tyll all the ſtormes were gone and paſt.

℀ Now at this time, for our gracious Queene,
　　Let vs geue harty prayes :
God may her defend, from enemies hand,
　　At this time and alwayes ;
And ſend her proſperous raygne,
With vs for to remayne,
　　For to defend Gods word ſo pure,
　　And euer with it for to endure :
　　That ſhe may be to vs a bower,
To kepe vs alway when it doth ſhowre ;
　　I pray God ſaue that princly flower !

　　　　　℀ Finis.　　　　John Symon.

℀ Imprinted at London by Richard
Johnes, dwellyng in the upper end
of Fleet Lane, 1572.

A Ballad againſt Slander and Detraction.

❦ Gar call him downe, gar call him downe, gar call him
 downe downe a :
❦ God ſend the faction, of all detraction, calld downe and
 caſt away.

LMYGHTY God
 Dooth ſhake his rod
  Of iuſtiſe, and all thoſe,
   That vniuſtly,
Detractyfly,
Detract their freends or foes.

He telthe eche one,
Thou ſhalt iudge none ;
 And if thou iudge unbiden,
Thyſelf, ſaith he,
Shall iudged be ;
 This leſſon is not hiden.

To this now ſturd,
This is concord,
 Whiche wilthe vs in eche dout ;
To deem the beſt,
That may be geſt,
 Till time the trueth try out.

Knowing by this,
That think amiſſe
 Againſt no man we may ;

Muche more muſt we
Ill langage flee,
　　And call it downe downe a ;
　　　Gar call him downe, &c.

❦ With ſwoord or ſkaine
To ſee babes ſlaine,
　　Abhorth to look upon ;
Attend to me,
And ye ſhall ſee
　　Murder and ſlaunder one.

Like as a knife
By reuing life,
　　So ſlaunder fame hath ſlain ;
And bothe ones doone,
Bothe alike ſoone
　　May be vndoon again.

Then what more ill
With knife to kill,
　　Or with the tung to ſting :
With knife or tung
Strike olde or yung,
　　Bothe in effect one thing.

Theſe woords are ſhort,
But they import
　　Sentence at length to way :
Of all whiche ſence,
To flee offence,
　　Call ſlaunder downe I ſay ;
　　　Gar call him downe, &c.

⁋ When vice is fought,
Al vice is nought,
  But fome vice wors then fome :
And eche man fees
Sundry degrees
  In eche vice felf dooth come.

Now fins the leaft,
We fhould deteft
  Vice or degree in vice :
If in the mofte
We fhowe our bofte,
  That fhoweth vs mofte unwice.

If I in thee
Suche faults ones fee,
  As no man ells doth knowe ;
To thee alone,
And other none,
  Thefe faults I ought to fhowe.

Then of intent
If I inuent
  Fauls tales, and them difplay :
That is mofte vile,
Whiche to exile,
  God calleth this down, downe a.
    Gar call him downe, &c.

⁋ Some count no charge
To talke at large
  Suche il as they doo heare ;
But Gods account
Dooth not amount
  To take fuche talkers heere.

Of woork il wrought,
When it is fought,
    In telling foorth the fame,
Though it be true,
The talke may brew
    Drink of damnable blame.

To frame excufe,
Of tungs mifufe,
    We haue no maner mene ;
So that by this,
No way ther is
    Il talles to cary clene.

Whiche makes me call
Vpon you all,
    As calling cal you may ;
Tales falfe or true,
Me to enfue,
    To call them downe, down a.
    Gar call him downe, &c.

❡ Chrifte crieth out ftil,
Say good for il,
    But we fay harme for harme ;
Yea ill for good
Ill tungs doo brood,
    Wrath is in them fo warme.

Slander to fere
And to forbere,
    This text ftands well in place ;
Wo by the tung,
Wherby is fprung
    Slander in any cace !

To fleke this fier
Of flanders yre,
  Repentance muft deuife
To fet all hands,
To quenche the brands
  With water of our eies.

Whiche brand then blowe
To make loue glowe,
  That loue by grace may ftay,
And by refort
Of good report,
  Call flander downe I fay.
    Gar call him down, &c.

FINIS,   q^d   Haywood.

Imprinted at
London, at the long Shop
adioining vnto Saint
Mildreds Churche
in the Pultrie, by
John Allde.

ᵡ   *A proper new Balad in praiſe of my*

Ladie Marques,

whoſe Death is bewailed to the Tune of New luſty gallant.

ADIES, I thinke you maruell that
        I writ no mery report to you,
        And what is the cauſe I court it not
        So merye as I was wont to dooe;
Alas! I let you vnderſtand,
    It is no newes for me to ſhow;
The faireſt flower of my garland
    Was caught from court a great while agoe.

For, vnder the roufe of ſweete Saint Paull,
    There lyeth my Ladie buryed in claye,
Where I make memory for her foule
    With weepinge eyes once euerye daye;
All other ſightes I haue forgot,
    That euer in court I ioyed to ſee,
And that is the cauſe I court it not,
    So mery as I was wont to be.

And though that ſhee be dead and gone,
    Whoſe courting need not to be tolde,
And natures mould of fleſhe and bone,
    Whoſe lyke now liues not to beholde,
Me thinkes I ſee her walke in blacke,
    In euery corner where I goe,
To looke if anie bodie do lacke
    A frend to helpe them of theyr woe.

Mee thinkes I fee her forowfull teares,
  To princelye ftate approching nye ;
Mee thinkes I fee her tremblinge feares,
  Lefte anie her fuites fhulde hit awrie ;
Mee thinkes fhe fhuld be ftill in place,
  A pitifull fpeaker to a Queene,
Bewailinge every poore mans cafe,
  As many a time fhee hath ben feene.

Mee thinkes I fee her modefte mood,
  Her comlie clothing plainlie clad,
Her face fo fweete, her cheere fo good,
  The courtlie countenance that fhee had ;
But, chefe of all, mee thinkes I fee
  Her vertues deutie daie by daie,
Homblie kneeling one her knee,
  As her defire was ftill to praie.

Mee thinkes I cold from morow to night
  Do no thing ells with verie good will,
But fpend the time to fpeake and writte
  The praife of my good ladies ftill ;
Though reafon faith, now fhe is dead,
  Go feeke and farue as good as fhee ; — α
It will not finke fo in my head,
  That euer the like in courte will bee.

But fure I am, ther liueth yet
  In court a dearer frinde to mee,
Whome I to farue am fo vnfit,
  I am fure the like will neuer bee ;
For I with all that I can dooe,
  Vnworthie moft maie feeme to bee,
To undoo the lachet of her fhooe,
  Yet will I come to courte and fee.

Then haue amongſte ye once againe,
    Faint harts faire ladies neuer win;
I truſt ye will conſider my payne,
    When any good veniſon cometh in;
And, gentill ladies, I you praie,
    If my abſentinge breede to blame,
In my behalfe that ye will ſaie,
    In court is remedie for the ſame.

❡ Finis, qᵈ W. Elderton.

❡ Imprinted at London in Fleteſtreat
beneath the Conduit, at the ſigne
of S. John Euangeliſt, by
Thomas Colwell.

The Priſoners' Petition.

To the worſhipful our good benefactor.

N all lamentable manner, moſt humbly beſeecheth your good Worſhip, wee, the miſerable multitude of very poore diſtreſſed priſoners, in the hole of Wood-ſtreet Counter, in nomber fiftie poore men or thereabouts, lying vpon the bare boordes, ſtill languiſhing in great neede, colde and miſerie, who, by reaſon of this daungerous and troubleſome time, be almoſt famiſhed and hunger-ſtarued to death; others very ſore ſicke, and diſeaſed for want of reliefe and ſuſtenance, by

reafon of the great number, which dayly increafeth, dooth in all humblenes moft humbly be-
feech your good worfhip, euen for Gods fake,
to pitie our poore lamentable and diftreffed cafes ;
and nowe helpe to relieue and comfort us with
your Chriftian and Godly charitie againft this
holie and bleffed time of Eafter. And wee, according to our bounden duties, do and will
dayly pray vnto Almighty God for your long
life and happy profperitie.

> We humbly pray, your Chriftian and
> Godly charitie to be fent vnto vs by
> fome of your feruants.

X

A moft pleafant Ballad of patient Griffell,

To the tune of the Brides Good-morrow.

NOBLE Marques as he did ride on
    hunting,
    Hard by a forreft fide ;
    A proper mayden, as fhe did fit a
    fpinning,
His gentle eye efpide.
Moft faire, and louely, and of curteous grace was
    fhe,
    Although in fimple attire ;
She fung full fweet with pleafant voyce melod-
    ioufly,
    Which fet the lords hart on fire.

c

The more he looked the more he might,
Beautie bred his hartes delight,
    And to this dainty damfell then he went;—
God fpeede, quoth he, thou famous flower,
Faire miftres of this homely bower,
    Where loue and vertue liues with fweete content.

With comely iefture and curteous milde behauiour,
    She bad him welcome then ;
She entertain'd him in faithful friendly maner,
    And all his gentlemen.
The noble marques in his hart felt fuch a flame,
    Which fet his fences at ftrife ;
Quoth he, faire maiden, fhew me foone what is
        thy name ?
    I meane to make thee my wife.
Griffell is my name, quoth fhe,
Farre· vnfit for your degree,
    A filly mayden and of parents poore.
Nay, Griffell, thou art rich, he fayd,
A vertuous, faire and comely mayd ;
    Graunt me thy loue, and I wil afke no more.

At length fhe confented, and being both contented,
    They married were with fpeed ;
Her contrey ruffet was changd to filk and veluet,
    As to her ftate agreed.
And when fhe was trimly tyred in the fame,
    Her beauty fhined moft bright,
Far ftaining euery other braue and comly dame,
    That did appeare in her fight.
Many enuied her therefore,
Becaufe fhe was of parents poore,
    And twixt her lord and fhe great ftrife did raife.

Some fayd this and fome fayd that,
Some did call her beggers brat,
　And to her lord they would her foone difpraife.

O noble Marques, quoth they, why doe you
　　wrong vs,
　Thus bacely for to wed,
That might haue gotten an honorable lady,
　Into your princely bed ?
Who will not now your noble iffue ftill deride,
　Which fhall hereafter be borne ?
That are of blood fo bafe by their mothers fide,
　. The which will bring them in fcorne ;
Put her therefore quite away,
Take to you a lady gay,
　Whereby your linage may renowned be ;
Thus euery day they feemde to prate,
That malift Griffelles good eftate,
　Who tooke all this moft milde and patiently.

When that the marques did fee that they were
　　bent thus
　Againft his faithfull wife,
Whom he moft deerely, tenderly and entirely,
　Beloued as his life ;
Minding in fecret for to proue her patient hart,
　Therby her foes to difgrace ;
Thinking to play a hard vncurteous part,
　That men might pittie her cafe.
Great with childe this lady was,
And at length it came to paffe,
　Two goodly children at one birth fhe had ;
A fonne and daughter God had fent;
Which did their father well content,
　And which did make their mothers hart full glad.

Great royall feaſting was at theſe childrens
  chriſtnings, ′.
And princely triumph made ;
Sixe weeks together, al nobles that came thither
  Were entertaind and ſtaid ;
And when that al thoſe pleaſant ſportings quite
  were done,
The Marques a meſſenger ſent
For his yong daughter, and his prety ſmiling ſon,
  Declaring his full intent,—
How that the babes muſt murdred be,
For ſo the Marques did decree,—
  Come, let me haue the children, then he ſayd.
With that faire Griſſell wept full ſore,
She wrung her hands and ſayd no more,—
  My gracious lord muſt haue his will obaid.

She tooke the babies, euen from their nurſing
  ladies,
  Betweene her tender armes ;
She often wiſhes, with many ſorrowful kiſſes,
  That ſhe might helpe their harmes.
Farewel, farewel, a thouſand times, my children
  deere,
  Neuer ſhall I ſee you againe ;
Tis long of me, your ſad and woful mother
  heere,
  For whoſe ſake both muſt be ſlaine.
Had I been borne of royall race,
You might haue liu'd in happy caſe,
  But you muſt die for my vnworthines ;
Come, meſſenger of death, ſaid ſhee,
Take my deſpiſed babes to thee,
  And to their father my complaints expres.

He tooke the children, and to his noble maifter
  He brings them both with fpeed ;
Who fecret fent them vnto a noble lady,
  To be nurft vp indeed ;
Then to faire Griffel with a heauy hart he goes,
  Where fhe fate mildly alone ;
A pleafant iefture and a louely looke fhe fhowes,
  As if this griefe fhe neuer had knowen.
Quoth he, my children now are flaine !
What thinkes faire Griffell of the fame ?
  Sweet Griffell, now declare thy mind to mee.
Sith you, my lord, are pleaf'd in it,
Poore Griffell thinkes the action fit ;
  Both I and mine at your command will be.

My nobles murmur, faire Griffell, at thy honor,
  And I no ioy can haue,
Til thou be banifht both from my court and pre-
    fence,
  As they vnjuftly craue ;
Thou muft be ftript out of thy coftly garments
    all,
  And as thou cameft to me,
In homely gray, infteed of biffe and pureft pall,
  Now all thy cloathing muft be ;
My lady thou fhalt be no more,
Nor I thy lord, which grieues me fore ;
  The pooreft life muft now content thy minde ;
A groat to thee I muft not giue,
To maintaine thee while I doe liue,
  Againft my Griffel fuch great foes I finde.

When gentle Griffell did heare thefe wofull
    tidings,
  The teares ftood in her eyes.

She nothing anſwered, no words of diſcontent
   Did from her lips ariſe ;
Her veluet gown moſt patiently ſhe ſlipped off,
   Her kirtles of ſilke with the ſame ;
Her ruſſet gown was broght again with many a
    ſcoffe,
   To beare them all herſelfe ſhe did frame.
When ſhe was dreſt in this array,
And ready was to part away,
   God ſeñd long life vnto my lord, quoth ſhee ;
Let no offence be found in this,
To giue my lord a parting kiſſe.—
   With watry eyes, Farewel, my deere, quoth he.

From ſtately pallace vnto her fathers cottage,
   Poore Griſſell now is gone ;
Full ſixteene winters ſhe liued there contented,
   No wrong ſhe thought vpon ;
And at that time through all the land the ſpeaches
    went,
   The Marques ſhould married be
Vnto a lady of high and great diſcent ;
   To the ſame all parties did agree.
The Marques ſent for Griſſell faire,
The brides bedchamber to prepare,
   That nothing therein ſhould be found awrye ;
The bride was with her brother come,
Which was great ioy to all and ſome ;
   And Griſſell tooke all this moſt patiently.

And, in the morning, when they ſhould to the
    wedding,
   Her patience now was tride ;
Griſſel was charged herſelf in princely maner
   For to attire the bride.

Moſt willingly ſhe gaue conſent to do the ſame ;
  The bride in her brauery was dreſt,
And preſently the noble Marques thither came,
  With all his lords, as he requeſt :
O Griſſel, I would aſke, quoth he,
If ſhe would to this match agree ;
  Me thinkes her lookes are waxen wondrous coy ;
With that they all began to ſmile,
And Griſſell ſhe replide the while,
  God ſend Lord Marques many yerès of joy !

The Marques was moued to ſee his beſt beloued,
  Thus patient in diſtreſſe ;
He ſtept vnto her, and by the hand he tooke her,—
  Theſe wordes he did expreſſe ;—
Thou art my bride and all the brides I meane to
    haue ;
  Theſe two thine owne children be !
The youthfull lady on her knees did bleſſing
    craue,
  Her brother as willing as ſhe ;—
And you that enuied her eſtate,
Whom I haue made my louing mate,
  Now bluſh for ſhame, and honor vertuous life ;
The chronicles of laſting fame,   *They will surely*
Shall euer more extoll the name,
  Of patient Griſſell, my moſt conſtant wife.

FINIS.

A Newe Ballade of a Louer extollinge his Ladye.

To the tune of Damon and Pithias.

LAS, my harte doth boyle,
 And burne within my brefte,
To fhowe to thee, myne onely deere,
 My fute and my requeft.
My loue no toung can tell,
 Ne pen can well defcrye;
Extend thy loue for loue againe,
 Or els for loue I dye.

❡ My loue is fet fo fuer,
 And fixed on thee fo,
That by no meanes I can abftaine,
 My faythfull loue to fhowe;
My wounded harte, theirfore,
 To thee for helpe doth crye;
Extend thy loue for loue againe,
 Or els for loue I dye.

❡ Although the gods were bent,
 With greedie mynde to flaye
My corpes with cruell panges of death,
 And lyfe to take awaye.
Yet fhould my faythfull harte
 At no tyme from thee flye;
Show loue therfore for loue againe,
 Or els for loue I dye.

❡ Although the fun were bent
　To burne me with his beames ;
And that mine eyes, throw greous pangs,
　Should fend forth bloudy ftreames ;
Yet would I not forfake,
　But ftyll to thee woulde crye,
To fhowe me loue for loue again,
　Or els for loue I dye.

❡ Ye though ech fterre were tournd
　Untyll a fiery darte,
And were all ready bent with payne,
　To perce throwe-out my harte ;
Yet coulde I not forfake
　To loue thee faythfullye ;
Extend thy loue for loue againe,
　Or els for loue I dye.

❡ Ye though eche foule were formde,
　A ferpent fell to be,
My corps to flay with bloudy wounds,
　And to deuower me ;
Yet would I be thine owne,
　To loue full hartelye ;
Extend thy loue for loue againe,
　Or els for loue I dye.

❡ Ye though the lyon were,
　With gapinge gredye jawe,
Readye with rygorus raggye teeth,
　My flefhe to teare and gnawe ;
Yet woulde I be thine owne,
　To ferue moft earneftlye ;
Extend thy loue for loue againe,
　Or els for loue I dye.

❡ Ye though the fifhes all,
    That fwymes in furginge feafe,
Should fwallowe me with gredy mouth,
    Yet could thee not apeafe.
My earneft harte to thee,
    To loue entyerlye ;
Extend thy loue for loue againe,
    Or els for loue I dye.

❡ Ye though the earth would gape,
    And fwallowe me there-in,
And that I fhould tormentyd be
    In hell, with euery fyn ;
Yet would I be thy owne,
    To faue or els to fpyll ;
Show me therfore lyke loue againe,
    Or els thou doft me kyll.

Finis, q M. Ofb.

Imprinted at London, in Fletftrete, at the
figne of the Faucon, by Wylliam
Gryffith, 1568.

*The true reporte of the forme and ſhape of a
monſtrous Childe borne at Muche Horkeſleye, a
village three myles from Colcheſter, in the
Countye of Eſſex, the* xxi *daye of Apryll in this
yeare* 1562.

> O prayſe ye God, and bleſſe his name;
> His mightye hande hath wrought the ſame.

THIS monſtrous world that monſters
     bredes as rife,
     As men tofore it bred by native
     kinde,
By birthes that ſhewe corrupted natures ſtrife,
Declares what ſinnes befet the ſecrete minde.
I meane not this, as though deformed ſhape
     Were alwayes linkd with fraughted minde with
     vice,
But that in nature God ſuch draughtes doth ſhape,
     Reſemblyng ſinnes that ſo bin had in price.
So groſſeſt faultes braſt out in bodyes forme,
     And monſter cauſed of want or to much ſtore
Of matter, ſhewes the ſea of ſinne, whoſe ſtorme
     Oreflowes and whelmes vertues barren ſhore;
Faultye alike in ebbe and eke in flowd,
     Like diſtaunt both from meane, both like ex-
     treames;
Yet greatſt exceſſe the want of meane doth
     ſhrowde,

And want of meanes exceſſe from vertues
   meanes.
So contraryeſt extreames conſent in ſinne,
   Which to bewray to blindeſt eyes by ſyght,—
Beholde a calfe hath clapt about his chinne
✗ His chauderne, reft whence nature placed it
   right,
And ruffd, driues doubtfull ſeers to proue by ſpeache
   Themſelues not calues, and makes the faſhion
   ſtale.
In him behold by exceſſe from meane our breache,
   And midds exceſſe yet want of natures ſhape.
To ſhowe our miſſe beholde a guiltleſſe babe
   Reft of his limmes,—for ſuch is vertues want—
Himſelfe and parentes both infamous made
   With ſinful byrth ; and yet a worldlyng ſcant.
Feares midwyfes route, bewrayeing his parentes
   fault
   In want of honeſtye and exceſſe of ſinne;
Made lawfull by all lawes of men, yet halt
   Of limmes by God, ſcapd not the ſhamefull
   marke
Of baſtard ſonne in baſtard ſhape deſcryed.
   Better, fare better, vngyuen were his lyfe,
Than geuen ſo.   For nature iuſt enuyed
   Her gyft to hym, and cropd wyth mayming
   knyfe
His limmes, to wreake her ſpyte on parentes
   ſinne ;
   Which, if ſhe ſpare vnwares ſo many ſcapes
As wycked world to breede wil neuer linne,
   Theyr liues declare theyr maims ſaued from
   their ſhapes,
Scorchd in theyr mindes.   O cruel priuye mayme
   That feſtreth ſtyll ! O vnrecured ſore !

a tiger chauderon". What is chaudron

Where thothers quiting wyth theyr bodyes fhame
  Theyr parentes guilt, oft linger not their lyues
In lothed fhapes, but naked flye to fkyes.—
  As this may do, whofe forme tofore thine eyes
Through want thou feeft, a monftrous vglye fhape,
Whom frendly world to finne doth terme a fcape.

On Tuyfday being the xxi day of Apryll, in
this yeare of our Lorde God a thoufand fyue
hundred thre fcore and two, there was borne a
man-childe of this maymed forme at Muche
Horkefley in Effex, a village about thre myles
from Colchefter, betwene a naturall father and a
naturall mother, hauing neyther hande, foote,
legge, nor arme, but on the left fyde it hath a
ftumpe growynge out of the fhoulder, and the
ende thereof is rounde, and not fo long as it fhould
go to the elbowe ; and on the ryghte fyde no mencion of any thing where any arme fhould be, but
a litel ftumpe of one ynche in length ; alfo on the
left buttocke there is a ftumpe comming out of
the length of the thygh almoft to the knee, and
round at the ende, and groweth fomething ouerthwart towardes the place where the ryght legge
fhould be, and where the ryghte legge fhould be,
there is no mencion of anye legge or ftumpe.
Alfo it hath a codde and ftones, but no yearde,
but a lytell hole for the water to iffue out.
Finallye, it hath by eftimation no tounge, by
reafon whereof it fucketh not, but is fuccoured
wyth liquide fubftaunce put into the mouth by
droppes, and nowe begynneth to feede wyth
pappe, beyng very well fauoured, and of good
and cheareful face.

⁅ The aforefayde Anthony Smyth of Much
Horkefley, hufbandman, and his wyfe, were both
maryed to others before, and haue had dyuers
chyldren, but this deformed childe is the fyrſt
that the fayd Anthony and his wyfe had betwene
them two ; it is a man chylde.   This chylde was
begot out of matrimony, but borne in matri-
monye ; and at the makynge hereof was liuing,
and like to continue.

⁅ Imprinted at London in Fleteſtrete nere
to S. Dunſtons Church, by
Thomas Marſhe.

A newe Ballade.

DERE Lady Elyfabeth, which art
our right and vertous Quene,
God hath endued the wᵗ mercy and
fayth, as by thy workes it may
be fene,
Wherefore, good Quene, I counfayle thee, Lady,
Lady,
For to beware of the fpiritualtie, moſt dere
Lady.

Haue you not rede of your progenitours, which
was before you many a yere,
How they endured many ſharpe ſhowers, as
by the cronicles it doth appere,

And many of them came to euell hap, Lady, Lady,
  And all was through the forked cap, moſt dere
  Lady ?

ℂ Haue you nat rede of Wyllyam Rufus the
  ſecond kyng hereof that name,
How he was ſlayne moſte maruelous, all through
  the curſſed ſeede of Caine ?
Tyrell kyllede hym with an arrowe, Lady, Lady,
  Yet ſome men ſayed he ſhot at a ſparow, moſte
  dere Lady.

ℂ Haue you not rede of good kyng John, how
  by them he was vndone ?
The Biſhop of Canterbury, yᵉ wicked man, ac-
  cuſed him to the court of Rome ;
They enterdyted his lande as the cronicle ſayeth,
  Lady, Lady,
  A monke poyſoned him to his death, moſte
  dere Lady.

ℂ Haue you not rede of the ſecond Richard,
  who was the black princes ſonne,
How they handled him full hard, and famiſhed
  him till lyfe was donne ?
In Powles they made him a funerall, Lady, Lady,
  To blinde the peoples eyes withall, mooſte dere
  Lady.

ℂ Haue you not rede of the ſixt Henry, which
  was a good and a ſimple man ?
The Cardinall of Wyncheſter truly made him
  loſe that hys father wanne,
The good Proteƈtor his vncle dere, Lady, Lady,
  The prieſtes kept war with him a longe yere,
  moſte dere Lady.

❡ Then came your father, King Henry y^e. viii.
    which was a prince of victory,
    And he depofed them all ftraight, when he had
      fpyed their idolatry ;
If this be trewe, as trewe it was, Lady, Lady,
    God graunt your grace may do no leffe, moft
    dere Lady.

❡ Then came your brother King Edward, which
    was a good and vertuous child,
    And to God's word he had regarde, but the
    wicked prieftes hath hym begilde,
And rayfed vp trentalles in euery place, Lady,
    Lady,
    And fome of them preached agaynft his Grace,
    moft dere Lady.

❡ Then came your fyfter Quene Mary, and for
    fiue yeres that fhe did rayne,
    All that was done (by) Edward and Hary her
    wicked prieftes made it but vaine ;
They brought in agayne the Romyfhe lore, Lady,
    Lady,
    Whiche was banifhed longe before, mofte dere
    Lady.

❡ Then God fent vs your noble Grace, as in dede
    it was highe tyme,
    Whiche dothe all Popery cleane deface, and
    fet vs forth God's trewe deuine,—
For whome we are all bound to praye, Lady,
    Lady,
    Longe life to raigne bothe night and day, mofte
    dere Ladye.

    Finis.   quod R. M.

The Pope in his fury doth anfwer returne
To a letter y^e which to Rome is late come.

DOE efteme your kyndnes much
   For fendyng worde fo fone,
   Your diligence it hath ben fuch,
     It is ariued at Rome :
But when I had pervfd your byl,
In that you fet thereto your wyl,
And eke your mynd applyed vntyl
   The writyng of the fame;·
I did beleue it to be true ;
But furely I muft fay to you,
It greued mee thofe lines to vew
   Were written in your name.

❡ And fure it is no maruell, loe !
   For daylye I doe heare,
The matter femeth to be fo,
   As amply doth appeare;
For euery man doth tell for true
The fame that late was fent of you,
But, out alas ! your tidynges new:
   Doth much appall my fpirite,
And makes me fweare and makes me teare,
To pull and hale, and rend my heare,
And brynges me dayly in difpaire
   To thinke on this defpite.

❡ But fith there is no remedye
   That mine obedient chylde

Is hanged vp vpon a tree,
  And to-to much reuylde :
What fhoulde I doe but curfe and ban,
And hurte them toe the worft I can,
For hanging vp fo good a man
  That bare mee fuch good wyll ?
But yf I had him here at Rome,
His body fhould be fhryued foone,
And maffe at mornyng and at noone,
  With chantyng of each bell,

℣ For euer fhoulde be fayd and foung
  The deuyls to controvle,
And prayers all aboute his tombe
  With fenceyng for his foule :
That neuer a deuyll fo deepe in hell
Shoulde once prefume with him to mell,
For once approch his body tyll
  To vexe him any way,
And I wolde kepe his body fo,
That it from hence fhould neuer go,
And dyuers of my fryers mo
  For him fhould dayly pray.

℣ And gladly wolde I be reuengd
  On England, yf I might,
Becaufe they haue toe much abufd
  My Bull with great defpight :
And make thereat a laughing game,
And fet but little by my name,
And much my holynes defame,
  And dayly me difpyfe.
Their queene hath chaft the rebels all
That loued to bow their knees to Ball,
And hanged their quarters on the wall
  As meat for crowes and pyes.

❡ But I wyll walke and dayly feke
    My purgatorie thorow,
And caufe all the deuyls at my becke
    To me their knees to bow :
And whereas I may any fynde
That to their prince haue ben vnkynde,
Be fure, with mee they fhall be fhrynde
    As they deferued haue.
And cheefly now John Felton hee
Shall euer be beloued of mee,
Becaufe that he fo louinglye
    My Bull did feeme to faue.

❡ But yf that I coulde haue at once
    The paryng of his toe,
His head, his quarters, or his bones,
    That with the wynde doe bloe :
Then fhoulde they be layd vp by mee
As reliques of great dignitie,
For euery man that comes to fee
    Thofe jewels of fuch grace.
The Nortons' bones fhould be fo fhrynd
That now hanges wauering in the wynd,
Yf that I coulde deuyfe or fynd
    To bryng them to this place.

❡ And I wyll curfe and ban them all
    That fpeake againft my powre,
And feekes to make my kyngdome fall,
    My curfe fhall them deuowre :
And yf that here I might you fee,
For wrytyng lately vnto mee,
Be fure, ye fhould rewarded bee
    As beft I coulde bethynke.
And as for Wylliam Elderton
That lately fent me worde to Rome,

Be fure that he fhould haue lyke dome
To bye him pen and ynke.

❡ Take this as written from our grace
That vnto you we fend,
Becaufe we want both time and place
To recompence you, frend :
As for the boyes that frump and fcoff,
And at my holynes doe laugh,
I mynd to dreffe them wel enough,
Yf cafe I had them here.
And for my feruants that abyde,
And long haue had their pacience tryde,
From Romaine faith that wyl not flyde,
I wyfh them all good chere.

❡ Finis.   S. P.

❡ Imprinted by Alexander Lacie for Henrie
Kyrkham, dwelling at the figne of the Blacke
Boy at the middle North dore of Paules
Church.

Lines underneath a Portrait of Queen
Elizabeth.

LOE here the pearle,
    Whom God and man doth loue :
Loe here on earth
    The onely ftarre of light :
Loe here the queene,
    Whom no mifhap can moue

To chaunge her mynde
From vertues chief delight !
Loe here the heart
That fo hath honord God,
That, for her loue,
We feele not of his rod :
Pray for her health,
Such as good fubiectes bee :
Oh Princely Dame,
There is none like to thee !

*Ane new Ballet fet out be ane fugitiue Scottif-
man that fled out of Paris at this
lait Murther.* ʃʃ ßaʊʃʃ ɾ auuʊ

OW Katherine de Medicis hes maid
fic a gyis,
To tary in Paris the papiftes ar
tykit,
At Baftianes brydell howbeit fcho denyis,
Giue Mary flew Hary, it was not vnlykit ;
ʒit a man is nane refpectand this number,
I dar not fay wemen hes wyte of this cummer.

ʒone mafk the Quene Mother hes maid thame in
France,
Was maikles and faikles, and fchamfully flane,
Bot Mary conuoyit and come with ane dance,
Quhill princes in fences was fyrit with ane trane ;
Baith treffonabill murtheris the ane and the vther,
I go not in mafking mair with the Quene Mother.

¶ Italianes ar tyranis, and treſſonabill tratoris ;
    For gyſours, deuyſours, the Guyſianis ar gude ;
Bot Frenche men ar trew men, and not of thair
     natouris ;
    Than, Charlie, I farlie thow drank thy awin
     blude,
I wyte bot thy mother wit, wemen ar vane,
In greis neir to Ganzelon, nor grit Charlie Mane.

¶ Thy ſtyle was Treſchriſtien, maiſt Criſten
    King,
    Baith hieſt and frieſt, and neiſt the impyre ;
Bot now Proueſt Marſchell in playing this ſpring,
    And reſſoun for treſſoun prouokis God to ire ;
Beleuis thow this trumprie ſall ſtabliſche thy
    ſtyle ?
Our God is not deed, ʒit be doand ane quhyle.

¶ Suppois that the Papiſtes deuyſit this at Trent,
    To ding vs and bring vs with mony lowd
     lauchter,
With ſic cruell murther is Chriſt ſa content,
    To take the and make the ane Sanct for our
     ſlauchter ?
Albeit he correct vs, and ſcurge vs in ire,
Be war with the wand ſyne he wapis in the fyre.

¶ For better is pure men nor princes periurit,
    Baith ſchameles and fameles, we find thame ſa
     fals ;
With ſangis lyke the ſeryne our lyfis thow
     allurit ;
    Ouirſylit vs, begylit vs, with baitis in our hals ;
Or as the fals fowler, his fang for to get,
Deuoiris the pure volatill he wylis to the net.

❡ In Ilis nor in Orknay, in Ireland Oneill,
   Thay dar not, thay gar not thair lieges be
   ftickit :
Solyman, Tamerlan, nor yit the mekle Deill,
   Proud Pharao, nor Nero, was neuer fa wickit ;
Nouther Turk nor Infidell vfis fic thing,
As be their awin burreo, being ane king.

❡ Baith auld men and wemen, with babis on thair
   breift,
   Not luking nor huking, to hurll thame in
   Sane,
All beand murdreift downe, quhat do ʒe neift ?
   Proceffioun, confeffion, and vp Mes agane ;
Proud King Antiochus was fum tyme als haly,
And yet our God gufchit out the guttis of his
   belly.

Thy fyfter thou maryit, thy faces was four,
   Sic cuikrie for luikrie was euill interprifit ;
ʒe maid vs the Reid Freiris, and rais in an hour,
   Abhorring na gorring that micht be deuifit ;
Thou playit the fals hypocreit fenzeing the fray,
But inwart ane rageing wolf waitand thy pray.

That France was confidderat with Scotland I grant,
   Baith aftit, contraftit and keipit in deid ;
The kyndnes of cutthrottis we cure not to want,
   Denyis thame, defyis thame, and al thair fals feid ;
It was bot with honeft men we maid the band,
And thou hes left leifand bot few in that land.

Our faith is not warldly, we feir not thy braulis,
   Thocht hangmen ouirgang men, for gaddaring
   our geir ;

ʒe kill bot the carcafe, ʒe get not our faulis,
   Not douting our fhouting is hard in Goddis eir;
The fame God from Pharo defendit his pepill,
And not ʒone round Robene that ftandis in ʒour
   ftepill.

❡ Now, wyfe Quene Elizabeth, luik to yourfelf,
   Difpite them, and wryte thame ane bill of de-
      fyance ;
The Papiftis and Spanʒards hes partit ʒour pelf,
   As newly and trewly was tald me thir tythance ;
Beleue thay to land heir, and get vs for nocht,
Will ʒe do as we do, it fal be deir bocht.

Giue pleis God we gre fa, and hald vs togidder,
   Baith furely and fturely, and ftoutly gainftand
      thame ;
They culd not weill conqueis vs, culd ʒe confidder,
   For our men are dour men, and likis weill to
      land thame ;
Quhen Cefar himfelf was chaift, haue ʒe forʒet,
And baith the realmes be aggreit, tak that thay
   get.

❡ For better it is to fecht it, defendant our lyfis,
   With fpeir men and weir men, and ventour our
      fellis,
Nor for to fe Frenchemen deflorand our wyfis,
   Difplace vs, and chace vs, as thay haue done ellis ;
I meane quhen the Inglifmen helpit at Leith,
And gart thame gang hame agane fpyte of thair
   teith.

❡ I cannot trow firmely that Frenchmen ar cummen,
   Perfayfand thame haifand thamefelfis into
      parrell ;

The Lord faue Elizabeth, thair ane gude woman,
  That cauldly and bauldly debait will our
    quarrell
With men and with money, baith armour and graith,
As fcho hes befoir tyme defendit this Faith.

Thocht France for thair falfet be drownit in
    dangeris,
  For caufis and paufis thay plait into Pareis,
ʒit we ar in war eſtait, waitand on ſtrangeris,
  Not gyding, deuyding our awin men from
    Mareis ;
So weid the calf from the corn, calk me thair dures,
And flay or ʒe be flane, gif fic thing occures.

Bot how can ʒe traiſt thame that trumpit ʒow ellis,
  Decoir thame, do for thame, or foſter thair feid ;
And thay may anis fe thair time, tent to ʒour-
    -fellis,
  Baith haitfull, diſſaitfull, ʒe deill with in deid ;
Anis wod and ay the war, wit quhat ʒe do,
And mak thame faſt in the ruit gif thay cum to.

❡ God blis ʒow, my brether, and biddis ʒow gud
    nicht,
  Obey God, go fay God, with prayer and faſting,
Chriſt keip this pure ile of ouris in the auld richt,
  Defend vs and fend vs the life euerlaſting ;
The Lord fend vs quyetnes, and keip our ʒoung
    king,
The Quene of Inglands Maieſtie, and lang mot
    thai ring.

    ❡ Finis, quod Simpell.

  ❡ Imprintit at Sanctandrois, be Robert
    Lekpriuik.   Anno Do. 1572.

A proper New Balad of the Bryber Gehefie.

Taken out of the fourth booke of Kinges, the v.
chapter ; to the tune of Kynge Salomon.

AS not the bryber Gehezie
     Rewarded iuftly of the Lord,
  Which for example verelie,
     The Holie Scripture doth recorde ?
If this be true, as true it was,
     Of his rewarde,
Why fhould not Chriftan men, alas,
     Than haue regarde ?

When that the prophet Elizae
     Had clenfed from the leprofie
Naaman of Affiria,
     Thorow the workes of God on hye,
Then Naaman wolde him conftraine
     To take rewarde ;
But Elizae from that refrainde,
     And had regarde.

But Gehezie of falfehed minde,
     When Naaman did paffe awaie,
Did hie him fafte that was behinde,
     And unto Naaman did faie,—
Beholde, my mafter hath me fente
     For a rewarde ;
To prophetes children he is bente
     To haue regarde.

With right good will, faid Naaman,
  Him to rewarde and did proceede ;
And Gehezie conuaide it then
  So preuilie in verie deede,
Forgetting that the prophete tho
  Of his rewarde
Could, by the fprite of God, it knowe,
  And haue regarde.

Alas, how was thou, Gehezie,
  Rauifhed in worldly gaine !
How was thou brought to mizerie,
  Of God appointed for thy paine,
And all thy ofspringe after thee,
  For thy rewarde !
The Lorde that hateth briberie
  Hath his regarde.

Then Gehezie deceitfulie,
  To-fore the prophet tooke his waie,
Who faid to hime, O Gehezie,
  Went not my harte with thee, I faie,
When Naaman from charret came
  Thee to rewarde,
And thou haft falfelie hid the fame,
  Without regarde ?

Gehezie, is it now a time
  Thy bribes (he faid) for to receaue ?
Beholde, for this thy wicked crime
  That leprofeie to thee fhall cleaue,
The which was vpon Naaman,
  For thy rewarde,
And to thy feede thee after than,
  To haue regarde.
  .

Incontinent then Gehezie
　Departed from his prefence fo,
As the Texte doth verefie,
　A leper white as is the fnowe;
Example to fuch bribers all,
　　To haue regarde;
With Gehezie at lengthe they fhall
　　Haue their rewarde.

If they doe not their faultes confeffe,
　Detefting of their bryberie,
Elfe God will fpie ther wickedneffe,
　Though they it cloke with Gehezie;
And can them paie accordinglie
　　The like rewarde,
As he hath done to Gehezie;
　　O haue regarde!

The Lord he is that fame God ftill
　That he was than vndoubtedlie;
Such Gehezies he punifh will,
　That bribes receiue fo wickedlie,
Though they fo preuilie do hide
　　Their falfe rewarde;
Yet of the Lorde it will be fpide,
　　Who hath regarde.

O Lorde, vs guide in all our waies,
　That we may leade our liues aright;
To deale with trueth at all affaies,
　Giue vnto us thy Holie Sprite;
And that our Queene and her Councell
　　Maie haue regarde,
In this lande bribers to expell
　　That take rewarde.

.

❡ Finis, quod George Mell.

Imprinted at London, in Flete Streate,
beneath the Conduit, at the figne
of S. John Evangelift, by
Thomas Colwell.

❡ *The fhape of ii monfters, M D lxii.*

THIS prefent yere of oure Lord God a
thoufande fiue hundred thre fcore and
two, one Marke Finkle, a joiner, dwelling befide Charing Croffe by Weft-
minfter, had a fow that brought forth one pigge
onely, vpon the feuenth of Maye, beinge Afcen-
tion daye, the whiche pigge had a head muche
lyke vnto a dolphines head, with the left eare
ftanding vp forked, and the right eare being like
as it were halfe a litle leafe, being deuided in the
middes, fharpe toward thend, lying downward flat
to the head, without any holes into the headward.
The two fore feet, like vnto handes, eche hande
hauinge thre long fingers and a thumbe, bothe the
thumbes growinge on the outfides of the handes,
the hinder legges growing very much backwarde
otherwife then the common natural forme hath
ben feen, beeing of no good fhape, but fmaller
from the body to the middle joint then they be
from the fame joint toward the foot. And the

taile growing an inche neare vnto the back then
it doth of any that is of right fhape.

Thefe ftraunge fights the Allmighty God
fendeth vnto vs, that we fhould not be forgetfull
of his mighty power, nor vnthankful for his fo
greate mercies ; the which hee fheweth fpecially by
geuing vnto vs his holy word, wherby our liues
ought to be guided, and alfo his wonderful
tokens wherby we are moft gentilly warned.

But if we will not be warned, neither by his
word, nor yet by his wonderful workes, then let vs
be affured that thefe ftraunge monftruous fightes
doe premonftrate vnto vs that his heauy indigna-
cion wyl fhortly come vpon vs for our monftruous
lyuinge. Wherfore let vs earneftly pray vnto
God that he wyl geue vs grace earneftly to repent our wickednes, faithfully to beleue his word,
and fincerely to frame our liues after the doctrine
of the fame.

❧ *An Admonition vnto the Reader.*

ET vs knowe by thefe vgly fights,
And eke confider well,
That our God is the Lord of mights,
Who rules both heauen and hell.

By whofe ftrong hand thefe monfters here
Were formed as ye fee,
That it mighte to the world appere,
Almightie him to bee.

Who might alfo vs men haue formde
  After a ftraunge deuife,
As by the childe of late deformde,
  Appeareth in plaine wife.

What might thefe monfters to vs teache,
  Which now are fent fo rife,
But that we haue Goddes wurd well preacht,
  And will not mend our life ?

At which ftraunge fightes we meruel muche,
  When that we doe them fee ;
Yet can there not be found one fuche,
  That fo will warned bee.

And loke what great deformitie
  In bodies ye beholde ;
Much more is in our mindes truly,
  An hundreth thoufand folde.

So that we haue great caufe in deede,
  Our finnes for to confeffe,
And eke to call to God with fpeede,
  The fame for to redreffe.

Which if we wyl not fayle to doo,
  And purely to repent,
He wyl, no doubt, vs comfort fo,
  As fhal our foules contente.

Now fith our God fo louing is,
  And ready to forgeue,
Why doe we not abhorre all vice,
  And only to him cleaue ?

Sith he alſo his hande can ſhake,
  And ſone deſtroy vs all,
Why doe we not then feare and quake,
  And downe before him fall?

Why doe we not amend, I ſaye,
  Either for loue or feare?
Why driue we of from day to daye,
  And ſinning not forbeare?

Good lawes of late renewde wee ſee,
  Much ſinne for to ſuppreſſe ;
God graunt that they fulfilde maye bee,
  To ouerthrow exceſſe."

O Lord, graunt vs alſo thy grace,
  That, by repentance pure,
In heauen to haue a dwelling place,
  For euer to endure.

Amen, quod W. F.

℃ Imprinted at London, at the Long Shop
  in the Pultry, by John Alde.

Ane Complaint vpon Fortoun.

INCONSTANT warld, fragill and friuolus,
  With feinȝeit Fortoun, quha con-
  fides in the
Sall find his lyfe cairfull and cruellus,
  Led in this vale of wofull miferie ;
Quhat potent princes in profperitie,
  Hes fho depofd from their imperiall places !
Hir craft quotidian we may cleirly fe,
  As men in mirrouris may behauld their faces.

The worthie Bocas, in his morall buke,
  The Fall of Princes plainly dois compyle ;
Amangs them all quha euer lykes to luke,
  Sall finde Dame Fortounis fauour for a quhyle ;
For with the one eye fho can lauch and fmyle,
  And with the vther lurke and play the loun ;
Sum to promotioun, and fome to plaine exile,
  Lyke draw-well bukkets dowkand vp and doun.

⦅ That variable witch makis all the warld ado !
  Quhat kingis and countreis hes fho brocht to end !
Affyrians, Perfians, Grekes, and Romains to,
  The monarches foure micht not hir force defend.
Bulworkis nor battellis bydis her nocht a bend ;
  Quha may withftand her ftraik, quhan fho lift
  ftryke ?
This nicht aneuch, the morne nathing to fpend ! .
  Imago in Luna, and fho lukis baith alyke.

E

To pen the fpeciallis it paffis mony a hunder,
    And makis the tyme ouer tidious to declare ;
Sum fho promouis and fum fho puttis to vnder,
    And fum rewardes with wandring heir and thair ;
And fum incaftrat captiues in the fnair,
    And fum for flatrie dois hir freindfhip find ;
To all eftates vntruethfull, quhat fould mair,
    Turnand her volt lyke woddercok in wind?

To paint her out it paffis mine ingyne,
    How wonderfully fhe wirkes in all thir thingis!
Sum fra thair birth brocht vp with doggis and
        fwine,
    Tane fra the pleuch and placit in fait of kingis.
The brutell beift ane barbour wolfe vpbringis
    The firft borne Romain callit Romulus,
Quhais blude as ʒit into that regioun ringis,
    By expeᵭatioun of auld Amelius.

Cyrus ficlyke was be ane bitche vpbrocht,   ·
    Cround as a king ane cruell man of weir.
Pareis in Troy that all the toun forthocht,
    Preferuit from flauchter be fouking of a beir.
And fwa was Thylaphus with ane hinde, I heir,
    Medas with imates and maid ane michtie prince ;
Plato with beis quha did fic prudence leir,
    That all men meruelled of his eloquence.

Without refpeᵭ to blude royall or clan,
    Pureanis promouit that na man wald prefume ;
Torquinius Prifcus, a baneift marchant man,
    Chaift out of Corinth and cround a king in
        Rome.
Siclyke was Seruius from ane fhipherd grome,
    And Tullus Hoftilius fand her fauour neift ;
Is, was, and falbe quhill the day of dome,
    Sic doubill dealing in Dame Fortounis breift !

Quha findis hir freindſhip of fauour hes aneuch,
  To warldly glore ſho gydes them all the gait ;
Tuke ſho not Gordias from the ſpaid and pleuch,
  And quickly placit him in a princes ſait?
How far may Darius bragge of her debait,
  Tane fra the ſtabil ouer Perſia to ring ;
Pure Agathocles from a law eſtait,
  Ane potteris boy to be ane potent King ?

Of Juſtine the ſuinehird ſho maid ane empriour,
  Ouer Conſtantinople ane king and cround him
    thair ;
Gyges the gait-hird ane michtie conquerour,
  To Lydia land ſhe maid him lord and aire ;
And Wallancianus from his landwart fair,
  Tane fra the pleuch to place imperiall ;
Cambyſes, Nero, be the contrair clair,
  Was thair awin burreois to thair buriall.

Sa Fortoun mountit neuer man ſa hie,
  Foſtered with folie,ſuppoſe ſhe make them faine;
Bot with ane tit ſho turnis the quheill, ȝe ſie,
  Doun gois their heid, vp gois their heillis againe !
Of Alexander to write I war bot vaine,
  Ouer fifty landis he lord was at the leiſt ;
ȝit threttie dayis lay efter he was ſlaine,
  Unbureit in Babell lyke a brutell beiſt.

Xerxes, quhoſe armeis maid the riueris dry,
  And ſchippis ſubumbragit all the ſeyis on breid,
Did ſho not wait him with ſic foule inuy,
  Pray to Pericles, that put him to his ſpeid ?
Of Julius Ceſar gif thow lykes to reid,
  In his triumphant toun victorious,
Slaine be his Senatis, ſchamefully in deid,
  By his awin kinſmen Brutus and Caſſus

Sum auld examples heir I man induce,
   To bring my purpofe to more fpeciall;
Quha was mair worthie git I wald make rufe,
   More ftout, more trew, nor hardy Hanniball?
Dauter of Romaines, to Carthage ane caftell
    wall,
The onely thing quhairin he maift reioyfit;
Do quhar he docht in deidis marciall,
   By his awin pepill petioufly depofed.

Siclyke was Sipio, faiklefly fchot furth,
   That vinqueift Hanniball lyke a warriour wicht,
His vailiant workes was weyit bot litils worth,
   Quhen he was baneift with a bair gude nicht;
Not lyke a captaine, nor a kindly knicht,
   Bot lyke ane beggar baneift in exile;
Sa Fortoun montit neuer man on hicht,
   Bot fho can law him within a litill quhyle.

Alchebead of Athenis was Duke,
   Of princely parents and ane royall race,
To keip his toun fic trauell undertuke,
   He maid his fo-men fle befoir his face;
To his rewarde he gat nane vther grace,
   Ingraitly baneift to their awin grit fkaith:
And Tymiftocles in that famin place,
   By their awin burgeffis thay wer baneift baith.

Experience teiches me not to flyte with Fortoun,
   With auld examples that dois na thing belang vs;
Marke James of Dowglas prefent Erle of Morton,
   Ane of the beft that euer was borne amang vs;
Danter of theuis that dayly dois ouer-gang vs,
   Key of this countre that kepit vs from fkaith;
I fpeik na farther in feir thay fould gar hang vs,
   Preichouris and poiettis are put to filence baith.

Few things wer done bot Mortoun interprifit them,
  Dumbar and Brichane and mony vthair bloke ;
Speik·quhat thay pleis, he wrocht them and deuifit
    them ;
He and his freindis ay formeſt in the flocke ;
He faucht ʒour querrell as kein as ony cok,
  Reuengit ʒour murthers ma nor twa or thrie ;
Ane nobillman and of ane ancient ſtoke,
  His valiant deidis demereitis not to die.

⁋ Ane of the ſpeciallis did mentene ʒour croun,
  ʒour ferme proteƈtour in ʒour tender ʒeiris ;
He maid ʒow vp and all ʒour fo-men doun,
  His marciall manheid did mentein ʒour weiris ;
Gif he did wrang, rewarde him as effeiris,
  Gif he did gud, God wald he ſould be tret ;
Bot as the prouerbe ſpeikis, it plaine appeiris,
  Auld men will die and barnes will ſone forʒet.

Was he not rewler ouer ʒour realme and
    rigioun,
  Quhill all was pacifeit be his prudent wit ?
Stude he not ſtoutly be the true religioun,
  Ane of the firſt that maid the freiris to flit ?
Franke on the feildis, and formeſt at the bit,
  Without refpeƈt to baggis or bodie to ;
ʒour faithfull fubieƈt, and fua he fal be ʒit,
  To do gude feruice, as I haue feene him do.

Than at Carbarrie hill he held a day,
  With litill bludeſhed Bothwell was put a-bake,
Quha ſlew ʒour father and fibilly fled away,
  Syne focht ʒourſelfe to bring this realme to ſake.
How mony clawbackes than ſuppofe thay crak,
  Conuenit with Mortoun quhan Bothwel tuk the
    chafe ?

Try or ʒe tine him and trow not all thay ſpak,
  Lat workes beir witnes, vaine wordis ſould haue
  na place.

Sone efter that the Counſell cround ʒourſell,
  Quhan godly Murray as a regent rang,
ʒit thair was ſome that bauldly did rebell,
  That to ʒour lawis wald nouther ryde nor
  gang.
Quha thair conuenit for to reuenge ʒour wrang,
  Albeit ʒour action was thocht innocent?
It was the Dowglaſſis douchtaly them dang,
  And pleit ʒour proces in that parliament.

Quha could declare our langſum lyfe in Leith,
  Fechtand all day and ſyne lay in our clais?
Gif Lindeſay lykes, that lord can tell ʒow eith,
  Quha was ʒour friendis or quha ʒour mortall fais,
Or quha gaid formeſt breiſtand vp the braies.
  I dar not pen the ſpeciallis, I do plaine ʒow;
Bot weill I wait, howeuer the warld now gais,
  Thai find maiſt freindſhip was fardeſt than again
  ʒou.

Syne at Langſyde feild ʒour grace may ken,
  Mortoun was thair ane man amang the reſt ;
In Striuiling toun, out of his dowie den,
  Maiſt lyke a fox thay ſyrit him in his neſt.
In Edinburgh Caſtell quhair thay war poſſeſt,
  He them deplaced that purpoſit to undo ʒow.
Quhan ʒe grow auld, I wait ʒe will confeſt,
  Mortoun hes bene ane faithfull ſaruand to ʒow.

Quhan Regentis deit and all the lytes inlaikit,
  The Counſell did conuene and ſet ane day ;

Thay cheifit him Regent in that rowme that waikit,
  With fad adwife, for few or nane faid nay ;
Bot ʒit I think thay playit ʒour grace foule play,
  Gif he was knawin than of thir crymes conuiƈt,
Gif he be faikles, furely I dar fay, .
  Thay haue defamit him with ane fulich trick.

To dant the theuis had he nocht mekill ado,
  Abandoned the borders that na man durft rebell?
The Armeftrangis, Eluottis and the Johneftons to,
  With twentie vther clans I can not tell,—
During his dayis thai durft not ryde ane ell ;
  The hirdis and hinde men in their labeis lay ;
Bot thair eftait, as now ʒe fie ʒourfell,
  All nicht to walke and fane to wirk all day.

Aganis grit lordis committing fmall offence,
  With iniuft challenge thay aucht na man to
    cheffoun ;
Mortoun hes ay bene vpricht with his prince,
  But fpot of cryme or ony point of treffoun.
Albeit gude faruice be not tane in feafoun,
  His workes may witnes he neuer fparit for
    perrell ;
Laitly accufit but outher ryme or reffoun,
  As findrie fchawis me for a faikles querrell.

Daft fulis defyis him becaufe thay finde him fage,
  And cowartis contrarious for his hardiment ;
Young men for glaikrie can not agrie with age,
  And waifteris inuyis him for his gouernement.
And facreit counfell can not be content
  To fuffer lorfhippis in equalitie ;
ʒit I befeik ʒour grace of gude intent,
  To play the prince but parcialitie.

Adwife ʒow weill, fen he hes not offendit ;
   To keip fic fenattis it fall decore ʒour land ;
Of rafche detreitis cums rew and may not
      mend it,
   As Scottifmens wifdome dois behinde the hand.
Wyfe lordis are ill ta make I vnderftand,
   And trewly in kingis is to abhorre ;
This fempill counfall, fyr, is na command,
   Bot wald to God that na man louit ʒow war.

FINIS, quod Sempill.

Imprintit at Edinburgh, be Robert Lekprewicke,
dwelling at the Netherbow.

The Plagues of Northomberland.

To the tune of Appelles.

HEN that the Moone, in Northom-
berlañd,
   Afterthechaynge, inage wellconne,
Did rife with force, then to withftande
The lyght and bright beames of the Sonne,
   The forowfull dolers foone began,
   Through Percies pryde, to many a man.

But then anone, the Weftmere Bull
   Behelde the ryfinge of this Moone ;
Thinking that fhee had byn at full,
   He haftyd then anone full foone,
With horfe and armes, and all his might,
From parfeᵈt daye to vncertaine lyght.

When they in one confent were pyght,
  With them was many an ignorant man ;
The Romyfhe lawes they wold redyght,
  Through councell of fome blind Syr John,
Who neuer knewe Godes veryte,
But to rebellion then dyd agree.

For if they would of Gods word knowen,
  Longe xxx yeres they haue had tyme,
Rebellion then had not byn fowen,
  To brynge ther countre in fuch cryme ;
Their poyfon now, all men may fee,
That vnder fuger longe did lie.

What myfchyfe mouid the Perfies hart,
  This enterpryfe to take in hand,
This for to playe a Rebelles parte,
  In raifinge vp Northomberland ?
But looke, what feede by hym is fowen,
With fharp fythes downe it was foone mowen.

❡ That countre is in full fore plyght
  That doth agaynft their prynce contend,
Seeking their owne dreames to redyght,
  The Popes precepts for to defend,
Lyke brutyfhe, peruerft, ignorant men,
That feekes before a lawe to ren.

❡ This venym longe a-breedinge was,
  Which in the Perfies brefte did growe ;
The Bull in bellinge did not ceaffe,
  Till that the poyfon oute did flowe ;
So farr abroade the ftreames did ronne,
That backe agayne cold not retourne.

❡ This hatefull poyſon longe was hyde,
  Under the cloake of amytie;
The outward treaſone was not ſpyde,
  But couerid with all courteſie;
Their cloſe vnlawfull conſpiracion
Hath brought them to great dyſolacion.

❡ The hope vnſure was tranſytorye,
  The which was in that clowdy Moone;
Her falſe eclypes with all the glorye,
  Her ioye vnſtable was endid ſoone;
Her ſudden chaynge now tells vs all
That ſuger ſweet was blent with gall.

❡ What ſtate now maye hymſelfe aſſure
  Longe here to lyue in quyetnes?
What worldely ioye maye here indure,
  In thoſe where is no ſtablenes?
Wher lords and yerles in welth doth flowe,
From their hye ſtate muſt fall downe lowe.

❡ Now by their fall learne to be wyſe,
  Both hye and lowe in eche degree;
Let no falſe lyght deceaue your eyes,
  As it hath done of late, you ſee.
The falſe beames of the glyſtringe Moone,
Now many a man it hath vndoone.

❡ For in the north ſhe did ſhine longe,
  But now eclypſyd is her lyght;
The Weſtmere Bull that held ſo ſtronge,
  Hee is depreuyd of his myght;
For many tongs of them will tell,
How theſe to yerles falſe did rebell.

And many a man more, as I heare,
 That with thefe rebelles did take part,
Which can not thinke themfelues now cleare,
 That in breft beares a doble hart ;
But as you haue begonne to brewe,
So are you found rebelles vntrue !

℣ The countre cleane you haue vndone ;
 The Lord graunt ther fome better ftaye,
Or els will many a mothers fonne
 For this curfſe you another daye !
You leaue your wyues and childrene deare,
Lamentinge in moft wofull cheare.

℣ Now let vs praye, as we are bound,
 All for our Queenes hyghe maiefte,
That fhee her enemies may confound,
 And all that to rebelles agre ;
And plant true men vp in their place ;
The Lord from heauen now gyue her grace !

Finis, quod John Barker.

℣ Imprinted at London, in Fleete Streate, beneath
 the Conduyt, at the figne of Saint John
 Euangelift, by Thomas Colwell.

A merry new Song how a Bruer meant to make a Cooper cuckold, and how deere the Bruer paid for the bargaine.

To the tune of, In Somer time.

IF that you lift, now merry be,
Lend liftning eares a while to me,
To heare a fong of a Bruer bold,
That meant a Cooper to cuckold.

The Cooper walked downe the ftreete,
And with the Bruer chanc'd to meete:
He called,—Worke for a Cooper, dame;
The Bruer was glad to heare the fame.

Cooper, quoth the Bruer, come hether to me,
Perchance I haue fome worke for thee :
If that thy doings I doe well like,
Thou fhalt haue worke for all this weeke.

The Cooper with cap and curtefie low,
Said, ready I am my tunning to fhow;
To doe your worke, fir, euery deale.
I doe not doubt to doe it well.

Then, quoth this luftie Bruer tho,
If thou my worke doeft meane to doe,
Come to me to morrow before it be day,
To hoope vp thefe olde tubs out of the way.

And ſo to make vp my merry rime,
The Cooper the next day roſe betime ;
To the Bruers gate he tooke his race,
And knocked there a great pace.

The Bruer leapt from his bed to the flore,
And to the Cooper he opned the dore ;
He ſhewed him his worke without delay ;
To the Coopers wife then he tooke the way.

The Cooper he called at mind at laſt,
His hatchet he had left at home for haſt :
And home for his hatchet he muſt goe,
Before he could worke ; the cauſe it was ſo.

But when he came his houſe ſomwhat nere,
His wife by fortune did him heare :
Alas ! ſaid ſhe, what ſhift ſhall we make ?
My huſband is come,—you will be take !

O Lord ! ſayd the Bruer, what ſhall I doe ?
How ſhall I hide me ? where ſhall I goe ?
Said ſhee,—if you will not be eſpide,
Creepe vnder this fat yourſelfe to hide.

The Bruer he crept vnder the ſame,
And blundering in the Cooper came :
About the ſhop his tubs he caſt,
To finde out his hatchet all in haſt.

Then his curſt wife began to prate,—
If thou let out my pig, ile breake thy pate !
A pig, ſaid the Cooper, I knew of none ;
If thou hadſt not ſpoke, the pig had bin gone.

If it be a fow-pig, faid the Cooper,
Let me haue him rofted for my fupper:
It is a bore-pig, man, faid fhe,
For my owne dyet, and not for thee.

It is hard if a woman cannot haue a bit,
But ftraightway her hufband muft know of it.
A bore-pig, faid the Cooper, fo me thinks;
He is fo ramifh,—fie, how he ftinkes!

Well, fayd the Cooper, fo I might thriue,
I would he were in thy belly aliue.
I thanke you for your wifh, good man ;
It may chance it fhall be there anon.

The Bruer that vnder the fat did lye,
Like a pig did affay to grunt and crie :
But, alas! his voice was nothing fmall ;
He cryed fo big that he mard all.

Wife, faid the Cooper, this is no pig,
But an old hog, he grunteth fo big !
He lift vp the fat then by and by ;
There lay the Bruer like a bore in a ftie.

Wife, faid the Cooper, thou wilt lie like a dog !
This is no pig, but a very old hog :
I fweare, quoth the Cooper, I doe not like him ;
Ile knock him on the head ere ile keepe him.

O Lord! faid the Bruer, ferue me not fo ;
Hold thy hand, Cooper, and let me goe,
And I will giue thee both ale and beere,
To find thy houfe this fixe or feauen yeare.

I will none of thy ale nor yet of thy beere,
For feare I be poifoned within feauen yeere !
Why, fayd the Bruer, if thou miftruft,
Hold here the keyes of my beft cheft ;

And there is gold and filuer ftore,
Will ferue thee fo long and fomewhat more :
If there be ftore, quoth the Cooper, I fay,
I will not come emptie-handed away.

The Cooper went and filled his hat ;
The Bruer fhall pay for vfing my fat !
The hooping of twentie tubs euery day,
And not gaind me fo much as I doe this way.

When he came againe his houfe within,—
Packe away, quod he, Bruer, with your broken fhin ;
And vnder my fat creepe you no more,
Except you make wifer bargaines before.

x

The true defcription of a monfterous Chylde,
borne in the Ile of Wight, in this prefent yeare
of oure Lord God M D lxiiij. the month of
Octobber, after this forme, with a clufter of longe
heare about the nauell: the Fathers name is
James Johnfun, in the parys of Frefwater.

OR mercy, Lorde, with one accorde,
    To the we call and crye,
That fo doth fhow, in earth below,
    Thy wonderous workes daylye.

Within the rafe of fyue yeres fpace
   Moche monfterous fights hath byn,
Of fundry kynde; man, bare in mynde,
   And fone turne from thy fyn.

Repent and pray, amende, I fay,
   Leue of thy wicked wayes;
The tyme drawes on, thou muft be gone,
   Beholde this later dayes.

Of infans yonge, agone not longe,
   With calues and pigges which were,
The tookens, loo, mifhappen foo,
   Whiche cryeth to vs great feare.

Now this late fyght in Ile of Wight,
   Straungely it is to tell,
Two children borne,—neuer beforne
   Suche wonders there befell.

The one I fynde, of woman kynde,
   Hauyng her fhape all right;
The other is tranfpofed this,
   As pleafeth the Lorde of myght.

Where natures art doth not her part,
   In workyng of her fkylle,
To fhape aright, eche lyuely wight;
   Beholde, it is Gods wyll!

Loo, here you fee, before your eye,
   A man-childe to beholde;
A babe gyltles, deformyd this,
   Mofte wonderous to be tolde.

No caruer can, nor paynter then,
  The fhape more ugly make,
As itfelfe dothe declare the truthe ;
  A fyghte to make vs quake !

Let vs all feare, and in mynde beare,
  This forme fo monfterous :
That no hurt wraught, nor euill hath thaught,
  What fhall become of vs.

That doth ftill fyn, and neuer lyn,
  As men heapyng vp treafure,
Agyanft the day of wrath, for aye,
  Of Gods heauy difpleafure.

Nowe praye wee all, bothe great and fmall,
  Unto the Lorde of might,
To gyue vs grace in heauen a place
  There to attayne his fight !

All ye that dothe beholde and fee this monftrous
    fight fo ftraunge,
Let it to you a preachyng be, from fynfull lyfe
    to chaunge :
For in this latter dayes trulye, the Lord ftraunge
    fyghts doth fhowe,
By tokens in the heauens hye, and on the yearth
    belowe.
This dothe demonftrate to vs, the lyfe whiche we
    lyue in ;
A monfter, oughly to beholde, conceyued was in fyn :
In fhape vnparfett here to vewe, that nature hathe
    not dreft,
A chylde now borne, by porte mofte true, this
    from the mothers breft :

F

For he that doth this fhape beholde, and his owne
  ftate will knowe,
Will make the proude pecocke fo bolde, beare
  downe his tayll full lowe :
Nowe, Lorde, fende downe thy Holy Spryte, the
  confortor of joye,
For to direct owr wayes aright, to dwell with
  thee for aye ;
And graunt we maye amende our lyfe, accordyng
  to thy worde,
In euery age, bothe manne and wyfe,—nowe
  graunt vs this, good Lorde !

Finis, quod John Barkar.

℄ Imprynted at London, in Flete Strete, at the
  fygne of the Faucon, by Wylliam Gryffith, and
  are to be folde at his fhop in Saint Dunftons
  churchyarde, in the weft of London, the viij.
  daye of Nouember.

*The firft part of the Marchants Daughter
of Briftow.*

To the tune of The Maydens Joy.

BEHOLD the touchftone of true loue,
    Maudlin the Marchants daughter
      of Briftow towne,
  Whofe firme affection nothing could
      moue,—
Such fauour beares the louely browne.

❡ A gallant youth was dwelling by,
  Which many yeeres had borne this mayden
    great good will;
She loued him as faythfully,
  But all her friendes withſtood it ſtill.

❡ The young man now, perceiuing well,
  He could not get nor win the fauour of her
    friendes,
The force of ſorrowes to expell,
  To view ſtrange countries he intendes.

❡ And now to take his laſt farewell
  Of his true loue, his faire and conſtant Maudlin,
With muſicke ſweete that did excell
  He playes under her window fine.

❡ Farewell, quoth he, my owne true loue!
  Farewell, my deare and cheefeſt treaſure of my
    hart!
Through fortunes ſpight, that falſe did proue,
  I am inforc't from thee to part.

❡ Into the land of Italy
  There will I waſte and wearie out my dayes in
    woe;
Seeing my true loue is kept from me,
  I hold my life a mortall foe.

❡ Faire Briſtow towne, therefore, adue,—
  For Padua muſt be my habitation now,—
Although my loue doth lodge in thee,
  To whom alone my hart I vow.

❡ With trickling teares thus did he ſing,
  With ſighes and ſobs deſcending from his hart
    ful ſore;

He fayth, when he his hands did wring,—
Farewell, fweete loue, for euermore !

℄ Faire Maudlin, from a window hie,
Beholdes her true loue with his muficke where
he ftood,
But not a word fhe durft reply,
Fearing her parents angry mood.

℄ In teares fhe fpendes the dolefull night,
Wifhing herfelfe (though naked) with her
faithful friend ;
She blames her friendes and fortunes fpight,
That wrought their loues fuch luckles end.

℄ And in her hart fhe makes a vow
Cleane to forfake her countrey and her kinsfolke
all,
And for to follow her true loue now,
To bide all chaunces that might fall.

℄ The night is gone, and the day is come,
And in the morning very early doth fhe arife ;
She gets her downe to the lower roome,
Where fundry feamen fhe efpies.

℄ A gallant maifter among them all—
The maifter of a faire and goodly fhip was he—
Which there ftood waighting in the hall,
To fpeake with her father, if it might be.

℄ She kindly takes him by the hand,—
Good fir, fhe fayd, and would you fpeake with
any heere :
Quoth he, faire mayde, therefore I ftand.
Then, gentle fir, I pray you come neere.

℡ Into a pleafant parlour by,
 With hand in hand fhe bringes this feaman all
 alone,
Sighing to him moft pitteoufly,—
 She thus to him did make her mone.

℡ She falles upon her tender knee,—
 Good fir, fhe fayd, now pitty you a maydens
 woe,
And proue a faythfull friend to me,
 That I to you my griefe may fhew.

℡ Sith you repofe fuch truft, he fayd,
 To me that am unknowne, and eke a ftranger
 heere,
Be you affured, proper mayde,
 Moft faythfull ftill I will appeare.

℡ I haue a brother, fir, quoth fhe,
 Whom as my lyfe I loue and fauour tenderly;
In Padua, alas! is he,
 Full ficke, God wot, and like to die.

℡ And faine I would my brother fee,
 But that my father will not yeeld to let me go;
Wherefore, good fir, be good to me,
 And vnto me this fauour fhow.

℡ Some fhip-boyes garments bring to me,
 That I difguifd may get away from hence un-
 knowne,
And vnto fea Ile goe with thee,
 If thus much friendfhyp may be fhowne.

℡ Faire mayde, quoth he, take here my hand,
 I will fulfill each thing that now you defire:

And fet you fafe in that fame land,
And in the place where you require.

℃ Then giues fhe him a tender kiffe,
And fayth, your feruant, gallant maifter, I will
    be,
And proue your faythfull friend for this,—
Sweete maifter, then forget not me.

℃ This done, as they had both decreed,
Soone after, early, euen before the breake of
    day,
He bringes her garments then with fpeed,
Wherein fhe doth herfelfe array.

℃ And ere her father did arife,
She meetes her maifter as he walked in the hall ;
She did attend on him likewife,
Euen till her father did him call.

℃ But ere the marchant made an end
Of all thofe matters to the maifter he could fay,
His wife came weeping in with fpeed,
Saying, our daughter is gone away.

℃ The marchant, much amazed in minde,
Yonder vilde wretch entic't away my child,
    quoth he ;
But well I wot I fhall him find
At Padua in Italie.

℃ With that befpake the maifter braue :
Worfhipfull marchant, thither goes this pretty
    youth,
And any thing that you would haue
He will performe it, and write the trueth.

℃ Sweete youth, quoth he, if it be fo,
  Beare me a letter to the Englifh marchants there,
And gold on thee I will beftow,—
  My daughters welfare I do feare.

℃ Her mother takes her by the hand,—
  Faire youth, quoth fhe, if there thou doft my
      daughter fee,
Let me thereof foone vnderftand,
  And there is twenty crownes for thee.

℃ Thus through the daughters ftrange difguife,
  The mother knew not when fhe fpake vnto her
      child :
And after her maifter ftraight fhe hies,
  Taking her leaue with countenance milde.

℃ Thus to the fea faire Maudlin is gone,
  With her gentle maifter,—God fend them a
      merry wind !—
Where we a while muft leaue them alone,
  Till you the fecond part do finde.   FINIS.

༺༻

x

*The fecond part of the Marchants Daughter
of Briftow.*

To the tune of The Maidens Joy.

ELCOME, fweet Maudlin, from the fea,
  Where bitter ftorms and cruel tem-
  pefts did arife :
  The pleafant banks of Italy
We may behold with ioyfull eies.

Thankes, gentle maifter, then quoth fhe,—
  A faithful friend in al my forows thou haft
    beene;—
If fortune once doth fmile on me,
  My thankfull heart fhall well be feene.

| Bleft be the land that feedes my loue,
  Bleft be that place whereas he doth abide ;
No trauell will I fticke to proue,
  Whereby my good will may be tride.

Now will I walke, with ioyfull heart,
  To view the town wheras my darling doth re-
    maine,
And feek him out in euery part,
  Untill I do his fight attaine.

/ And I, quoth he, will not forfake
    Sweete M. in al her iorneys vp and downe ;
In wealth and woe thy part Ile take,
  And bring thee fafe to Padua towne.

And, after many weary fteps,
  In Padua they fafe ariued at the laft ;
For verie ioy her heart it leapes,—
  She thinkes not on her perills paft.

But now, alas, behold the lucke !
  Her own true loue in woful prifon doth fhe find,
Which did her heart in peeces plucke,
  And greeude her gentle mind.

| Condemnd he was to die, alas,
    Except he would his faith and his religion turne :
| But rather then he would go to maffe,
    In fiery flames he vowed to burne.

Now doth faire Maudlin weepe and waile,
  Her ioy is changd to weeping, forow, greefe
    and care ;
But nothing can her plaints preuaile,
  For death alone muft be his fhare.

She walkes vnder the prifon walles,
  Where her true loue doth ly and languifh in
    diftreffe ;—
Moft wofully for foode he calls,
  When hunger did his heart oppreffe.

He fighes, and fobs, and makes great mone ;
  Farwel, faid he, fweet England, now for euer ;
And al my friends that haue me known
  In Briftow towne with wealth and ftore !

But moft of al, farewel, quoth he,
  My owne true loue, fweete M., whom I left
    behind !
For neuer more I fhal thee fee ;
  Woe to thy father moft unkind !

How wel were I, if thou waft here
  With thy fair hands to clofe vp both thefe
    wretched eyes ;
My torments eafie would appeere,
  My foule with ioy fhould fcale the fkies.

When M. heard her louers mone,
  Her eies with tears, her hart with forow filled was ;
To fpeak with him no means was known,
  Such grieuous . . . on him did paffe.

Then caft fhe off her ladies attire,
  A maidens weede upon her back fhe feemly fet ;

To the iudges houfe fhe did enquire,
    And there fhe did a feruice get.

She did her dutie there fo wel,
    And eke fo prudently herfelf fhe did behaue,—
With her in loue her maifter fell,—
    His feruants fauour he doth craue.

Maudlin, quoth he, my hearts delight!
    To whom my hart in firme affections tide,
Breede not my death through thy difpight,—
    A faythful friend I will be tride.

Graunt me thy loue, faire maide, quoth he,
    And at my hands defire what thou canft deuife,
And I wil grant it vnto thee,
    Whereby thy credite may arife.

O fir, fhe faid, how bleft am I,
    With fuch a kind and gentle maifter for to meete!
I will not your requeft denie,
    So you will grant what I do feeke.

I haue a brother, fir, fhe faid,
    For his religion is now condemnde to die ;
In loathfome prifon he is laide,
    Oppreft with care and miferie.

Graunt me my brothers life, fhe faid,
    And to you my loue and liking I wil giue:
That may not be, quoth he, faire maide,—
    Except he turne, he may not liue.

An Englifh friar there is, fhe faid,
    Of learning great, and of a paffing pure life ;

Let him be to my brother fent,
   And he will finifh foone the ftrife.

Her maifter granted this requeft.
   The mariner in friars weed fhe doth aray,
And to her loue, that lay diftreft,
   She doth a letter ftraightway conuay.

When he had read her gentle lines,
   His heauy hart was rauifhed with inward ioy ;
Where now fhe was ful wel he finds,
   The friar likewife was not coy,

But did declare to him at large /
   The enterprife his loue for him had taken in
      hand :
The yong man did the friar charge,
   His loue fhould ftraight depart the land.

Here is no place for her, he faid,
   But woful death and danger of her harmles life ;
Profeffing truth I was betraid,
   And feareful flames muft end our ftrife.

For ere I wil my faith denie,
   And fweare myfelf to follow damnde antichrift,
Ile yeeld my bodie for to die,
   To liue in heauen with the higheft.

O fir, the gentle friar faid,
   For your fweete loue recant and faue your
      wifhed life :
A wofull match, quoth he, is made,
   Where Chrift is loft, to winne a wife.

When fhe had wroght al means fhe might
　To faue her friend, and that fhe faw it wold not
　　be,
Then of the iudge fhe claimd her right
　To die the death as well as he.

For looke what faith he doth profeffe,
　In that fame faith be fure that I wil liue and dy ;—
Then eafe vs both in our diftreffe,
　Let vs not liue in miferie.

When no perfwafion would preuaile,
　Nor change her mind in anything that fhe had
　　faid,
She was with him condemnd to die,
　And for them both one fire made.

And arme in arme, moft ioyfully,
　Thefe louers twain vnto the fire then did go,—
The mariners, moft faithfully,
　Were likewife partners of their woe.

But when the iudges vnderftood　　　　　·
　The faithful frindfhip in them al that did re-
　　maine,
They faude their liues, and afterward
　To England fent them home againe.

Now was their forrowes turnde to ioy,
　And faithful louers had now their harts defire ;
Their paines fo wel they did imploy,
　· God granted what they did require.

And when they were in England come,
　And to mery Briftow arriued at the laft,

Great ioy there was of al and fome,
That heard the dangers they had paft.

Her father he was dead, God wot,
And eke her mother was ioyful of her fight ;
Their wifhes fhe denied not,
But wedded them with hearts delight.

Her gentle maifter fhe defirde
To be her father, and at church to giue her then;
It was fulfild as fhe requirde,
Unto the ioy of all good men !

Finis.

Printed at London for William Blackwall.

A briefe ſonet declaring the lamentation of
Beckles, a Market Towne in Suffolke, which
was in the great winde vpon S. Andrewes eue
pitifully burned with fire, to the value by eſti-
mation of tweentie thouſande pounds, and to the
number of foureſcore dwelling houſes, beſides a
great number of other houſes, 1586.

To the tune of Labandalaſhotte.

Y louing good neighbours, that comes
to beholde
Me, ſillie poore Beckles, in cares many-
folde;
In ſorrow all drowned, which floated of late,
With teares all bedewed, at my wofull ſtate :
With fire ſo conſumed, moſt wofull to vewe,
Whoſe ſpoyle my poore people for euer may rue ;
When well you have vewed my dolefull decay,
And pittie haue pierced your heartes as it may,
Say thus, my good neighbours, that God in his ire
For ſinne hath conſumed me, Beckles, with fire.

For one onely pariſh myſelfe mought vaunt,
To match with the braueſt for who but will graunt ;
The ſea and the countrey me fitting ſo nye,
The freſh-water river ſo ſweete running by,
My medowes and commons ſuch proſpect of health,
My fayers in ſomer ſo garniſht with wealth,
My market ſo ſerued with corne, fleſh, and fiſh,
And all kinde of victuals that poore men would
wiſh ;

That who but knewe Beckles, with fighing may
   faye,
Would God of his mercie had fparde my decaye !

But, O my deftruction ! O moft difmall day !
My temple is fpoyled, and brought in decay,
My marketfted burned, my beautie defaced,
My wealth ouerwhelmed, my people difplaced !
My muficke is wayling, my mirth it is moone,
My ioyes are departed, my comfort is gone ;
My people, poore creatures, are mourning in woe,
Still wandring, not wotting which waye for to goe,
Like fillie poore Troians, whom Sinon betrayde ;
But, God, of thy mercy releeue them with ayde !

O daye moft vnluckie ! the winde lowde in fkie,
The water harde frofen, the houfes fo drye ;
To fee fuch a burning, fuch flaming of fire,
Such wayling, fuch crying, through fcourge of
   Gods ire,
Such running, fuch working, fuch taking of payne,
Such whirling, fuch haling, fuch reauing in vaine ;
Such robbing, fuch ftealing, from more to the lefle,
Such difhoneft dealing, in time of diftreffe ;
That who fo hard-hearted, and worne out of grace,
But pittie may pierce him to thinke of my cafe.

But, O my good neighbours, that fee mine eftate,
Be all one as Chriftians, not liue in debate ;
With wrapping and trapping each other in thrall,
With watching and pryeng at each others fall,
With houing, and fhouing, and ftriuing in lawe,
Of God nor his Gofpell once ftanding in awe ;
Lyue not in heart-burning, at God neuer wreft,
To Chrift ance be turning, not vfe him in ieft,

Liue louely together, and not in difcorde ;
Let me be your mirrour to liue in the Lorde !

But, though God haue pleafed, for finne to
plague me,
Let none thinke there liuing is caufe they fcape
free ;
But let them remember how Chrift once did tell,
Their finnes were not greater on whom the wall
fell :
But leaft you repent ye, thus much he doth fay,
Be fure and certaine ye alfo decaye.
Let none, then, perfwade them fo free from all
thrall,
But that their ill-liuing deferueth a fall ;
Thus, farewell !   Forget not my wofull annoye ;
God fend you good new yeare and bleffe me with
ioye !

Finis quod D. Sterrie.

Fœlix quem faciunt aliena pericula cautum.

Ech ftately towre with mightie walles vp prope,
Ech loftie roofe which golden wealth hath raifed,
All flickering wealth which flies in firmeft hope,
All glittering hew, fo haught and highly praifde,—
I fee, by fodaine ruine of Beckles towne,
Is but a blaft if mightie Ioue doe frowne.

At London :
Imprinted by Robert Robinfon, for Nicholas
Colman of Norwich, dwelling in S.
Andrewes Church Yarde.

A proper newe ſonet declaring the lamentation of Beckles [a market towne in] Suffolke, which was in the great winde vpon S. Andrewes eue laſt paſt moſt pittifully burned with fire, to the loſſe by eſtimation of twentie thouſande pound and vpwarde, and to the number of foure ſcore dwelling houſes, 1586.

To Wilſon's Tune.

WITH ſobbing ſighes, and trickling teares,
My ſtate I doe lament,
Perceiuing how God's heavie wrath
Againſt my ſinnes is bent ;
Let all men viewe my woefull fall,
And rue my woefull caſe,
And learne hereby in ſpeedy ſort
Repentaunce to embrace.

For late in Suffoclke was I ſeen
To be a ſtately towne,
Repleniſhed with riches ſtore,
And had in great renowne ;
Yea, planted on a pleaſant ſoyle,
So faire as heart could wiſh,
And had my markets, once a weeke,
Well ſtorde with fleſh and fiſh.

A faire freſh riuer running by,
To profite me withall,
Who with a criſtall cleered ſtreame
About my bankes did fall ;

G

My fayres in fomer welthely
    For to increafe my ftore ;
My medowes greene and commons great,—
    What could I wifh for more ?

But now beholde my great decay,
    Which on a fodaine came ;
My fumptuous buildings burned be
    By force of fires flame :
A careleffe wretch, moft rude in life,
    His chymney fet on fire,
The inftrument, I muft confeffe,
    Of God's moft heauie ire.

The flame whereof increafing ftil
    The bluftering windes did blowe,
And into diuers buildings by
    Difperft it to and fro ;
So, kindling in moft grieuous fort,
    It waxed huge and hie ;
The riuer then was frozen, fo
    No water they could come by.

Great was the crye that then was made
    Among both great and fmall ;
The wemen wept, and wrong their handes,
    Whofe goods confumed all ;
No helpe was found to flacke the fyre,
    Theyr paines was fpent in vaine ;
To beare theyr goods into the fieldes
    For fafegarde they were fayne.

And yet, amid this great diftreffe,
    A number fet theyr minde
To filtch, and fteale, and beare away
    So much as they could finde ;

Theyr neighbors wealth, which wafted lay
　About the ftreetes that time,
They fecretly conuayde away,—
　O moft accurfed crime !

Thus, from the morning nyne a clocke
　Till four aclocke at night,
Fourefcore houfes in Beckle's towne
　Was burnd to afhes quite ;
And that which moft laments my heart,
　The houfe of God, I fay,
The church and temple by this fyre
　Is cleane confumde away.

The market-place and houfes fayre,
　That ftood about the fame,
Hath felt the force and violence
　Of this moft fearefull flame ;
So that there is no Chriftian man
　But in his heart would grieue,
To fee the fmart I did fuftaine
　Vpon faint Andrewes eue.

Wherefore, good Chriftian people, now
　Take warning by my fall,—
Liue not in ftrife and enuious hate
　To breed each other thrall ;
Seeke not your neighbors lafting fpoyle
　By greedy fute in lawe ;
Liue not in difcord and debate,
　Which doth deftruction draw.

And flatter not yourfelues in finne,
　Holde not Gods worde in fcorne,
Repine not at his minifters,
　Nor be not falfe forfworne ;

For, where fuch vices doth remaine,
    Gods grace will neuer be ;
And, in your health and happie ftate,
    Haue yet fome minde on me,—

Whofe fonges is changd to forrowes fore,
    My ioyes to wayling woe,
My mirth to mourning fighes and grones,
    The which from griefe doth growe ;
My wealth to want and fcarfetie,
    My pleafure into payne,
All for the finne and wickednefſe
Which did in me remaine.

If then you wifh profperitie,
    Be louing, meeke and kinde,—
Lay rage and rancour cleane afide,
    Set malice from your minde ;
And liue in loue and charitie,
    All hatefull pride deteft,
And fo you fhall with happie dayes
    For euermore be bleft.

And thus I ende my wofull fong,
    Befeeching God I may
Remaine a mirrour to all fuch
    That doe in pleafure ftay ;
And that amongeft their greateft mirth
    And chiefeft ioye of all,
They yet may haue a heart to thinke
    Of Beckles fodaine fall.   .

Finis, T. D.

At London :
Imprinted by Robert Robinfon, for Nicholas
Colma[n], of Norwich, dwelling in S.
Andrewes church yard.

Franklins Farewell to the World. ×

With his Chriſtian Contrition in Priſon, before

his Death.

FARWELL, vaine world, whoſe com-
forts all are cares,
Whoſe gaines are loſſe, whoſe liberty
are ſnares,
Whoſe gold is droſſe, whoſe wiſedome is meere
folly,
Whoſe wealth is woe, whoſe ſeruice is vnholly,
Whoſe life is death, whoſe ioy is griefe and
ſadnes,
And all that's in thee is a map of madnes.
Who ſo (like me) long in the world hath beene,
And hath ſo many alterations ſeene,—
How ſome from greatnes fall, ſome riſe from little,
How mans foundation ſlip'ry is and brittle,
How tranſitory things doe mount and fall
At His great pleaſure, that created all?
Who ſo doth note, and beare theſe things in minde,
Shall ſee how Fortunes breath, like wau'ring winde,
Doth blow vp men like bladders with ambition,
And caſt them headlong downe to black perdition.
That this is true the world may plainly ſee,
And view a fearefull ſpectacle in mee ;
For I that had enough of fading pelfe,
And need not want (except I would myſelfe),—
I that had ſence, diſcretion, reaſon, wit,
And could diſcerne things fitting and vnfit,

I whom my high Creator made a creature,
Adorning me with guifts of art and nature ;—
Yet of all this I made no further vſe,
But Gods, kings, countryes, and my ſoules abuſe.
From crime to crime ſtill plundging further in,
With my continuall adding ſinne to ſinne,
Till ſinne on ſinne at laſt brought ſhame on ſhame,
And ſhame on ſhame paid the deſert of blame.
My thoughtsſurmis'd th' Almighties eyes were hid,
And that he ſaw not what I ſecret did,
But He (whoſe ſight eclipſeth moone and ſun)
Hath brought to light the deeds in darknes done ;
He, in his iuſtice, iuſtly hath reueal'd
My hainous faults, which I had long conceal'd ;
He hath laid open my notorious crimes
To bee a warning to enſuing times ;
That they ſhall neuer dare to doe the like,
Leaſt (like to me) his vengeance them doe ſtrike.
Then let a dying friend good counſell giue
To all eſtates and ſexes how they liue :
Oh, let my ending of my loathed breath
Make all men care to ſhun eternall death !
And though my life hath bin polluted foule,
Yet iudge with charity my ſinfull ſoule ;
For were the ſinnes of all the world in me,
Yet (with the eye of faith) I cleerely ſee
That Gods great mercy, like a boundles flood,
Through my bleſt Sauiour and Redeemers blood,
Hath freely pardon'd all that I haue done,
(By th' interceſſion of his onely Sonne,)
So that my ſtedfaſt faith doth me perſwade
My peace for euer with my God is made.
Hee that raiſ'd Lazarus from out his graue,
He that vpon the Croſſe the theife did ſaue,
'Tis he alone, and onely none but hee,

Hath raifd me vp from death, and faued me.
Yea, though I all my life-time haue liu'd euill,
A feruant and a flaue vnto the deuill,
Yet heer's the ioy that makes my courage bolde,—
My Sauiour Chrift hath tooke me to his folde;
Hee true repentance vnto me hath giu'n,
And for me (through his merits) purchas'd Heau'n.
Then world, flefh, Sathan, and grim death, auaunt!
Doe all your worft, my faith you cannot daunt:
He, that for me hath conquer'd death and hell,
Hath granted me that I with him fhall dwell;
And though my life eternall fire did merit,
Yet God in mercy hath receiu'd my fpirit.
Farwell, my countrey, by whofe iuftice I
For mine vniuft and bloody action dye!
Farewell, moft facred and renowned king,
Whofe equall iudgement through the world doth
　　ring,
Whofe zeale to right, and whofe impartiall hand
Are the maine prop on which this ftate doth ftand!
Long may he raigne in his maieftick feate,
And, as on earth, bee made in Heau'n more great.
Let his pofterity and royall race
Be all infpir'd with the fupernall grace,
And of his feed let vs haue alwaies one
To fway the fcepter of Great Britaines throne!
Defend them, Lord, from foule and body harmes,
From home-bred traytors, and from foreigne
　　armes,
That in thy fauour they may liue and dye,
And dye to liue with thee immortally!

FINIS.

Printed at London, for Henry Goffon.

ℂ *The xxv. orders of Fooles.*

TAY a while with pacience, my freends,
        I you pray,
Of the orders of fooles fomewhat I
    wyll fay :
Fiue and twentie iuft a quarterne is, ye know,—
Euery foole in his foolifhnes wyll I fhow.
    And, as the prouerbe doth fhow very playne,
    A hood for this foole, to kepe him from the
        rayne.

ℂ Many fooles the carte of fin now-a-dayes doth
        draw,
Nowrifhyng their finne againft all right and law ;
Though that the way to hell be very playne,
Yet lyke a foole I aduife thee to returne agayne.
    If thou in foolifhnes ftyll doeft dwell,
    Thou fhalt haue a bable and a bell.

ℂ He is a foole that his finnes can not hate,—
Naught young, worfe olde, fuch is his eftate :
This olde foole is glad of that name,
Defiryng all men to take parte of the fame.
    This foole muft haue in hand, without fayle,
    A bable, a bell, or els a fox-tayle.

ℂ Of fooles yet I fynd another forte,
Which are caufers of lying and yll reporte ;
And he is a foole, both euen and morrow,
That nothyng wyll lend, but all thynges borrow ;

And, as the prouerbe doth fhow very playne,
A hood for this foole, to kepe him from the
rayne.

⦅ Of fooles yet another forte doth come,
Which neuer feketh for to haue wifedome;
Many fuch fooles wifedome difdayne,
Yet for their foolifhnes they fhall fuffer payne;
   And, as the prouerbe doth fhew very playne,
   A hood for this foole, to kepe him from the
   rayne.

⦅ He is a foole which to others doth preach and
   tell,
And yet this foole is ready himfelf to go vnto hell:
Liue thou vprightly, be caufe of no blame,
If thou doo not, the more is thy fhame;
   And, as the prouerbe doth fay very playne,
   A hood for this foole, to kepe him from the
   rayne.

⦅ He is a foole, and euer be fhall,
That others iudgeth, and himfelf worft of all:
This foole is blynd, frantike, and wood,
Without all reafon iudgeth bad thinges good;
   And, as the prouerbe doth fhew very playne,
   A hood for this foole, to kepe him from the
   rayne.

⦅ He is a foole that wifedome doth efchue,
For no good counfell can bring him to vertue:
This foole, which fcorneth his neighbour faft,
Shall be fcorned iuftly himfelf at the laft;
   And, as the prouerbe doth fhew very playne,
   A hood for this foole, to kepe him from the
   rayne.

❡ Another foole yet I doe here fynd,
Which can not kepe clofe the fecrets of his mynd :
This is a naturall foole, and vndifcrete,
Which can not hyde his owne counfell and fecrete;
   And, as the prouerbe doth fhew very playne,
   A hood for this foole, to kepe him from the
     rayne.

❡ He is a foole that in youth wyll not prouyde,—
In age muft he fterue, or in pouertie abyde :
This is a foole, and of the number one,
Which in the fommer can make no prouifion ;
   And, as the prouerbe doth fhew very playne,
   A hood for this foole, to kepe him from the
     rayne.

❡ He is a foole that getteth his goods wrongfullye,
For his heires after him wyll fpend it vnthriftelye:
This fooles golde is his God, wrongfullye got,—
Why, thou foole! thy golde is muk and clay,
     knoweft thou not?
   And, as the prouerbe doth fhew very playne,
   A hood for this foole, to kepe him from the
     rayne.

❡ He is a foole, whether he be man or wyfe,
Whiche ftyll deliteth in difcorde and ftryfe :
Such fooles their owne flefh to the bones may gnaw,
That contendeth in matters fcant worth a ftraw ;
   And, as the prouerbe doth fhew very playne,
   A hood for this foole, to kepe him from the
     rayne.

❡ He is a foole that on meffage is fent,
And, when he is on his way, forget whether he went:

This foole is worthy of the bable and the bell,
For of all other fooles he doth excell ;
   And, as the prouerbe doth ſhew very playne,
   A hood for this foole, to kepe him from the
      rayne.

❡ Yet of fooles a whole dozen I haue eſpyed,
And lead in a ſtryng, together they are tyed :
Theſe fooles you may know by their fauour,
For, lyke the aſpen leafe, with euery wynd they
      wauer ;
   And, as the prouerbe doth ſhew very playne,
   A hood for theſe fooles, to kepe them from
      the rayne.

❡ He is a foole that thinketh it great wonder,
When God ſtryketh by lightnyng and thunder :
Alas ! we dayly, without all dread, commit
Much curſed vice, for lacke of godly wit ;
   And, as the prouerbe doth ſhew very playne,
   A hood for this foole, to kepe him from the
      rayne.

❡ All youth I doo lyken vnto fooles blynd,
That vnto their parents are rebels vnkynd ;
Thow vnkynd chylde, and foole diſobedient,
Remember what goods thy freends on thee ſpent ;
   And, as the prouerbe doth ſhew very playne,
   A hood for theſe fooles, to kepe them from
      the rayne.

❡ He is a foole that greatly doth flatter and boaſt,
When he thinks leaſt, he ſhall taſt of the roſt !
This foole at laſt is caſt out of fauour,
For flatteryng pleaſeth no wiſe man of honour ;

And, as the prouerbe doth fhew very playne,
A hood for this foole, to kepe him from the
rayne.

❡ He is a foole, and voyd of all prudence,
Which to vayne tales doth geue all his credence :
Therfore remember this, both low and hye,
That flatterers fpeake fayre when they doo lye ;
    And, as the prouerbe doth fhew very playne,
    A hood for this foole, to kepe him from the
    rayne.

❡ He is a naturall foole, and a very daw,
That from doing good his neighbour doth with-
    draw :
Such froward fooles, all goodnes they defile,
If their neighbours doe good, then they reuile ;
    And, as the prouerbe doth fhew very playne,
    A hood for this foole, to kepe him from the
    rayne.

❡ He is a foole, and greatly vnprouable,
That in all his doings he is vnfortunable,
But in his misfortune he is fo blynd,
He neuer confidereth no remedy in mynd ;
    And, as the prouerbe doth fhew very playne,
    A hood for this foole, to kepe him from the
    rayne.

❡ He is a foole, that himfelf doth applye
Behynd his neighbours backe to fclander with
    enuye :
Such beaftly fooles commonly are well apayd,
Which thinke all is well, that falfely is wayd ;

And, as the prouerbe doth ſhew very playne,
A hood for this foole, to kepe him from the
rayne.

❡ Yet more fooles there be, which be vncom-
mendable,
That vſeth yll manners alway at the table:
Of pleaſant nurtour they haue no heede,
But beaſtly entend as ſwyne alway to feede;
    And, as the prouerbe doth ſhew very playne,
    A hood for theſe fooles, to kepe them from
    the rayne.

❡ Many fooles there be, in theſe our dayes,
Which ſeeme to be wyſe, yet folow fooliſh wayes;
Therfore I haue tolde vnto you very playne,
What foolifhnes in theſe dayes in many doth re-
mayne;
    And, as the prouerbe doth ſhew very playne,
    A hood for theſe fooles, to kepe them from
    the rayne.

❡ He is a foole, that wyll ſtyll deſyre
His owne death, to runne into the fyre:
And he is a foole, that hath no mynd deuoute,
But in the temple ſtyll walketh aboute;
    And, as the prouerbe doth ſhew very playne,
    A hood for theſe fooles, to kepe them from
    the rayne.

❡ GOD grant that all fooles wiſedome may learne,
And that they may good from yll alway diſcerne;
Then no more fooles we may them call,
But wyſe men, and wiſedome ſhew they ſhall.

God grant that on all partes we may now begin
To repent of our follye, and flye from our fin !

FINIS quod T. Gr.

❮ Imprinted at London by Alexander Lacie, for
Henrie Kyrkham, dwellyng at the figne of the
Blacke Boye, at the middle North dore of
Paules church.

The wonders of England.

1559.

WHEN date of (1553) was expirde ful,
And Gods wrath rypt, ready to fall,
His fworde from fheath did ferce out
pul,
And to the heauens beganne to call,
Saying :—on England now I fhall
Plage prince, prophet, and people all,
For contemptes fake !
Go, Death, inclofe their kyng in clay,
And, Sunne, withdraw the light of day,
And darkenes make.

No fooner fayd, but ftraight was done,—
The Englifh kyng Edward God tooke ;—
Light of foule from England gone,
Darkenes made them blyndely looke ;

Truth and fayth of people forfooke,
Their prophetes taken from the booke,
And pryfoners made ;
The bats and owles from holes out came,
Wolues and beares, and cruel Caim
Did England inuade.

When darknes thus echwhere was fen,
And nightly vermin rulde the roft,
No birds might fyng in that late euen,
By land, by fea, or by the coaft,
But ftraight were brought to firy poft,
Or els to Lolers tower toft,
And kept in cage,—
From meate and frend fomtimes fo bard,
That lomy wales they fed on hard,
Hunger to fwage.

Thys darkenes fo extremely bode,
That none from other fcarce were known ;
On noble, fage, learned and good,
Thefe wormes of darknes fpared none,
And pourde their poifon abrod fo flowne
On prophet, people, and prince their own,
Whych is by name
Elizabeth,—by God nowe Quene,
To Englands ioy ryght wel is fene,— ·
They fought to fhame.

The fun thus quentch, and day made dark,
And cockes in coopes from croing kept,
Then ftraight thefe owles began to wark,
And to the churches fearcely lept,
And with new broumes them clene out fwept,
From God, from king and Scripture fet

Vpon the wall,
And in their ftede fet ydols long,
And made people, with prayfe and fong,
    On them to call.

Thus vermin darke the maftry had
    Of realme, of prince, of noble and all :
And yet not herewith fully glad,
    Away they fought to faue theyr fall,
    And counfayle gaue a forayne, to call
    To match our quene and crowne royal,—
        All for their pope
To haue their kingdome raygne alway,
And they themfelues to beare the fway,
    And blindly grope.

Al this not yet their mindes fyllyng,
    For no regarde to natiue land,
Fearing again Gods light fhould fpring,
    Brought merfhial law forthwith in hand
    Againft al fuch as would withftand
    Their wicked raygne and cruell band,
        And Gods part take ;
Or els in priuye places founde,
Praying to God proftrate on ground,
    His wrath to flake.

Thus, rulyng all in darkenes blynde,
    Came miferies with heape on heape ;
No lore was taught to fyl the mynde,
    Godly to lyue, and good fruite reape,
    But al for Church they cride and threape,—
    Reftore, reftore, euen as good cheape,
        As ye dyd take !
And be ye fure ye fhall attayne
To heauens blyffe wythout more payne,
    And fo mendes make.

Loſſes of townes and holdes came on,
  Ruine of people beganne eche-where ;
Rich men made beggers, and captains bond,
  Armour for warre our enmyes toke clere ;
  When al thys was fene in this realme here,
  Yet, fayd thefe owles, we nede not feare,
    For all was well.
No loſſe haue we by heritikes gone,
Ne for Calis for whych ye mone
    Whych here do dwell.

Yet God as God, ſtyll alwaies one,
  Though angry, yet began to ſtay,
Plaging the realme and people eche one,—
  At laſt with teares beganne to faye :
  Oh England! England! fore doeſt thou ſtray ;—
  My martirs bloud ſhed out thys day,
    In wofull plyght !
The infantes yong that fatherles be,
Wyth wydowes poore crying to me,
    Wythdrawes my fpyte.

With that the ſkies their hue did change,
  And light out-ſhone in darkenes ſteede ;
Up, faid this God with voice not ſtrange,
  Elizabeth, thys realme nowe guyde !
  My wyll in thee doo not thou hyde,
  And vermine darke let not abyde
    In thys thy land !
Straightway the people out dyd cry,—
Prayfed be God and God faue thee,
    Quene of England !

Finis, quod I. A.

❡ Imprinted at London by Iohn Awdeley.

H　　.

A Ballad without title, having a large cut reprefenting five figures, that of Death with his dart purfuing them, with legends underneath each, as follows :—

> *The Priest.* " I praye for yov fower."
> *The King.* " I defende yov fower."
> *The Harlot.* " I vanquefh yov fower."
> *The Lawyer.* " I helpe yov iiij to yovr right."
> *The Clown.* " I feede yov fower."
> *Death.* " I kill yov all."

In the background in a bower are feated the foldier, the harlot, the lawyer, and prieft. A feftive board furnifhed with viands is fupported on the back of the clown, who refts on his hands and knees. Death approaching with his dart clutches at fomething on the table. Birds of prey are hovering in the air.

ARKE well the effect purtreyed here
    in all :
The prelate with his dignities renowne,
The king that rules, the lawyer in the
    hall,
The harlot and the countrey toyling clowne,
Howe and which way together they agree, ·
And what their talke and conference might bę.
Ech to their caufe, for gard of their degree,
And yet death is the conquerour, you fee.,

The bifhop vaunts to pray for thother fower,
As who wold fay, he holds the palme and prife,
And that in him and his moft holy power
It doth depend their caufes to fuffife ;—
I pray, faith he, that Chrifts continual grace
May them conduct and guide in euery place.

The puiffant king, he claimeth to defend,
The bifhop and the other three like cafe,
In all conflictes or broyles vnto the end,
Who but his power their enemies doth deface ;
He mufters men, and fends them forth afarre
In their behalf to maintaine deadly warre.

The fmiling queane, the harlot cald by name,
Stands ftiffe vpon the blafe of beauty braue ;
To vanquifh all fhe makes her prized clame,
And that fhe ought the golden fpurs to haue,
For by her flights fhe can bewitch the beft,
The ftrong, the lawyer, and the reft.

The lawyer he, in title of his clame,
Prefumeth next, by law and iuftice true,
Somwhat the more to eleuate his name.;
For law, faith he, all difcord doth fubdue,—
It endeth ftrife, it giues to ech his right,
And wholy doth contention vanquifh quight.

The contry clowne, full loth to lofe his right,
Puts in his foot and pleads to be the chiefe ;
What can they do, faith he, by power or might,
If that by me they haue not their reliefe ?
For want of food they fhould all perifh than ;
What fay you now to me, the countrey man ?

For want of me they fhould both liue and lacke,
For want of me they could not till the earth,
And thats the caufe I cary on my backe
This table here of plenty not of dearth ;
I feaft them all, their hunger I appeafe,
For by my toyle they feede euen at their eafe.

Death that aloofe in ftealing wife doth ftand,
Hearing the vaunts that they begin to make,
Straight fteppeth forth, with piercing dart in hand,
And boldly feemes the quarell vp to take,—
Are they, faith he, fo proud in their degree?
Lo, here by me foone conquered fhall they bee!

And ftanding by to giue their later foode,
He entreth ftraight, the conqueft to attaine;
Thers none of them, faith he, the chiefeft bloud,
That valiant death intendeth to refraine.
Ile crop their crowne and garlands frefh and gay,
And at the laft Ile fhrine them all in clay.

I pray for you all,   I vanquifh you all,
I help you all to your right, I feede you all,
I defend you all,   I will kill you all.

(***) The authors apoftrophe to the reader.

Here may you fee what as the world might be,
The rich, the poore, Earle, Cefar, Duke and King,
Death fpareth not the chiefeft high degree,—
He triumphes ftill on euery earthly thing;
While then we liue, let vs endeuour ftill
That all our works agree with Gods good will.

*⁋ A godly ballad declaring by the Scriptures
the plagues that haue infued whordome.*

EFRAIN of youth thy vain defire,
   Subdue thy lufts inordinate ;
Suppreffe the fparks, left in the fire,
   To quenche them it wilbe to late.

Thou knowfte not what a poifon ftrong,
   Thou letteft breed within thy breft,
Whiche, if thou keep within thee long,
   Wil caufe thee care and muche vnreft.

Though it feem fweet in thy conceit,
   Beware thou neuer nurifh it ;
The fifh is by a plefant bait
   Conftrained to the deadly bit.

Like as the woorm, in Affrick bred,
   Whofe fting deftroith with venem colde,
Is not fo noifome to be fled,
   As luft that reigneth vncontrolde.

If reafon cannot rule thy wil,
   But vice wil reign through appetite,
Then let the harmes, that happen ftil
   Through lufts, refrain thy fond delight.

Remember eke that in Noes dayes,
   When vice through luft was rifly growne,
The whole world by fuche wicked waies,
   By rage of rain was ouerthrowne.

The king of Egipt, Pharao,
   Was he not plagued of God moſte iuſt?
Bothe he and all his houſe alſo,
   Onely for he gaue place to luſt.

So read we of Abimelech,
   The mighty king of Gerera,
That God gaue him a greuous check
   For luſting after Saraa.

Luſt did deſtroy the Sodomites,
   As is in Scripture manifeſt;
For luſt were ſlain the Sichamites,
   When Sichem Dina had oppreſt.

Luſt did the wits ſo muche inchaunt
   Of Putipher, thegipcians wife,
That Joſeph, for he would not graunt
   Her ſute, ſhe brought nigh from his life.

Bethſaba, naked in bath,
   Bewitched ſo king Dauids brain,
That giltles he procured hath
   Her huſband Vry to be ſlain.

The cheef among the Iſraelites,
   For noughty luſt and eke offence,
Wrought by the meanes of Moabites,
   Were hanged vp by Gods ſentence.

For luſt Zimry the Iſraelite,
   As witneſſeth Gods holy woord,
And Coſby eke the Madianite,
   Periſhed bothe through Zimphas ſwoord.

The Ifraelites, through flefhly luft
Towards their enmies doughters, were
Alluerd by them falfe Gods to truft,
Whiche all their thraldomes caufed clere.

Sampfon the fonne of Monoa,
That mighty judge in Ifrael,
For luft he had to Dalila,
Himfelf to kil greef did compel.

Lo, him that none coulde foil in fight,
Whofe puiffant arme the lion flew,
Whofe ftrength put thoufands vnto flight,
By luft one woman ouerthrew.

Luft in the tribe of Beniamin
Caft twenty thoufand down and fiue ;
So that in all, for that one fin,
Were but fix hundred left on liue.

If Ammons luft had not defilde
His fifter Thamar with inceft,
He had not of his life been fpoild,
At Abfolon his brothers feaft.

If luft had not impaird the name
Of Salomon, that witty king,
He had not loft his roiall fame,
Nor fallen to idolls worfhiping.

If Herod, in his finful life,
Had not by luft been fore mifled,
He had not kept his brothers wife,
Nor ftricken of John Baptifts head.

❡ Now what be thefe but tokens fure,
    That God wil plage all thofe that vfe
To lead their liues in luft vnpure,
    And without fear themfelues abufe?

But fome doo think God dooth not fee,
    To eche mannes dooing in all things,
Becaufe fome feem ful fafe to be,
    And profper ftil in il liuings.

But if fuche wil geue ear vnto
    Gods woord, which dooth the truth vs tel,
Shal foon perceiue thofe that liue fo
    Shall fudenly go down to hel.

Therfore to God now let vs pray
    That he wil gide our harts aright,
To flee from filthy lufts alway,
    And him to pleafe with all our might.

And alfo for our gracious Queene,
    That God long profper her, and then
Good dayes among vs may be feene,
    Whiche unto vs he graunt.   Amen!

Finis, A. I.

❡ Imprinted at London, at the long fhop adioining vnto Sainct Mildreds churche in the Poul-
trie, by John Allde, Anno Domini 1566,
Nouembris 25.

A merie newe Ballad intituled, the Pinnyng of the Baſket : and is to bee ſonge to the tune of the doune right Squire.

WAS my hap of late to heare
 A pretie ieſte,
The which by me, as may appeare,
 Is here expreſte,—
With tantara, tantara, tantara,—
 For this belonges thereto ;
With bitter broyles, and bickeryng bloſe,
 And ſtrife, with muche adoe.

Marke then, for now this maruell ſtrange
 I will declare :
A joigner ſent his man to change
 Money for ware,—
Tantara, tara, tantara ;—
 Unto the toune he goſe,
And haſted to the chandlers ſhop,
 His money to diſpoſe.

But ſee the chaunce, the chandler drie
 Was gone to drinke,
Or els, poore ſoule, to plaie thereby
 At ſice and ſincke,—
Tantara, tara, tantara,—
 Whereat his wife did chafe,
And out ſhe went then, in a rage,
 To ſeeke her good man, Rafe.

She ranged forthe, and could not refte
   Vpon the molde,
When fhe hym founde, the bedlam beafte
   Beganne to fcolde,—
Tantara, tara, tantara ;—
   Quoth fhe,—Vnthriftie knaue,
If thou be at the good ale tappe,
   Thou haft that thou wouldeft haue !

This quiet man acquainted was
   With her rough talke,
And paciently doeth with her paffe,
   And homeward walke,—
Tantara, tara, tantara ;—
   At home fhe founde hym plaie,
Till he had ferued his cuftomer,—
   And then beganne the fraie.

For hauyng doen,—Hold here, quoth he,
   The bafket, dame ;
Goe, goffip, giue it hym, and fee,
   You pinne the fame,—
Tantara, tara, tantara ;—
   Now doeth the fporte beginne ;
Knowe thou, quoth fhe, fir knaue, that I
   The bafket will not pinne !

Her houfebande, fore infenfte, did fweare
   By ftockes and ftones,
She fhould, or els he would prepare
   To bafte her bones,—
Tantara, tara, tantara ;—
   Quoth he, Ile tame your tongue,
And make you pinne the bafket to,
   Doubt not, ere it be long.

Then with a baftian that ftoode by,
  Whiche he did fmell,
At her he freely did let flie,
  And bumbde her well,—
Tantara, tara, tantara,—
Vnguentum Bakaline
Did make this houfwife quickly pinne
  The bafket paffyng fine.

This paftyme pleafed well the page,
  That all this while
Sat on his horfe, and fawe this rage
  And bitter broyle,—
Tantara, tara, tantara ;—
The good wife doeth retire,
And fwears fhe will no more deny
  Her houfebandes iuft defire.

The bafket pinde, the page departes,
  When all is paied ;
He fpurres his cutte, the jade ftartes,
  He was fo fraied,—
Tantara, tara, tantara ;—
In hafte he homewarde rides,
Yet when he comes, for tariyng long,
  His maifter chafes and chides.

His miftres too, as one halfe madde,
  Beganne to raue ;
Becaufe too long he taried had,
  She calde hym knaue,—
Tantara, tara, tantara ;—
He fpake his miftres faire,
And tolde her fhe fhould knowe the caufe
  Of his long tariyng .there.

Then boldly he began his tale,
  And tolde them all,
Betwixt thefe two, how Beaudly Ale
  Had bred a braull,—
Tantara, tara, tantara ;—
  Quoth he, the chandlers wife
Would not intreated be to pinne
  The bafket for her life,

Till he to beate her did beginne,
  With bounfyng bloofe,—
Then quickly fhe in pofte to pinne
  The bafket goofe,—
Tantara, tara, tantara ;—
  The joigner ioyes at this,
But fure his wife, to heare this tale,
  Was quite bereft of bliffe.

The joigners wife . . . . . . ame,
  Whofe gallant grace
Was chaunged, now beganne to frame
  A frounyng face,—
Tantara, tara, tantara ;—
  Quoth fhe,—For all his bloofe,
The knaue the bafket fhould haue pinde
  Hymfelf, fpight of his nofe !

Here then her houfebande did beginne,—
  Quoth he,—If I
Should bid you, wife, the bafket pinne,
  Would you deny ?—
Tantara, tara, tantara ;— .
  To hym fhe plainly tolde
That fhe the bafket would not pinne,
  Thereof he might be bolde !

Then thei hereof for to conferre
  Doe hafte to bedde,
And here you fee a feconde iarre,
  The bafket bredde,—
Tantara, tara, tantara ;—
  The thirde doeth now beginne,—
The fillie page, to get fome meate,
  In hafte doeth hye hym in.

No whit amazde, vnto the maide
  He ftraight doeth goe,
The queane of hym no more afraide,
  Beganne to crowe,—
Tantara, tara, tantara,—
  Caulyng hym knaue and fot,
And vfed hym, that, in the ende,
  A broken head he got.

Henceforthe take heede of makyng ftrife,
  Thou knaue, quoth fhe,
Betwixt thy maifter and his wife,
  Where loue fhould be,—
Tantara, tara, tantara ;—
  With greef her wordes he heares ;
But yet it grieued hym more to feele
  The blood about his eares.

Yet vp he ftept full ftoutly then,
  And bomde me Jone ;
That fhe lent he fo paide againe,
  He made her grone,—
Tantara, tara, tantara,—
  And getts his fupper too,
And made her fitte and eate with hym,
  Although with muche adoe.

His maiſter on the morowe nexte
    Of this was glad ;
His miſtres was herewith ſo vexte,
    It made her mad,—
Tantara, tara, tantara ;—
    This happe brynges ioye and care,
For now the joigners wife to pinne
    The baſket muſt prepare.

Her houſebande by his mans good happe
    Doeth hope to winne,
And makes her now, ſpite of her cappe,
    The baſket pinne,—
Tantara, tara, tantara,—
    Againe he doeth replie ;
Will you the baſket pinne or no ?
    She ſtoutly doeth denie.

Then with a bedſtaffe he to baſte
    Her doeth beginne :
Yet would ſhe not, for all his haſte,
    The baſket pinne ;—
Tantara, tara, tantara,—
    This combate beyng doen,
Unto a Juſtice houſe hard by,
    In haſte this dame doeth runne.

And to this ioylly Juſtice wife
    Diſcoueryng all,
Betwixt her ſpouſe and her what ſtrife
    Did late befall,—
Tantara, tara, tantara,—
    Whom ſhe would faine haue bounde
Unto the peace, if by the happe
    There might ſuche meanes be founde.

Of this her frende the francke confent
  She fone had wone,
To doe for her incontinent
  What might be doen,—
Tantara, tara, tantara,—
  This Juftice wife now gofe,
Her goffipps fute in hafte vnto
  Her houfebande to difclofe.

Her houfebande, hearyng by this tale
  How all thynges ftood,
In mynde he at this iefte fo ftale
  Did laugh a-good;
Tantara, tara, tantara,—
  A little more adoe,
This Juftice would have taught his wife
  To pinne the bafket too.

Now all good wiues, beware by this
  Your names to blot;
The bafket pinne with quietneffe,
  Denie it not,—
Tantara, tara, tantara,—
  Be counfailed by your frende;
And of this bafkettes pinnyng now
  Enough, and fo an ende.

Finis, quod T. Rider.

Imprinted at London, for Henrie Kirkham,
and are to be fold at his fhop, at the little North
doore of Paules, at the figne of the Blacke Boye.

❡ *The defcription of a monftrous pig, the which was farrowed at Hamfted befyde London, the xvi day of October, this prefent yeare of our Lord God, M.D. lxii.*

HIS prefent yeare of our Lord God, a thoufand, fyue hundred, three fcore and two, one Robert Martin of Hamfted, in the countie of Mid. befyde London, had a fow, the which brought forth viii piggs, the xvi day of October, whereof vii were of right fhape and faffion, but the eight was a wonderous monfter, and more monftrous then any that hath bene feene before this time, as you may fe by this picture. It hath a head contrary to all other of that kynd ; it hath a face without a nofe or eyes, fauing a hole ftanding directly betwen the two eares, which eares be broad and long, lyke the eares of a bloude-hound, and a monftrous body, like vnto a thing that were flean, without heare. It hath feet very monftrous with the endes of them turning vpwards, lyke vnto forked endes. This monfter lyued two houres, and the reft of them lyued about halfe a day.

❡ Thefe ftraunge and monftrous thinges Almighty God fendeth amongeft vs, that we fhuld not be forgetfull of his almighty power, nor vnthankeful for his great mercies fo plentifully powred vpon vs, and efpecially for geuyng vnto vs his moft holy word, whereby our lyues ought to be guyded: and alfo his wonderful tokens, wherby we ought to be warned. But if we will not be inftructed by his worde nor warned by his wonderfull workes, then let vs be affured that thefe ftraunge monftrous fightes do forefhew vnto vs that his heauy indignation wyl fhortly come vpon vs for our monftrous liuyng. Wherefore let vs earneftly pray vnto God that he wyll geue vs grace fpedely to repent our wickedneffes, faithfully to beleue his holy Gofpel, and cencerely to frame our lyues after the doctrine of the fame, to whome be all prayfe, honour, and glory. Amen.

❡ Imprinted at London, by Alexander Lacy, for Garat Dewes, dwellyng in Poules church yarde, at the eaft end of the church.

❡ *A very proper Dittie :*

To the tune of Lightie Loue.

❡ Leaue lightie loue, Ladies, for feare of yll name,
And true loue embrace ye, to purchace your Fame.

Y force I am fixed my fancie to write,
Ingratitude willeth mee not to re-
fraine :
Then blame me not, Ladies, although I indite
What lighty loue now amongft you doth raigne.
Your traces in places, with outward allurements,
Doth mooue my endeuour to be the more playne :

I

Your nicyngs and ticings, with fundrie procure-
   mentes,
To publiſh your lightie loue doth mee conſtrayne.

❡ Deceite is not daintie, it coms at eche diſh,
   Fraude goes a fiſhyng with frendly lookes;
Throughe frendſhip is ſpoyled the feely poore fiſh,
   That hoouer and ſhouer vpon your falſe hookes;
With baight you lay waight, to catch here and
      there,
   Whiche cauſeth poore fiſshes their freedome to
      loſe:
Then loute ye and floute ye, wherby doth appere
   Your lighty loue, Ladies, ſtyll cloaked with
      gloſe.

❡ With DIAN ſo chaſte you feeme to compare,
   When HELLENS you bee, and hang on her
      trayne:
Mee thinkes faithfull Thiſbies be now very rare,
   Not one CLEOPATRA, I doubt, doth remayne;
You wincke and you twincke, tyll Cupid haue
      caught,
   And forceth through flames your louers to ſue:
Your lyghtie loue, Ladies, too deere they haue
      bought,
   When nothyng wyll mooue you their cauſes
      to rue.

❡ I ſpeake not for ſpite, ne do I diſdayne
   Your beautie, fayre ladies, in any reſpect:
But ones ingratitude doth mee conſtrayne,
   As childe hurt with fire, the ſame to neglect;
For proouing in louyng, I finde by good triall,
   When beautie had brought mee vnto her becke,

She ftaying, not waying, but made a deniall,
  And, fhewyng her lightie loue, gaue mee the
  checke.

℃ Thus fraude for frendfhip did lodge in her breft;
  Suche are moft women, that, when they efpie
Their louers inflamed with forowes oppreft,
  They ftande then with Cupid againft their replie:
They taunte, and they vaunte; they fmile when
  they vew
  How Cupid had caught them vnder his trayne;
But warned, difcerned the proofe is moft true
  That lightie loue, Ladies, amongft you doth
  reigne.

℃ It feemes, by your doynges, that Creffed doth
  fcoole ye,—
  Penelopeys vertues are cleane out of thought:
Mee thinkes, by your conftantneffe, Heleyne doth
  rule ye,
  Whiche both Greece and Troy to ruyne hath
  brought.
No doubt, to tell out your manyfolde driftes,
  Would fhew you as conftant as is the fea fande:
To trufte fo vniuft, that all is but fhieftes,
  With lightie loue bearyng your louers in hande.

℃ If ARGVS were lyuyng, whofe eyes were in
  nomber
  The peacockes plume painted, as writers replie,
Yet women by wiles full fore would him cumber,
  For all his quicke eyes, their driftes to efpie;
Suche feates, with difceates, they dayly frequent,
  To conquere mennes mindes, their humours to
  feede,
That bouldly I may geue arbittrement
  Of this your lightie loue, ladies, indeede.

❡ Ye men that are ſubieƈt to Cupid his ſtrooke,
  And therin ſeemeth to haue your delight,
Thinke, when you ſee baight, theres hidden a
      hooke,
Whiche ſure wyll bane you, if that you do bight:
Suche wiles and ſuche guiles by women are wrought,
  That halfe their miſchefes men cannot preuent;
When they are moſt pleaſant vnto your thought,
  Then nothyng but lightie loue is their intent.

❡ Conſider that poyſon doth lurke oftentyme
  In ſhape of ſugre, to put ſome to payne,
And fayre wordes paynted, as dames can define,
  The olde prouerbe ſaith, doth make ſome fooles
      faine !
Be wiſe and preciſe, take warning by mee;
  Truſt not the crocodile, leaſt you do rue;
To womens faire wordes do neuer agree,
  For all is but lightie loue, this is moſt true.

❡ Anexes ſo daintie example may bee,
  Whoſe lightie loue cauſed yong Iphis his woe;
His true loue was tryed by death, as you ſee,
  Her lightie loue forced the knight therunto;
For ſhame then refrayne, you ladies, therfore,
  The cloudes they doo vaniſh, and light doth
      appeare;
You cannot diſſemble, nor hide it no more,
  Your loue is but lightie loue, this is moſt cleare.

❡ For Troylus tried the ſame ouer well,
  In louyng his ladie, as Fame doth reporte;
| And likewiſe Menander, as ſtories doth tell,
  Who ſwam the ſalt ſeas to his loue to reſorte,
So true, that I rue ſuch louers ſhould loſe
  Their labour in ſeekyng their ladies vnkinde,

Whofe loue thei did prooue, as the prouerbe
    now goes,—
Euen very lightie loue lodgde in their minde.

❧ I touche no fuche ladies as true loue imbrace,
    But fuche as to lightie loue dayly applie ;
And none wyll be grieued, in this kinde of cafe,
    Saue fuche as are minded true loue to denie ;
Yet frendly and kindly I fhew you my minde ;
    Fayre ladies, I wifh you to vfe it no more ;
But fay what you lift, thus I haue definde,
    That lightie loue, ladies, you ought to abhore.

❧ To truft womens wordes in any refpeÒt
    The danger by mee right well it is feene,
And loue and his lawes who would not negleÒt,
    The tryall wherof mofte peryllous beene ?
Pretendyng the endyng if I haue offended,
    I craue of you, ladies, an anfwere againe ;
Amende, and whats faid fhall foone be amended,
    If cafe that your lightie loue no longer do rayne.

❧ Finis.   By Leonarde Gybfon.

❧ Imprinted at London, in the vpper end of
Fleetlane, by Richard Jhones ; and are to be
folde at his fhop, ioyning to the South-wefte
Dore of Saint Paules church.

Sapartons Alarum to all fuch as do beare
the name of true fouldiers, in England or elf-
wheare.

L Mars his men, drawe neere,
    That warlike feates embrace,
Sit downe a while, and harken heere,
    A feruinge fouldiers cafe.

Laye downe the fhiuered fpeare,
    And eke the battered fhielde ;
From trumpets found withdraw thine eare,
    And harke, in open field,

The true complaint of one,
    Whofe gaine by feruice got
Will fcarfely yelde a hungry boone
    To caft into the pot.

If euer warlike wighte
    Hath ferued his time in vaine,
In hope to haue bin well requighte,
    And hath receiued difdaine,—

In faith, then, I am he,
    Such one that for my parte
Haue ready bin full willinglye,
    With hand and eeke with harte,

To ferue my prince in fielde,
    Whiles life had bearing breath,—
As one that minded not to yelde,
    Nor forced life or death.

The fiery cannons thump
The cragged fcull that riues,
Whofe force by inwarde charge is wonte
To fpoyle poore fouldiers liues,

Could neuer force me yet
The enemies face to fhonne,
If captaines courage femed fit
The conqueft to haue wonne.

And for the time, perchaunce,
I was accepted then,
And promifed to haue aduaunce
As foone as other men.

I fpeake as founde I haue ;—
What thoe? I am contente,—
For Saparton now waxeth graue,
Some youthfull yeares are fpente.

Tis not the curled head,
Nor yet the frifled heare,
That courage giues in time of neede
To weld thunweldy fpeare.

Some youthfull imps I knowe,
That beares a paffing grace,
If they to pitched fielde fhould goe,
Durft fcarfly fhew their face.

But when that all is don,
Tis manhood makes the man ;—
Match not the candell with the funne,
No praife deferue you than.

If courage craues a fame,
Remaining in the breaft,

Then manhood needes muſt make his claime
For to excell the reſte.

Though Venus ſtriue with Mars
    To get the vpper grounde,
At length yet ſhall the barded horſe
    Exceede both hauke and hounde.

And, luſtie laddes, to you,
    Let not your courage quell;
Good hap hereafter may enſue,
    Though I good hap do fell.

℃ Coaſte on apace, althoe
    Light horſeman trace the ſoyle;
Encounter ſharpely with thy foe,
    Make hauocke of the ſpoyle.

Eſteeme not my yll hap,
    Nor weye it ought at all;
The wight that ſcapes the cannons clap
    Runnes yet to further thrall.

O Mars, bewaile thy man,
    Becauſe he hath ſuche wronge!
In dolefull tunes, O ruſtick Pan!
    Now helpe to waile this ſonge.

So thus my leaue I take;—
    O ſouldier, now farewell:
No more to do now will I make,
    But God preſerue Queene EL.

Finis.   Iohn Saparton.

Imprinted at London, in Fleeteſtreete, by William
    How, for Richard Johnes, and are to be ſolde
    at his ſhoppe vnder the Lotterie houſe.

*A godly ditty or prayer to be song vnto God
for the preferuation of his Church, our Queene
and Realme, againſt all Traytours, Rebels, and
papiſticall enemies.*

Preferue thy feruaunt, Lord,
 Elizabeth, our Queene ;
Be thou her ſhield and ſword,—
 Now let thy power be feene.
That this, our queene annoynted,
 May vanquiſh al her foes ;
And, as by thee appoynted,
 Let her lay ſword on thofe.

Geue, Lord, true faythful hartes
 To vs, her fubieêtes al,
That we play not the partes
 Of thefe traitours that fal
Both from their God and prince,
 And from their lawful othes ;—
All fuch, O Lord, conuince,
 And geue them ouerthrowes.

Syng this after the tune of the cxxxvij Pfalme, which begins,
When as we fat in Babilon ;—or fuch lyke.

UR liuyng God, to thee we cry,
 Now tend vnto our playnt ;
Behold thy church and family,
 Which enmies feeke to faynt ;
And though our fyns haue moued thee
Juſt plagues on vs to poure,
Yet let thy Chriſtes death ſhortly
Thy wrath vp cleane deuour.

Correct vs, Lord, by thine own hand,
　And leaue vs not to thofe
That do thee and thy truth withftand,
　Like diulyfh deadly foes ;
For better is it for vs, Lord,
　Into thy handes to fall,
Then vnto them for to accord
　Which in hell perifh fhall.

Behold, O Lord, thine enmies rage
　Againft thee and thy Chrift ;
Not our fyns they feeke to afwage,
　But thy truth to refift.
And fhall our fyns then be a let
　For thee them to withftand,
Seing againft thee they be fet ?
　No, Lord, fet to thy hand.

For thine the glory is, not ours,
　Which they feeke to fuppres ;
Bend, therfore, Lord, thine hoft of powrs,
　And this thy caufe redres ;
Refift thefe rebels and traytours,
　With papiftes euery one,
Which thy poore people fo deuours
　In euery nacion.

Let not the wicked thus preuayle,
　To vexe thy church and fayntes ;
But ftroy them from the head to tayle,
　Let none bewayle their playntes !
Lord, heare the cry of fatherles
　And wyddowes, which do mone,
The which thefe enmies do oppres
　With mifchiefes many one !

Defend, O God, our gracious queene
   From pope, rebel, and all;
And as by her thy woorkes be feene,
   So let thy wrath now fall
Upon all thofe that vexe thy truth,
   Our queene, our realme and ftate,
And let their vicious prankes of ruth
   Light vpon their own pate!

So fhall thy name be magnified;
   So fhall thy power be knowne;
So fhall our Chrift be fanctified
   By them that be his owne:
Wherefore, O Lord, graunt our requeftes,
   Which here to thee we make,
And make vs loue and lyue thy heftes
   For thy Chrift Jefus fake!

Finis, quoth Ioh. Awdely.

☙ Imprynted at London, by Iohn Awdely.

*The Groome-porters lawes at Mawe, to be
obferued in fulfilling the due orders
of the game.*

1.

IF you chaunge hands, it is the loffe of
the fet.
   2. If you renounce, it is the loffe of
the fet.
   3. If you leade when your mate fhoulde, it is
the loffe of that game and vied cardes.

4. If you lofe dealing, it is the loffe of fower cardes; but if the lofer of the dealing deale not againe, you acquite the fower, and no gaine to either of both parties.

5. If you looke either on the afked carde or the bottome carde, it is the loffe of that game and vied cardes, in whom the fault is found.

6. If you roub (not hauing the ace) you lofe fower and al the vied cards, although you lay downe the fame carde which you tooke vp.

7. If you make out the carde when your mate rubbeth, it is the loffe of fower, for the roubber muft make out the carde himfelfe.

8. If you turne vp the ace of hartes, you gaine fower thereby.

9. If you turne vp the ace of hartes, and thereby make either partie aboue xxvj, the contrary part muft haue liuings; but if the contrary parte bee xxv, by meanes whereof liuings fets them out, then is he who turned vp the ace of hartes to make for the fet, fo that he make not one game nor the firft tricke, without the confent of both parties.

10. The partie that afketh a carde may not vie any carde before the firft tricke be played.

11. You may not vie it after your card is led, but the contrary part may.

12. Three cardes croffed, no carde by any meanes giuen backe.

13. Neither partie may giue backe his owne vied card, though none be croffed.

14. You may not afke a carde to fet the contrary parte or your felfe at liuings or out.

15. Prouided alwaies that, if the contrary parte bee xxiij or aboue, by reafon that fower fets the

other partie behinde the liuinges, it fhalbe lawfull for the partie which is behinde to afke a carde,
although the carde fo afked put the other to liuings.

16. Prouided alfo that, if you meane to lead
a helpe, you may vie it vpon your owne afked
carde, fo as it be done before the helpe be out of
your hand; the contrary part may pledge you a
card after he feeth your helpe vpon the boord, fo
as it be done before his owne card be played.

⟨ Of the horrible and wofull deſtruction of Sodome and Gomorra.

To the tune of the Nine Mufes.

HE Scripture playne doth fhow and
  tell
How Lot in Sodome towne did dwell,
  Amongſt the Sodomites vile;
He did rebuke their noughty liues,
Both yong and olde, both men and wiues,—
Why do you yourfelues defile?
He often times, with watry eyes,
  Their caufe he did lament.
He wept in hart, in greeuous wife,
  And bad them to repent,—
Defiring, and praying,
  From finne they fhould refrayne,
Leaft body and foule bee
  In euerlaftyng payne.

❡ God doth abhorre that whoriſh bed,
Whiche thouſands now therin are led,
    And therin ſtyll doth dwell ;
They yeld their ſoules for ſacrifice
To filthy ſinne in diuers wiſe,
    Vnto the paynes of hell.
You rauenyng needy men, quoth he,
    That riches haue in ſtoare,
Geue to the poore, I ſay to thee,
    The whiche coms to thy doore ;
To fatherleſſe and wydowes, too,
    To pyttie them take payne ;
You ſurffetters and dronkardes, now
    From this your ſinne refrayne.

❡ Then all in vayne Lot preached ſtyll,
They all did folow their ſelfe wyll,
    For that was their deſire ;
For his counſell good they paſſed ſmall,
In filthy ſinne they wallowed all,
    As filthy ſwyne in myre ;
Then did the Lorde commaund that Lot,
    That he ſhould ſoone depart
From amongſt the Sodomites ſo whot,
    For they ſhould feele great ſmart ;
The angell then to hym he ſaide,—
    Come, Lot, and haſte awaye,
For tyll the tyme that thou be gone,
    Nothynge be done there maye.

❡ The angell ſaid, Looke you not backe,
To ſee that wofull ſight and wracke,
    Which on them now ſhall light ;
For you out of the towne are brought,
And are eſcaped from their wicked thoughts,
    Wherin they do delyght :

Yet Lots wyfe ſhe turnde backe agayne,
  As ſoone as ſhe was gone ;
For her offence ſhe turned was
  Into a huge ſalt ſtone,
Where ſhe doth ſtande continually,
  By Goddes decreed judgement,
Becauſe ſhe brake, and did forſake
  Goddes good commaundement.

❡ The gates of Heauen God opened than,
So fyer and brymſtone from thence came,
  And on Sodome downe did rayne :
Gomorra towne they did excell,
As thicke as hayle the fyre it fell,
  And deſtroyed was euery man ;
Both man and beaſt were burnd to mucke,
  And babes in mothers lap,
And eke the chyldren that did ſucke
  On mothers tender pap ;
With fier were they burned,—
  O wofull, grieuous ſight !—
They cryed and ſhryked,
  To healpe no boote it might.

❡ The damſelles teare their coſtly guyſe,
Their yelow lockes downe to their eyes,
  And their heare like ſiluer wyer ;
Their ſownde did reach vnto the clowdes,
With bitter teares they cryed alowde,
  All burnynge in the fier !
Theſe townes like gold that ſhyned ſo bright,
  With flamyng fier is conſumed ;
The mighty God hath deſtroyed quite,
  And brought it to the grounde,
That nought is left, the trueth to ſay,
  But ſtinkynge pooles and welles,

Whiche was a place of braue delyghtes,
   And eke of pleafant fmelles.

℃ Thus were thefe towns brought to decay,
Both all and fom, the trouth to fay,
   Sauyng Lots houfeholde then :
And Lot hymfelfe was counted iuft,
Tyll his doughters tempted hym to luft,
   As the ftory fheweth playne ;
Loe, wanton girles whiche fo doth burne
   In Venus pleafant games,
If that they may content their turnes,
   And eake their youthfull flames,
They do defire their fathers bed,
   The cankred flefh to pleafe :
Alas, that ye fo wanton bee,
   That you wyll neuer ceafe !

℃ Thou mightie God that fitteft on hie,
O turne our hartes for thy mercie,
   That now amend we may !
O Lorde, thou faydft, and it may fo be,
The Sodomits fhould witnes be
   Againft vs at the latter day :
O heauy fayng ! yf that thefe men
   Shall fooner mercy craue,
Then we which know Gods fainges, then
   What iudgement fhall we haue ?
O let vs bewayle vs,
   Our finnes doth fo abound,
For in fhort fpace, I feare, the Lorde
   In wrath wyll vs confound !

℃ O England, thou like Sodome art,
In filthy finne doth play thy part,—

What finnes are found in thee!
Thou dooeft exceede Sodome in finne,
Thou careft not for Lots preaching;
O, thefe heauy newes wyll be!
Ye, be thou fure, and fure agayne,
The ftones that lieth in wall,
Becaufe we doo fo fore offend,
To God for plagues wyll call;
Therfore let fee, amends to be,
And euery one amende:
Good Lorde, I fay, graunt this allway,
And thus I make an end.

❧ Finis.

❧ Imprinted at London, by Richard Johnes, for
Henrie Kyrkham, dwellyng at the figne of the
Blacke Boy, at the middle North dore of Paules
church.

❧ * ❧

❧ *A mery balade, how a wife entreated her
hufband to haue her owne wyll.*

N May, when floures fwetely fmel,
  The people romyng abrode ful ryfe,
A mery tale I fhal you tel,
  That then was herd, but no great
  ftrife;

K

In clofe a yong man and his wife
  Sate reafonyng fore, but for none yl ;
She faid, I am wery of this lyfe,—
  Good hufband, let me haue mine owne will.

❡ Wyfe, quoth he, then muft I nedes know
  What is your wyll, then, for to haue :
At me you muft neither mocke nor mow,
  Nor yet loute me, nor call me knaue ;
Nor VENVS game vpon me craue,
  Nor yet your honeftye for to fpill,
And make me neyther boy nor flaue,
  But do good, and therin take your owne wyl.

❡ Tufh, quoth fhe, fir, as for that
  I wyll be honeft, to dye therefore ;
But, hufband, hufband, wot ye what ?
  I haue bene your wyfe this month and more,
And haue not gone but to the dore,—
  Such keping in my heart doth fpyll ;
By houfe-kepers neighbours fet no ftore,—
  Good hufband, let me haue mine owne wyll !

❡ Wyfe, quoth he, be you content ;
  You fhall to church and to market go,
And to neighbours to, at time conuenient,
  But not to goffip, the truth is fo ;—
Tauernes to haunt ? no wyfe, no, no !
  Nor yet alehoufes, with Jacke nor Gyll ;
You know my mynd for friend or fo,—
  Doe good, and therein take your owne wyll.

❡ Hufband, quoth fhe, you be to blame
  To kepe me in, and fo playne withall ;
Me thinke I fhuld be a fyne dame,
  Whereby great prayfe to you might fall :

I being fayre, nice, and fmall,
Yf I had gay clothes my body to hyll,
Then gentlewomen for me wold call,—
Good hufband, let me haue myne owne wyll.

❧ No, wyfe, quoth he, it wyll not be borne
For you to go fyne and gayly clad;
To go as I will haue you, thinke ye no fcorne,
That is, comely and cleane, fober and fad;
Wherefore, be you neyther ficke nor yet mad,
Becaufe ye may not your mynd fulfyll,
For your defyre is wicked and bad,—
Doe good, and therein take your owne wyll.

❧ Not mad, quoth fhe; alas, good man,
What woman culd your wordes abyde?
I entreatyng you as fayre as I can,
And yet my wordes you fet afyde;
Though I be fayre, I loue no pryde,
For I ferue your fwyne with draffe and fwyl;
Unto my friendes I wold fayne ryde,—
Good hufband, let me haue myne owne wyll.

❧ Wyfe, quoth he, what nedeth all this?
You craue a great deale more then neede;
Your friendes haue no need of vs, I wis,
Wherefore be ftayed, good gentle Beede:
Now let vs plow and fow our feede,
Our wynter land is yet to tyll;
How to thryue let vs firft take heede,
And do good, and therin take your owne wyl.

❧ Oh hufband, quoth fhe, I am but yong,
Wherefore, I pray you, graunt me one thyng,
At libertie let me haue my toung,
Eyther to chyde, or els to fyng;

To daunce, to kyffe, not ouer-workyng,
　　But once a weke to go to myll;
My time is fhort, my death is cumming,—
　　Good hufband, let me haue mine owne wyll.

❡ No, wyfe, quoth he, I am your head,
　　Wherefore, I pray you, my counfell take,
And let fuch tricks in you be dead,
　　Leaft that for it your bones doe ake;
Therefore learne betime to brue and bake,
　　And liue no longer in ydleneffe ftyll;
Wherefore, for your owne eafe fake,
　　Doe good, and therein take your owne wyll.

❡ Alas, quoth fhe, what chaunce haue I,
　　To couple myfelfe with fuch a one,
That had rather to fee me dye,
　　Then to decke me gay, as I wold haue gone,
To chyde, nor fyng, nor to daunce alone?
　　I wold I had maried John Goofequyll,
Then nede I not to haue made this mone,
　　For by him I might haue had all my wyll.

❡ No more of thefe twayne culd be hard,
　　But home they went together playne;
But let no wyues this wyfe regard,
　　For her requeft was all in vayne.
And yet with fhrewes fome men take payne,
　　And abydeth the iob of the deuylles byll,
From the which, all good wyues, refrayne!
.　　God geue vs all grace to doe his wyll.　Amen

❡ Finis, quod T. W. T.

❡ Imprinted at London by Alexander Lacy.

The Othe of euerie Freeman of the City
of London.

E ſhall ſweare that yee ſhall bee good
and true to our Souereigne ladie Queene
Elizabeth, &c, and to the heires of
our ſaid ſouereigne ladie the Queene.
Obeyſant and obedient ye ſhall be to the Mayor and
Miniſters of this citie. The franchiſes and cuſtomes
thereof yee ſhall mainteine, and this citie keepe
harmeles in that that in you is. Ye ſhall be con-
tributorie to all manner of charges within this
citie, as ſummons, watches, contributions, taſkes,
tallages, lot and ſcot, and all other charges, bearing your part as a freeman ought to doo. Yee
ſhall colour no forreines goods, vnder or in your
name, whereby the Queene or this citie might or
may looſe their cuſtomes or aduantages. Ye
ſhall know no forreine to buy or ſell anie mar-
chandiſe with any other forreine within the citie
or the franchiſe thereof, but yee ſhall warne the
Chamberlaine thereof, or ſome miniſter of the
chamber. Yee ſhall implead or ſue no freeman
out of this citie, whiles yee may haue right and
law within the ſame citie. Yee ſhall take none
apprentice, but if hee bee free borne (that is to ſay)
no bond man's ſonne, nor the childe of any alien,
and for no leſſe terme then for ſeuen yeeres; within the firſt yeere yee ſhall cauſe him to be enrolled,
and at his termes end ye ſhall make him free of
this citie, (if he haue well and truely ſerued you.)
Ye ſhall alſo keepe the Queenes peace in your

owne perfons; ye fhall know no gatherings, con-
uenticles, nor confpiracies made againft the Queenes
peace, but ye fhall warn the Mayor thereof, or let
it to your power.   All thefe points and articles
yee fhall well and truely keepe, according to the
lawes and cuftomes of this citie to your power.
So God you help, and by the holie contentes of
this Booke.   God faue the Queene.

Printed at London, by Hugh Singleton.

† *A Balade declaryng how neybourhed, loue,*

and trew dealyng is gone.

OW ftraunge it is to men of age,
The which they fe before their
face,
This world to be in fuch outrage,
It was neuer fene in fo bad cafe.
Neibourhed nor loue is none,
Trew dealyng now is fled and gone.

Where fhall one fynde a man to truft,
Alwaye to ftande in tyme of neede?
The moft parte now they are vniuft,
Fayre in wordes, but falfe in deede.
Neybourhed nor loue is none,
True dealyng now is fled and gone.

Who can flatter now beft fhall fpeede ;
Who can deceyue is gaynes well won : ✓
Of deceytfull tongues who can take hede ?
Many a man they haue undone.
Neibourhed nor loue is none, &c.

The wickedneffe that doth abounde,
More then I can with tongue expreffe,
To fee vnfaithfull men are founde ;
Of frendfhip there was neuer leffe.
Neiborhed nor loue is none, &c.

On couetoufneffe moft men defyre ;
Their neibours houfe fome doth procure,
And ouer his hed they wyll it hyre,
Or bye a leace to make it fure.
Neiborhed nor loue is none, &c.

To pourchace and bye, for lucre and gaine,
Both leace and houfe, both wood and grounde,
Thei double the rent, to poore mens payne ;
Of landlordes nowe fewe good are founde.
Neiborhed nor loue is none, &c.

This is vfed now euery where,
And wyll be tyll we haue redreffe ;
With them I thought the Lorde dyd fere,
Becaufe his worde they doo profeffe.
Neiborhed nor loue is none, &c.

What neiborhed is this you call,
That one another doth backbite,
And daily wyll both fkolde and brall
With flaunderous wordes in moft defpite ?
Neyborhed nor loue is none, &c.

For matters fmall fome fuffre wronge,
    Upon difpleafure in prifon caft,
And there fhall lye, without pitie, long,
    Tyll that his goodes are fpent and waft.
        Neyborhed nor loue is none, &c.

Thungodly riche the poore oppreffe,
    On them few haue compaffion ;
Their caufe is here remedileffe,
    Without all confolacion.
        Neyborhed nor loue is none, &c.

If any membre be hurte in man,
    The whole body lamentes therfore ;
The poore oppreft, who cureth than
    Or helpes him for to falue his fore ?
        Neiborhed nor loue is none, &c.

The percialneffe that now doth raigne
    With fome that haue fuche caufe in hande,
The riche men doth the poore difdayne,
    And fekes the meanes to make them band.
        Neyborhed nor loue is none, &c.

Truly to deale one with another
    In thefe dayes now ar very fewe ;
The fifter wyll begyle the brother,
    The brother agayne deceyte wyll fhewe.
        Neyborhed nor loue is none, &c.

The father wyll deceyue the chylde,
    The chylde the father likewife agayne ;
Thus one another dothe begylde,
    By falfe deceyt that now doth raigne.
        Neyborhed nor loue is none, &c.

To fpeake fomwhat of vfurye,
    The whiche the Lorde doth daily curfe ;
Yet fome doo vfe it priuely
    To fyll their vncontented purfe.
        Neyborhed nor loue is none, &c.

To ftriue or fpeake it is no boote,
    In couetoufneffe there is no order ;
Of mifchiefe it is the very roote,
    All thinges it fpoyles in euery border.
        Neyborhed nor loue is none, &c.

Our preachers with Gods word doth cry
    On couetoufmen that wyll not ceffe ;
Their wordes are herde with yeres fo flye,
    Their filthy gaynes they ftyll encreffe.
        Neybourhed nor loue is none, &c.

How many doth their rentes abate,
    Or now a dayes their tenentes eafe ?
They fet their rentes at a new rate,
    Both fines and leaffes they daily reafe.
        Neybourhed nor loue is none, &c.

Couetoufneffe hathe now the way,
    Wronge and briberye dothe not refrayne ;
In euery coft pride bereth the fway,
    Amonges the whole now it doth raygne.
        Neybourhed nor loue is none, &c.

What is the caufe neibourhed is gone,
    Which here hath reigned many a daye ?
I heare the poore men make great mone,
    ·And fayth hit is falne in decaye.
        Neibourhed nor loue is none, &c.

True dealyng dare not once appeare,
   Deceit hath put him out of place ;
Euery where, both farre and nere,
   He raigneth now in moſt mens face.
   Neibourhed nor loue is none, &c.

Graunt, oh God, for thy mercyes ſake,
   That neigbourhed and dealyng trewe
May once agayne our ſprites awake,
   That we our lyues may chaunge a-new ;
   That neybourhed and loue alone
   May come agayne to euery one.

quod Jhon Barker.

Imprinted at London, by Richard Lant.

*A proper newe Ballad ſheweing that philoſo-
phers learnynges are full of good warnynges.
And ſonge to the tune of my Lorde Marques
Galyarde, or the firſte traces of Que paſſa.*

HILOSOPHERS learnings are ful of
     good warnings,
   In memorye yet left to ſcoole vs,
So be ther contayned, in poietries
     fained,
   Great documentes to rate and rule vs ;
As well for continuance of life, helth, and ſubſtance,
   Whoſe vanities the world requireth,
As for the dereĉtion of life by correĉtion
   From lyberties that luſt deſireth.

Menander being afked what life was, he anfwered,
A miferie that neuer ceafeth,
Tormenting minds worldly for goods goton hardly,
With contraries as time increafeth,—
Wherin is no furance of hope nor induraunce,
But jeoberdies as fortune fendyth ;
Now ficklie, now helthie, now poorelie, now welthy,
With cafualties as life contendith.

Of Chilo thus reed we, whofe councel moft need
we,
No memorye ought more to moue vs,
Then for to know throwly ourfelues and our dewty,
To notifie what doth behoue vs ;
And as we feeme faultie, reiecte folyes noughtie,
With·practefinge all waies to fhone them ;
So may we, triumphing, geue praife to ech good
thing,
Recomfortinge that we haue done them.

Exceffe that delighteth, as Plutarche well writeth,
In greedines that life requireth,
In furfeitinge difshes, ill workinge, ill wifhes,
Suche filthines as flefhe defyrethe ;
Withdraw wyth their pleafurs dame natures dew
meafures,
Whofe gouernaunce is fo defaced ;
What man can difpofe them when luft ouerthrows
them,
To temperaunce that fhould be placed ?

Periander of liuinge good counfell once geuinge,
Said merilie, Looke well within thee ;
If confience accufe thee, ill reft will abbufe thee,
No libertie hath leaue to win thee.

Kepe concience then clearly, that life may liue
    chearly,
As Socrates doth wifelie will thee ;
No corzye fhall greeue thee, found fleepes fhall
    reliue thee,
Unquietnes can no waye fpill thee.

If fortune difpleafe vs, whofe wrackes may difeafe
    vs,
Let Sophacles his doctrine fkoole vs,—
Who writes that no furetie on earth getteth victrye,
    But pacience in paines to rule vs ;
In fuche pointes prefifely, good counfel moft wifely
    Exuperate blinde fortunes fcourges,
As the marriner fteareth the fhip when he feareth
    The violence of falt fea fourges.

Ten thoufand and ten to of theafe and like men to,
    Lyke documentes haue left behinde them ;
Methinks that thefe pagons may counfel good
        Chriftians
    With diligence to heare and mind them.
Sith life hath no fuertie, nor longe time of puertie,
    For accedence that can preuaile vs,
Let wifdome now win vs to plant vertue in vs,
    With penitence, eare life doth faile vs.

        ❡ Finis, qd W. Elderton.

❡ Imprinted at London, in Fleeteftreet, beneath
    the Conduit, at the Signe of Sainte John
    Evangelift, by Thomas Colwell.

A Balade of a Preiſt that loſte his noſe,
For ſayinge of maſſe, as I ſuppoſe.

HO ſo liſt, heare of a wonderous
   chaunce !
   Of late I mette with one did me tell,
   The craftieſt prieſt in England or
   Fraunce,
Hath loſt his noſe, and how ſhould he ſmell ?
He went to his freinde his mynde to diſcloſe,
And, as he came home, one cut of his noſe.

It is a gentleman, a prieſt he tolde me,
   To tell you his name I do not much paſſe ;
It is olde ſyr John, the vycar of Lee,
   Which rayles at Gods boke and reeles at his
      maſſe.
His cankarde mynde he cannot kepe cloſe,
Yet he ſerued him ſhrewdly that cut of his noſe.

His ſmeller is ſmitten cleane from his face,
   Yet was there but one, as he did ſaye,
Which caught him and pluckt of his noſe in that
      place ;
   A hie man, a lowe man, a foxe or a graye ?
Tenne ſhillinges, he ſaith, in his purſe he did loſe ;
I thinke he lied therof, but not of his noſe.

Great ſerching was ſence that ſmeller to ſeke ;
   Some for haſt left their ſcabbert at home,
Some had gunnes, ſome halberts, ſome forked
      pikes,
   Some in ſhyrts of maile like a luſty mome :

There was neuer fene before, I fuppofe,
Such toffing and tombling for a prieftes nofe.

Som men that thought him no harme in ther life,
    But becaufe they feare God and do go about
To liue with pure confcience and be without ftrife,
    Thei ar bound to the peas now for a priefts
        fnout ;
But becaufe he can kepe mens horedom fo clofe,
Therfore they make fuch a worke for his nofe.

Becaufe his fcollers did mock at his maffe,
    He faid he wolde make bloud run by their heles,
But God hath turned the plage from their arfe,
    And he with his nofe did bloudy the ftiles.
With bloud, I hard faye, as red as a rofe ;
He dronke well, belike, before he loft his nofe.

What maner of nofe was it, fir, ye fought for ?
    A black nofe, a red nofe, or one like my fift ?
To be without nofe was the marke of an whore,
    And now it is the marke of an whorifhe prieft.
And now you are ryd right well of the pofe,
Why do you make fuche a worke for your nofe ?

Or was your nofe fomewhat wan or pale ?
    A blewe nofe, a bottle nofe, or was it yellowe ?
Nos autem haue fene it fometime at the ale ;
    Libera nos, falua nos, from the fwap of the
        fwalowe.
But why did ye vfe, fyr, to lye fo and glofe ?
Was it any meruayle though ye loft your nofe ?

Some men are liuing to whom he did fay,
    Seing he knew the truth, if euer he fayd maffe,

He wifht that fome membre might be cut away ;
  Now at his requeft it is come to paffe.
Much work he doth make for the lomp he did
    lofe—
Well, what will ye geue, fyr, for a newe nofe ?

But what fhal we fay, yf men do not lye ?
  Who cut of the prieftes nofe it is harde to iudge,
But he himfelf, I think, did it of enuy,
  And then to bewite it to them he did grudge,
That therby they might ther kingdom vp clofe,
As fometime Sopirus did fnap of his nofe.

For fometime he fayth it was but a mome,
  And eftfone a talle man this he doth name ;
But ftyll he affyrmeth it was but one,
  Which caught him and brought his nofe oute
    of frame.
Could one man fo do it, as you fuppofe,
Except he were willing to haue of his nofe ?

Remedie is none, but this thinge is true,
  His fnout is fnapt of, howfoeuer it was ;
I thinke it were beft to make him a new,
  As fone he may do it as God at his maffe ;
Yf he cannot make him a fnout, I fuppofe,
He can not make God no more then his nofe.

Seing the true God is gone from your towne,
  And god Pean and Baccus doth rule in his ftede,
With hoyfty and foyfty ouer fhoulder and crowne,
  Yet hath he no more life then a lompe of leade ;
Yf he haue, then charge him that man to difclofe,
Which met you and caught you, and cut of your
    nofe.

But yf you do vfe the true God to mocke,
   And geue his honor to your god in the purfe,
Loke whom ye bleffe, and in blyndneffe rocke,—
   The liuing God will you and your bleffinges
      curfe ;
And at length your falfehed to all men difclofe,
And then, no dout, your head wyl folow your
      nofe.

Take hede, I faye, you chaplyns of Balle,—
   Though ye haue fed longe at Jefabels borde,
Not longe but Helias fhall geue you a fall ;
   Repent and returne to the liuinge Lorde.
Though ye pricke till bloud runne by your toes,
Ther wil a worfe chance com then lefing your
      nofe.

I wyll not pray for you,—let them do that lifte,—
   For feare God with me fhould be mifcontent,
Seyng of purpofe the Holy Ghoft you refifte;
   And if ye haue cleane forgotten to repent,
When God fhall the fecretes of all men difclofe,
Ye fhal haue as much help as the preift of his nofe.

But you haue a vauntage, fyr, if you mark all ;
   If a mous catch your god, when ye haue made it,
Then ye may catche the moufe faft by the walle,
   For how can you hurt your nofe except ye
      had it ?
The prouerbe is true in you, I fuppofe,—
He cannot tell where to turne his nofe.

FINIS.

God faue the Quene.

The true difcripcion of this marueilous ftraunge Fifhe, whiche was taken on Thurfday was fen-night, the xvj. day of June, this prefent month, in the yeare of our Lord God, M.D.lxix.

¶ A declaration of the taking of this ftraunge Fifhe, with the length and bredth, &c.

OOING you to vnderftande that on Thurfdaye, the xvj. daye of this prefent month of June, in the yeare of our Lord God M.D. lxix. this ftraunge fifhe was taken betweene Callis and Douer, by fertayne Englifh fisfher-men whych were a fyfh-ynge for mackrell. And this ftraunge and mer-ueylous fyfhe, folowynge after the fcooles of mackrell, came rufhinge in to the fifher-mens netts, and brake and tore their nettes marueilouflie, in fuch forte, that at the fyrft they weare muche amafed therat, and marueiled what it fhould bee that kept fuche a fturr with their netts, for they were verie much harmed by it with breking and fpoyling their netts.

And then they, feing and perceiuyng that the netts wold not ferue, by reafon of the greatnes of this ftraung fifhe, then they with fuch inftrue-ments, ingins, and thinges that they had, made fuch fhift that they tooke this ftraung fifhe. And vppon Fridaye, the morowe after, brought it vpp to Billyngefgate in London, whyche was the xvij. daye of June, and ther it was feene and vewid of manie, which marueiled much at the ftraungnes of

L

it ; for here hath neuer the lyke of it ben feene :
and on Saterdaye, being the xviij. daye, fertayne
fifhe-mongers in New Fifhftreat agreeid with them
that caught it, for and in confideracion of the
harme whych they receiued by fpoylinge of ther
netts, and for their paines, to haue this ftraunge
fifhe.   And hauinge it, did open it and flaied of
the fkinn, and faued it hole.   And, adiudging the
meat of it to be good, broyled a peece and tafted
of hit, and it looked whit like veale when it was
broiled, and was good and fauerie (though fum-
what ftraung) in the eating, and then they fold of
it that fame Saterdaye to fuche as would buy of
the fame, and they themfelues did bake of it, and
eate it for daintie ; and for the more fertaintie
and opening of the truth, the good men of the
Caftle and the Kinges Head in new Fifhftreat did
bui a great deale and bakte of it, and this is mofte
true.

The ftraunge fifhe is in length xvij. foote
and iij. foote broad, and in compas about the
bodie vj. foote ; and is round fnowted, fhort
headdid, hauing iij.ranckes of teeth on eyther
iawe, maruaylous fharpe and very fhort, ij. eyes
growing neare his fnout, and as big as a horfes
eyes, and his hart as big as an oxes hart, and likewyfe his liuer and lightes bige as an oxes ; but all
the garbidge that was in hys bellie befides would
haue gone into a felt hat.   Alfo ix. finns, and ij. of
the formoft bee iij. quarters of a yeard longe from
the body, and a verie big one on the fore parte
of his backe, blackifh on the backe, and a litle
whitifhe on the belly, a flender tayle, and had but
one bone, and that was a great rydge-bone, run-
ninge a-longe his backe from the head vnto the

tayle, and had great force in his tayle when he was in the water. Alfo it hath v. gills of eache fide of the head, fhoing white. Ther is no proper name for it that I knowe, but that fertayne men of Captayne Haukinfes doth call it a fharke. And it is to bee feene in London, at the Red Lyon in Fletestreete.

Finis, quod C. R.

Imprynted at London, in Fleetstreate, beneathe the Conduit, at the figne of Saint John Euangelist, by Thomas Colwell.

❦ The fantafies of a troubled mannes head.

Y fortune, as I lay in bed, my fortune was to fynd
Such fancies as my careful thought hath brought into my mynd ;
And when each one was gone to reft, all fofte in bed to lye,
I would haue flept, but that the watch did folow ftyl mine eye.
And fodeinlie I faw a fea of wofull forrowes preft,
Whofe wicked wayes of fharpe repulfe bred mine vnquiet reft :
I faw this world, and how it went, ech ftate in his degree,
And that from Wealth ygraunted is both lyfe and libertie :

I faw eke how Envie did raigne, and bare the
    greatift price,
Yet greatter poifon is not found within the cock-
    atrice:
I faw alfo how fowle Difdaine oft times, to forge
    my woe,
Gaue me the cup of bitter fweete, to pledge my
    mortal foe:
I faw alfo how that Defier to reft no place could
    fynd,
But ftyl conftraind, in endles paine, to follow
    natures kynd:
I faw alfo (moft ftraunge of all) how Nature did
    forfake
The bloud that in her womb was wrought, as doth
    the lothed fnake:
I faw how fancie would retaine no longer then
    fhee luft,
And as the wynd how fhee doth chaunge, and is
    not for to truft:
I faw how fteadfaftnes did flye with wynges of
    often chaunge,—
A flyeng bird but feldome feen, her nature is fo
    ftraunge:
I faw how pleafaunt times did paffe, as flowers do
    in the mede,
To-day that rifeth red as rofe, to-morow falleth
    deade:
I faw my time how it did run, as fand out of a
    glaffe,
Euen as each owre appointed is from time and
    tide to paffe:
I faw the yeares that I had fpent, and loffe of all
    my payne,
And how the fporte of youthly plaies my follie
    did retayne:

I faw how that the little ants in fomer ftyl doth
   rome,
To feke their foode, wherby to liue in winter for
   to come.
I faw eke Vertue how fhee fate, the threede of
   life to fpin,
Which fheweth the end of euery worke before it
   doth begin;
And when all thefe I thus behelde, with manie
   mo pardie,
In me, me thought, each one had wrought a
   perfect propertie;
And then I faid vnto myfelfe, a leffon this fhall bee
For other that fhall after come, for to beware by
   mee.
Thus all the night I did diuife which way I might
   conftrayne
To forme a plot that wit might worke thes
   braunches in my brayne.

❧ Finis. I. C.

Of euyll tounges.

EUYLL tounges, which clap at euerie
   wynd,
   Ye flea the quicke, and eke the dead
   defame;
Thofe that liue well fome fault in them ye fynd,

Ye take no thought in fclaundring their good
    name.
Ye put iuft men oft times to open fhame ;
Ye ryng fo lowde, ye found vnto the fkyes,
And yet in proofe ye fowe nothyng but lyes.

❡ Ye make great hatred where peace hath ben of
    long,
You bring good order to ruine and eke decaye ;
Ye plucke downeright, ye doe enhaunce the wrong,
Ye tourne fwete myrth to wo and wallawaye.
Of mifcheifs all you are the ground, I faye,—
Happie is he that liueth on fuch a forte,
That nedes not feare fuch tounges of falfe reporte.

❡ Finis, quod I. Canand.

❡ *Of Truft and Triall.*

WHO trufts before he tries may foone
    his truft repent,
Who tries before he trufts doth fo his
    care preuent ;
Thus truft may not be caufe of triall, then, we fee,
But triall muft be caufe of truft in ech degree.

❡ Finis. B. G.

A Strife betwene Appelles and Pigmalion.

HEN that Appelles liued in Grece,
Pigmalion alfo raigned than :
Thefe two did ftriue to frame a pece,
Which fhould amaze the fight of
   man,
Whereby they might win fuch a name,
As fhould deferue immortall fame.

ℂ Appelles then ftrayed euerie where,
   To marke and viewe ech courtlie dame,
And when he heard where any were
   Did well deferue the prayfe and fame,
He thither rode, with willyng harte,
Of her to take the cumlieft parte.

ℂ And when he had, with trauaile great,
   A thoufand wights knit vp in one,
He found therewith to wurke his feat,
   A paterne fuch as earft was none ;
And then with ioye retourned backe,
For to thofe limmes but lyfe did lacke.

ℂ Pigmalion eke, to fhew his arte,
   Did then conclude in iuorie white
To forme and frame in euerie parte
   A woman fayre to his delighte,
Wherein was euerie limme fo coucht,
As not a vayne he lefte vntoucht.

℄ When their two cunnings ioyned were,
    A worlde it was to fee their wurke;
But yet it may greue euerie eare,
    To heare the chaunce did therein lurke;
For through the pece they framed had,
For loue Pigmalion did run mad.

℄ Which feene, Appelles fhut his booke,
    And durft no longer viewe that fight;
For why? her comelie limmes and looke
    In one did paffe ech other wight;
And while Appelles wiped his eye,
The pece did mount vnto the fkye.

℄ Whereas Dame Nature toke it ftraight,
    And wrapt it vp in linnen folde,
Efteeming it more then the waight
    Had ten times ben of gliftryng golde;
Shee lockt it vp faft in a cheft,
To pleafure him that fhee loued beft.

℄ Appelles then, difmayed much,
    Did throw his booke into the fire;
He feared left the gods did grutch
    That wurkemen fhould fo high afpire;
Yet once agayne he trauailed Grece
With leffe effect, and made a pece,

℄ Which long time did hold great renowne,
    For Venus all men did it call,—
Tyll in our dayes gan Nature frowne,
    And gaue the workemannes worke a fall;
For from her cheft, t'auoyde all ftryfe,
Shee tooke the pece, and gaue it lyfe;

❡ And for a token gaue the fame
   Vnto the higheft man of ftate,
And faid, Since thou art crownd by Fame,
   Take to thee here this worthie mate,—
The fame which kyld the caruers ftrife,
Before that Nature gaue it life.

❡ Lorde! yf Appelles now did know,
   Or yf Pigmalion once fhould heare,
Of this their worke the worthie fhow,
   Since Nature gaue it life to beare ;
No doubt at all her worthie prayfe
Thofe felie Grekes from death wold rayfe.

❡ Then thofe that daylie fee her grace,
   Whofe vertue paffeth euerie wight,—
Her comelie corps, her chriftall face,—
   They ought to pray, both day and night,
That God may graunt moft happie ftate
Vnto that Princeffe and her mate.

❡ Finis.   Ber. Gar.

❡ Imprinted at London without Alderfgate, in
   Little Britaine, by A. Lacy.

❦

A new Ballad againft Unthrifts.

HEN raging louts, with feble braines,
   Mofte wilfully wyl fpend awaye,
   And eke confume more then their
      gaines,
   In riotyng al the longe day,
And fpend with him that wil fpend mofte,
Yet of their gaine they need not bofte.

When drunken drunkerds will not ſpare
  The alehous daily for to plye,
But ſit and tipple there full ſquare,
  And to their gaines will haue no eye,
Nor will not ceaſe, I warrant ye,
So long as they haue one penny.

When rufling roiſters wil beſtowe
  Vpon their backs ſuche fine aray,
And be not wurth that whiche they owe,
  Falling therby into decay ;
Yet wil they ſet theron a face,
And bragge and crake it out a-pace.

When liuely lads wil plye the dice,
  Conſuming there away their good,
No man wil count them to be wice,
  But rather to be mad or wood ;
For when that all their money is gone,
Then are they dreſſed like a mome.

When laſie loiterers will not wurk,
  And honeſtly their liuings get,
But had rather in corners lurk
  Then that they wold with labor ſwet,
Therfore no welth they can attain,
But liue in trouble and in pain.

When doting doltes wil enterpriſe
  To wurk ſuche feates as I haue tolde,
Not ceaſſing for to exerciſe
  Worſe deeds then thoſe with courage bold,
Then ſome do lay their cotes to gage,
Til that they haue receiued their wage.

Then fome the Counter oft doo kiffe,
  If that the money be not paid,
Or if that they their day doe miffe,
  For whiche to gage their cote was laid ;
Yet wil they not by this take heed,
But ftil continew to proceed.

Then fome therby their credit lofe,
  So that no wife man wil them truft,
Wherfore they can no lenger glofe,
  But rub and reuel not they muft,
For wherfoeuer they be come,
They are not fo wel truft as knowne.

Then fome at length do beg their bread,
  Who, if in time they had been wife,
Might wel haue had inough to fed
  Themfelues, their children, and their wiues ;
But when that all is gone and fpent,
It is to late then to repent.

Then fome to pilfer doo begin,
  But affone as they be efpied,
With whips they are laid on the fkin,
  At a carts ars being wel tied ;
But al this can not thofe amend,
That wil doo mifchefe to the end.

Then fome proceed to rob and kyl,
  Counting al fifh that comes to net ;
And yf that they might haue their wil,
  For right or wrong they wuld not let,
Til at the laft they fall in bands,
And can not efcape out of hands.

Then fome at Newgate doo take fhip,
    Sailing ful faft vp Holborne Hil;
And at Tiborn their anckers piche,
    Ful fore indeed againft their wil ;
But then it is to late, I fay,
To cal againe the yefterday.

Wherfore al ye that vfe this trade,
    Leaue of betimes, yf ye be wife,
Left that perchaunce this way ye wade
    Ful fore againft your owne deuife ;
For heer ye fee the end of fuche,
As litle haue and wil fpend muche.

℃ Finis, quoth W. F.

℃ Imprinted at London, at the long fhop adioining vnto Saint Mildreds Churche, in the
Poultry, by John Alde.

A newe Secte of Friars, called Capichini.

HESE newe frefhe come Friars, being
    fprong vp of late,
    Doe nowe within Andwarpe keepe
        their abidinge,
Seducinge muche people to their damned eftate,
    By their newe falfe founde doctrine the Gofpel
        deridinge ;
Sayinge and affirminge, which is no newe falfe
    tidinge,

That all fuche as doe the Popes doctrine
difpife,
As damned foules to hell mufte be ridinge ;
For they doe condemne them with their newe
found lies.
Thefe be the children of the worlde counted wife,
Whofe wifedome is folly to God and his elect ;
But let Sathan worke all that he can deuife,
God it is alone which the Gofpel doeth protect.

X

*The firft part of the faire Widow of Watling
ftreet and her 3 daughters, and how her wicked
fonne accufed her to be a harlot, and his fifters
baftards, only to deceiue them of their portions.*

To the tune of *Bragandary.*

F' the kind Widdow of Watling ftreet
I will the ftory tell,
Who by her hufband deere was left,
In fubftance rich and well;
A prodigall fonne likewife had fhe,
And faire yong daughters louely three ; —
Great mifery, forrow and mifery,
Commeth for want of grace.

⁋ For by his dayly practifes,
Which were both lewd and ill,
His fathers hart from him was drawne,
His loue and his good will;
But yet, what chance fo ere befell,
His mother loued him deerely well.

℃ When he in prifon lay full poore,
    For debt which he did owe,
His father would not ftur out of doore,
    For to releafe his woe ;
But when his mother his griefe did fee,
She found the meanes to fet him free.

℃ And when her hufband fell full fick,
    And went to make his will,—
O hufband, remember your fonne, fhe faid,
    Although he hath beene ill ;
But yet no doubt he may returne,
Repenting the euill that he hath done.

℃ Remember, wife, what forrow and care
    Through him I dayly found ;
Who, through his lewd vngratious deeds,
    Hath fpent me many a pound ;
And therefore, let him finke or fwim,
I meane not for to deale with him.

℃ And therefore fole executor here
    I do thee onely make,
To pay the debts and legacies,—
    The reft vnto thee take.
Not fo, my hufband deare, quoth fhe,
But let your fonne be ioynd with me ;

℃ For-why he is our child, fhe faid,—
    We can it not deny,—
The firft that euer graced you
    With fathers dignity ;—
O, if that euer you did me loue,
Graunt this requeft for his behoue.

❡ Thy loue, deere wife, was euermore
  Moſt precious vnto me,
And therefore, for thy ſweet loues ſake,
  I·graunt thy ſuite to thee ;
But, ere the yeare is fully ſpent,
I know thou wilt the ſame repent.

❡ Now was his ſonne receiued home,
  And with his mother deere
Was ioyn'd executor of the will,
  Which did his courage cheare.
The old man dying, buryed was,—
But now behold what came to paſſe.

The funeral being ended quite,
  It fel vpon a day
Some friends did fetch the widdow foorth,
  To driue conceits away.
While ſhe was forth, and thought no ill,
Her wicked ſonne doth worke his will.

Poſſeſſion of the houſe he took
  In moſt deſpitful wiſe,
Throwing his ſiſters out of dores,
  With ſad lamenting cryes.
When this they did his mother ſhow,
She would not beleeue he would do ſo.

But when ſhe came vnto her houſe,
  And found it true indeed,
She cald vnto her ſon, and ſaid,—
  Althogh her hart did bleed,—
Come down, my ſonne, come downe, quod ſhe,
Let in thy mother and ſiſters three.

❡ I will not let in my mother, he faid,
  Nor fifters any one ;
The houfe is mine, I will it keepe,
  Therefore, away ! be gone !
O fonne, canft thou indure to fee't,
Thy mother and fifters to lie in the ftreete ?

❡ Did not thy father, by his will,
  For terme of this my life,
Giue me this houfe for to enioy .
  Without al further ftrife ;
And more, of all his goods, quoth fhe,
I am executor ioynd with thee.

❡ My father left you the houfe, he faid,
  But this was his intent,—
That you therefore, during your life,
  Should pay me yearely rent ;
A hundred pound a yeare, therefore,
You fhall me giue, or giue it ore.

❡ And fith the citties cuftome is,
  That you the thirds muft haue
Of all my fathers moueables,
  I graunt what law doth craue ;
But not a peny more will I
Difcharge of any legafie.

❡ O wicked fonne, quoth fhe, that feekes
  Thy mother thus to fleece,—
Thy father to his daughters gaue
  Three hundred pound a peece :
Tell me who fhall their porcions pay,
Appointed at their marriage day.

❡ Then, with a fcornefull fmile, he faid,
  What talke you of fo much?
Ten pound a peece I will them giue,—
  My charitie is fuch.
Now fie vpon thee, beaft, quoth fhe,
That thus doth deale with them and me!

❡ But ere that they and I will take
  This iniury at thy hand,
The chiefeft peeres of England fhall
  The matter vnderftand.
Nay, if you go to that, quoth he,
Mark well what I fhall tell to thee :—

Thou haft a fecret harlot bin,
  And this ile proue full plaine,
That in my fathers lifetime did
  Lewd ruffians entertaine,
The which did then beget of thee,
In wicked fort, thefe baftards three.

❡ No daughters to my father then
  Were they in any wife,
As he fuppofd them for to be,
  Thou blinding fo his eyes ;
Therefore no right at all haue they
To any peny giuen this day.

❡ When fhe did heare her fhameles fonne
  For to defame her fo,
She with her louely daughters three,
  With griefe away did goe ;
But how this matter forth did fall,
The fecond part fhall fhew you all.
  Great mifery, forow, &c.   Finis.

Imprinted at London for T. P.
M

The ſecond part of the Widdow of Watling-ſtreete and her three Daughters.

To the tune of the Wanton Wife.

HE beautifull widdow of Watling
　　　ſtreete,
　　　Being thus falſly accuſde by her
　　　ſonne,
With her three daughters of fauor ſo ſweet,
　　Whoſe beauty the loue of ſo many had wonne,
With her daughters three, for ſuccour went ſhe,
Vnto the kings counſaile of noble degree.
　　　Now fie vpon falſhood and forgerie fraile,
　　　For great is the truth, and it ſhall preuaile !

❡ Her ſonne by a writ now ſommoned is
　　At the Star-chamber with ſpeed to appeare,
To anſwere there the abuſes of his ;—
　　The Lords of the Counſel the matter will heare.
The news was brought ; his wits he ſought,
Which way his villanie beſt might be wrought.

❡ Then vp and downe the citty ſo faire
　　He ſeeketh companions to ſerue his turne,—
A ſort of vacabonds, naked and bare,
　　The which to worke murders for money is won :
Theſe wretches behold, for money and golde,
He hired for witneſſes his lyes to vphold, &c.

❡ My maiſters, quoth he, my mother by name
　　To be a lewd ſtrumpet accuſed I haue ;

And, hauing no witneſſe to proue that ſame,
  Your ayde and aſſiſtance herein I do craue :
Therefore, without feare, before the Lords there,
Yet this thing is certaine, you ſixe ſhall it ſweare.

❡ The firſt two, quoth he, ſhal ſweare on a booke,
  That ſixteene yeares paſt they plainely did ſee,
As they through the garden hedge ſadly did looke,
  That ſhe in one houre was abuſed by three ;
And how it fell, as they markt it wel,
That iuſt nine moneths after ſhe had hir firſt
    girle.

❡ The ſecond couple ſhall ſweare in this ſort,
  That at Briſtow Faire, about xvij. yeares paſt,
She with her owne apprentiſe did fal in ſuch ſport,
  That her ſecond daughter was got at the laſt.
Now truſt vs, quod they, weele ſweare what you
    ſay,
Or anything elſe for money, this day, &c.

And thus the third couple their oath now ſhal
    take,
  That as at the bath ſhe ſtaid on a day,
For ach in her bones, as the ſcuſe ſhe did make,
  How ſhe with a courtier the wanton did play ;
And how well you wot, in the pleaſant plot,
Her deareſt yong daughter for certaine was got.

But now, you maſters, your names let me know,
  That I may prouide you apparell with ſpeed ;
Like ſixe graue cittizens ſo muſt you go,
  The better your ſpeeches the Lords will heed ;
So ſhal I with ſcorne, ere Saturday morne,
Proue her a harlot, my ſiſters baſe borne, &c.

❡ My name is Make-fhift, the firft man did fay;
    And Francis Light-finger, the fecond likewife;
Cutbert Creepe-window, the third to difplay;
    And Rowland Rob-man, with foule ftaring
        eyes;
Jack Shameles comes then, with Hary Steale-hen.
You are, quod the widdow, fome right honeft
    men!

❡ Before the lords moft prudent and graue,
    This wretch doth with his witneffe come:
The mother complains, and juftice doth craue
    Of all the offences that he hath her done.
My Lords, then quod he, I pray you heare me,—
The law for my deeds my warrant fhall be.

I fay, fhe is a harlot moft vilde,
    And thofe be her baftards that ftandeth in
        place,
And that fhe hath often her body defilde
    By very good witnes ile proue to her face.
This thing of thy mother thou oughtft for to
    fmother,—
'Tis fhame for a child to fpeake [fo] of his mother!

❡ But if this matter be proued vntrue,
    And thou a falfe lyar be found to thy face,
Worfe then an infidell, Pagon, or Jew,
    Thou oughtft to be punifht and plagd in this
        cafe;
And therefore draw neere, and now let vs heare
What faies the witnes that here doth appeare.

❡ When the firft couple did come for to fweare,
    They quiuerd and quakt in moft wondrous fort;

The lords very countenance did put them in feare,
  And now they knew not what to report ;
The fecond likewife ftard fo with his eyes,
They ftamberd and knew not what to deuife.

❧ The lords, perceiuing the cafe how it went,
  Did afke the laft couple what they had to fay,
Who fell on their knees incontinent,
  Saying, they were hird for mony that day :
Quoth they, it is fo, the truth for to fhow,
Againft the good widow no harme we do know.

❧ Thus was the widow deliuered from blame,
  With her three daughters of beauty moft bright,
Her fonne reproached with forrow and fhame,
  Hauing his iudgment appointed him right,—
To loofe, at the leaft, the goods he poffeft,
To loofe both his eares, and banifht to reft.

When he heard this iudgment pronounced to be,
  The teares full bitterly fell down from his face,—
To mother and fifters he kneeled on his knee,
  Confeffing that lucre had wrought his difgrace ;
That for my own gaine I fought to detaine
My fifters three portions, this lye I did faine !

Therefore, deare mother, forgiuenes I craue
  Of you and my fifters, offended fo fore ;
My body from perill if you will but faue,
  I fweare I will grieue and offend you no more.
The lords then replide,—the law iuftly tride,
The punifhment now thou art like to abide :

❧ Therefore to prifon now thou fhalt go,
  Where thou fhalt the king's pleafure abide ;

From thence to be brought, with fhame and with
   wo,
To fuffer the punifhment due to thy pride :
Then out of hand, thou fhalt vnderftand
That prefently thou fhalt be banifht the land.

❡ Now, while in prifon this prifoner did reft,
   Himfelfe he hanged in defperate wife—
Such horror of confcience poffeffed his breft ;
   And being caft forth, the rauens pickt out his
   eies.
All children, behold what here hath bin tolde,
Accufe no man falfly for lucre of golde !

Now fie vpon falfhood and forgerie fraile,
For great is the truth, and it will preuaile.

FINIS.

Imprinted at London for T. P.

❡ *Almightie God I pray his Holy Spirite to fend,*
The iuft mannes hart ftedfaft to ftay, and wicked
liues to mend.

RUE tryall touchyng truth time
trimly here doth trye,
E xcept the fcribes therfore we paffe
in righteoufnes, we dye.
M yndes many mooued bee all truth to eftablyfh ;
P apes popifh, puft in Plutoes pride, all popery
here doe wyfh ;—

V oyde from them all, good men, which godly
    be in mynde,
S ith Sathan affaileth fome fo fore, and ftyl their
    harts doth blynde.

E mbrace and loue the truth; on Chrifts fyde
    ftifly ftand ;
D eny the Pope, Sathan, the Turke, reiect them
    quite from hand.
A nd neuer wifh in wyll with wicked men t'agree,
X pe faith we can not their wayes hould, and
    eke his feruaunts be.

R eiect and expell quite that which difpleafe
    God may ;
E ncline to Chrift, the truth embrace, be fure
    thereon to ftay ;
R eioyce, though rigour raunge, and run for to
    obtayne ;
V pon thee perfecution beare, great ioyes to haue
    agayne ;
M ufe nothyng on thefe dayes, but wey the time
    now frayle.

T he tryed truth time vndertreades,—in time truth
    wyl preuayle,
I n time the wicked laugh, in time the iuft lament:
M ufe not, therfore, the iuft to trie, the Lordes
    wyl now is bent ;
E mploy thy wyll and mynd to the Scriptures
    deuine.

B e not feduced in no wyfe, from truth doe not
    decline;
R efufe (yf faith thou haft) a Chriftian dumme to
    bee ;

Y elde out thy talent with encreaſe, and looke thy
  faith be free.
N o doubt, yf dumme thou lurke, clokyng thy
  faith for feare,
G od wyl thee plague, and to good men thy faint
  faith wyl appeare ;
E nclyne thine eare hereto, and this well vnderſtand ;—
T rie out the ſence hereof by truth,—all wickedneſſe withſtand ;
H eauen with the Lorde of Lordes we ſhall not
  inherite
E xcept our righteouſnes far paſſe the ſcribe and
  hipocrite.

A ll wicked men we ſee now glorie much in
  mynd,
L ookyng for maſſe, an idoll which to them hath
  ben full kynd.

T ruely thoſe naughtie men thinke now, within
  ſhort time,
H ere, for Jeſus Chriſtes true worde, to plant
  Sathans doctrine ;
Y ea, ſtyll they hope indeede, and ſtyll looke for
  a day,
N o doubt, Chriſts goſpel to exclude, and popes
  lawes to beare ſway.
G od ſaue our noble queene, Lorde, graunt this,
  we requyre ;
E mong vs here long ſhee may raigne, and cut
  ſhort papes deſyre ;
S end out thy wrath, O Lorde, confound with
  open ſhame

T hofe which in hart vnto her grace long lyfe
  doe not proclaime !
O ut pull thofe hatefull harts, which in fpight
  rage and boyle

A gainft thy truth, her grace, good men; O Lorde,
  thou canft them foyle.
N othyng but wickedneffe, fuch in their hartes
  embrace,

E mong vs here although they fay, and beare out
  a fmooth face.
N ow, Lorde, thy flocke defend ; Lorde, bleffe
  thine heritage ;
D ireft thy fpirit ouer vs all, in this our time and
  age ;
E ncourage vs againft rageyng Sathan alway.

Q uicken our myndes, ftrength vs herein, O
  Lorde, to thee we pray ;
V ouchfafe eke on thofe men thy heauenlie fpirite
  to fend ;
O Lorde, enfpire them with thy grace, their err-
  yng liues t'amend ;
D eftroy all errours here, illuminate their hart.

C all home all thofe which haue run wyde, to the
  truth them conuart ;
H eale thofe which broken be, O Lorde, I fay,
  in mynd !
R educe and bryng to thee in truth all wicked
  Jewes vnkynd,
I nfidels and eke Turkes, Paganes which know
  thee not :
S o fhall we all be to thee one inheritaunce and
  lot.

T read vnder and fuppreffe all vice, and eke
    expell
O ur hollow-harted hipocrites, which loue not
    thy Gofpell;
P ut in their harts fuch grace, O Lorde, that they
    may now
H ope in thee, their eternall God, and to thee
    their hartes bow!
E uer to watch and pray, as thou haft taught the
    fame,
R eady to be with oyle in lampe, heauen with thee
    to attaine.

W ee, hopyng on thee thus, all vayne hope now
    confound,
I n heauen with thee at length wyl we thy worthy
    praife forth found.
L orde, graunt that we may raigne in ioyes ce-
    leftiall;
S uch as wyl ftyl thy foes remaine, fhall to paynes
    infernall.
O Lorde, graunt this requeft,—Lorde, let thy
    kyngdome cum :
N ow watch and pray we wyll ;—for whye? Tem-
    pus edax rerum.

    ❡ Finis, quod Chriftopher Wilfon.

A Song againſt the Maſs.

OME hope you ſee,—
  The more pitie,—
    Not in the Lorde of might ;
  Whoſe harts and mynd
His wayes ſhould fynd,
  To prayſe him day and night.

℃ With hart and voyce
They ſhould reioyce
  Onely in Chriſt, I ſay ;
And not to hope
To ſee the pope,
  With his lawes to beare ſway.

℃ Lament I doe,
Here to ſee nowe,
  The ioyes that ſome be in,—
Wyſhyng for Maſſe,
I ſay, alas !
  The cloke of filthy ſin !

℃ I may here write,
And truth endite,
  Affyrme plainely, and ſay :
The worde of truth,—
The more is ruth,—
  Is ſowne in ſtonie way.

℃ For all teachyng
And true preachyng,

Some harts be hard as fteele ;
There is no way
Their harts to ftay,
    Or caufe them truth to feele.

℅ But ftoute they be
In all poperie,
    As by this man doth feeme ;
Whofe fhameleffe face
Put forth this cafe,
    And bad his neighbours deme :

℅ Where beft fhould be,
To make, quod he,
    An aulter for our Maffe ?
Let vs firft be
Herein, quod he,
    It wyll thus come to paffe.

℅ This freend of popes
Offred ten grotes
    This aulter there to make,
Where maffe fhould be ;
Haue here, quod he,
    This money mine here take.

℅ Lorde, our Queene faue,
We cry and craue,
    In godlie ftate alway ;
Defend her grace
Long time and fpace
    Emong vs here, we pray !

℅ Imprinted at London without Alderfgate, in
little Britaine, by Alex. Lacy.   The 16 of
Auguft, 1566.

The Daunce and Song of Death.

At the four corners four engravings, with verſes.

1. Under a picture of the Miſer (or rich man) counting his gold, with Death at his elbow, the following quatrain.

From your gold and ſiluer
To graue ye muſt daunce ;
Though you loue it ſo deare,
And haue therein affiaunce.

2. Over a picture of a Priſoner fettered to an iron ring, with Death at his ſide.

Thy pryſon and chaynes·
From graue cannot keepe ;
But daunce, though in paynes,
Thou ſhalt thereto creepe.

3. Engraving of a Judge upon the bench of juſtice, with Death beſide him, theſe lines under :—

From trone of iuſt iudgement,
Syr Judge, daunce with vs ;
To graue come incontinent
From ſtate ſo glorious.

4. A Man careſſing a Lady in a bower, a table ſpread with wine and fruit, Death ſeated behind them ; the following inſcribed.

Ye dallying fyne louers,
In mydſt of your chere,
To daunce here be partners,
And to graue draw ye nere.

In the centre a figure playing the pipe and tabor upon a feat
made of crofs-bones, mattock, and fhovel, acrofs a yawning
grave, with this placard, " Sycknes, Deathes minftrel."
    Around him in a circle, joined hand in hand, are the
following figures, Death leading the dance, the king,
the begger, the old man, the childe, the wyfe man, the
foole, with thefe lines.

Come, daunce this trace, ye people all,
    Both prince and begger, I fay ;
Yea, old, yong, wyfe, and fooles I call,
    To graue, come, take your way.
        For ficknes pipes thereto,
        By griefes and panges of wo.

A Ballad intituled, Prepare ye to the plowe.

To the tune of Pepper is blacke.

℃ The queene holdes the plow, to continew good feede;
    Truftie fubieftes, be readie to helpe, if fhe neede.

OOKE vp, my Lordes, and marke my
        wordes,
    And heare what I fhall fing ye :
    And fubiefts all, both great and fmall,
Now marke what word I bring ye.
Parnafo Hill, not all the fkill
    Of Nimphs or Mufes fayned,
Can bring about that I finde out,
    By Chrift himfelfe ordayned.

Let wifdom be, as it is, I fee,
  A gift moft worth the telling,
Which neuer was fo brought to paffe
  Where Pagans haue ben dwelling,
Is now, in fine, by power deuine,
  Among vs Englifh planted;
Which many a day was kept away,
  And many a one it wanted.

And by that wifdom haue we had
  Such proofe as yet was neuer,
To judge and deeme both good and bad,
  To our great comfort euer.
Which fithes we haue, now let vs hold,
  This tutchftone is the triall,
To beate the baggage from the gold,
  And truth from falfe deniall.

And by this knowledge we do know
  That euery thing is vaine
Beneath the fonn, which heare below
  We couet to attaine.
Let not the fpright geue vs delight
  To labour and attend vs,
To feke to haue before our graue
  The ioy that Chrifte may fend vs.

In feking that, then, muft we nat
  Build on the fandy furges,
Nor fow our feede where euery weede
  His grace and bounty vrges;
Nor put our hope in Preefte or Pope,
  In maffe or other matters,
Or, by our dole, to faue our foule
  With filling empty platters.

Or by a pardon to appeafe
    The furfits of our finning,
Although our fathers had all theafe
    By wicked mens beginning.
Nor let vs make our flock and flore
    A burden to accufe vs ;
For, doing fo, fo much the more
    We tempt GOD to refufe vs.

Neither let vs once prefume fo far,
    Of mercy or of meekenes,
To counterfait, to make or mar
    This image or this likeneffe,
That our forefathers did beleue
    Were Gods to giue and guide them :
Such follies did the Chriftians greeue,
    And Pagans now deride them.

Remember once the latter law—
    Left yet in Moyfes table,—
That neighbourly to liue in awe
    It is moft commendable :
Then fhouldft thou not defire to craue
    Thy neighbours loffe or lacke ;
Neither exceffe defire to haue,
    That puts thy foule to wracke.

Neither vfery, nor vfe at all
    Of women, wealth, or wine ;
Neither of aboundance, great or fmall,
    Ill gotten, fhould be thine :
Neither fhould contencion, craft, increafe,
    Nor fwearing beare the fway,
Nor God vnferued—men as beafts
    Would break the Sabboth day.

Then would the honour duly hit,
  To parents, lord, or king ;
Then would ther be no doubt a whit
  To haue ftore of euerything :
All this the new law, with the old,
  Doth nip vs to remember,
Euen as the froft, that waxeth cold,
  Doth nip vs in December.

And as, vpon a fodain heat,
  We foone forget that freefing,
When God doth of his mercy great
  Spare vs for lack of leefing,—
So let vs think, as Sommer fhows
  Grene graffe to our deliting,
We fe that all the graffe that growes
  Goth down with litle fmiting ;

And when the mowyer coms to mowe,
  'Tis fone both ripe and rotten :
This tale, I truft, of hye and low
  Will neuer be forgotten.
On Gods good booke then let vs loke
  For that which neuer faileth ;
Without which boke, by hooke or crooke,
  No worldly wit preuaileth.

God faue her Grace that holds the plow,
  To fowe this trufty treafure ;
Though many a one be ftubborn now,
  And harrow it but at leafure :
God graunt that he that harrowed Hell
  In guardon ftill may haue her,

N

And fend you grace that thinke not well
Of God, that fo doth faue hir.

W. Elderton.

❧ Imprinted at London, in Fleeteftreete, by
William How for Richard Johnes : and are
to be folde at his Shop, ioyning to the
fouthweft doore of Paules Church.

*An Epitaph on the death of the vertuous Mat-
rone the Ladie Maiorefle, late wyfe to the right
Honorable Lorde (Alexander Auenet,) Lord Maior
of the Citie of London, who deceafed the vij. daie
of July,* 1570.

ELPE nowe, ye Mufes nyne, powre
out your noates of woe!
Aide me, with pitious piercing plaints,
the loffe of her to fhoe,
Whofe virtues, maugre Death! fhall lyue and
laft for aye,
As fliyng Fame in golden trump doth cherefully
difplay.
Ye ladyes, leave your fportes, your paftymes fet
afyde ;
To weepe this ladyes fatall fine, conduictes of
ftreames prouide :
Caft off your coftly filkes, your juelles nowe forfake,

To decke yourſelues in mournynge weedes, now
poaſtynge haſte do make.
Helpe now, ye faythfull wyues, to wayle this
faythfull wyfe,
Whoſe flowynge vertues were not hyd whyle ſhe
enioyed lyfe ;—
As well to frende as foe her curteſie was knowne ;—
But now the goddes haue thought it good to
clayme agayne their owne.
Lvcina hath forgot her chardge, the fatall Fates
haue don ;
Clotho hath left the rocke of lyfe, and Lachas
longe hath ſpon.
Theſe werie of their wonted toyle, at mightie
Ioves decree—
To whom the heauens, the earth, and ſea, and
all thynges ſubieƈt bee,—
The ſiſter dire, fearce Atropos, with ſchortchyng
cuttynge knyfe,
Hath ſhred the threede that longe dyd holde this
godly ladies lyfe;
Whoſe loſſe, deare dames, bewayle, and weepe
with many a teare,
For you ſhall miſſe a matrone graue in daunger
you to cheare,
Whoſe counſell in their neede her neighbours
could not want.
Her helpe vnto the comfortleſſe could neuer yet
bee ſcant ;
Vnto the poore, oppreſt with ſickeneſſe, griefe and
payne,
To miniſter and giue reliefe her hart was euer
fayne.
The poore haue loſt a nurſe to helpe their nedie
ſtate,

The ritche fhall want a perfecte frende, as they
    can well relate.
Thus ritche and poore fhall want her aide at
    euerie neede ;
For both eftates in daunger deepe fhe laboured to
    feede,—
The ritche with counfelles fwete to chearifh ftyll
    fhe thought,
The poore by almes and lyberall giftes to tender
    longe fhe fought.
But who fhall haue the greateft loffe I knowe is
    not vnknowen,—
Her beft beloued, the wight whom fhee accompted
    for her owne,
The Lorde MAIOR, whiche nowe doth rule in
    LONDON, noble citie,
Shall want her fight,—the greater griefe to miffe
    a mate fo wittie ;
A phenyx rare, a turtell true, fo conftant in her
    loue,
That Nature nedes muft fhowe her force, her
    hufbandes teares to moue.
Who for the loffe of fuche a wyfe can fobbyng
    fighes refrayne,
In whom fo many vertues dyd continue and
    remayne ?
You damfelles deare domefticall, whiche in her
    houfe abyde,
Haue caufe to wayle, for you haue loft a good and
    godly guide,
Whofe lenytie and gentell hart you all haue
    knowen and felt,
For vnto you in courteous forte her giftes fhe
    euer dealt.
You officers, that dayly ferue her lorde at euery
    neede,

Can teſtifie that you haue loſt a ladie kynde in
   deede,—
So gentell, graue, demure, and wife, as ye yourfelues expreſſe,
That needes ye muſt guſh foorth your teares, and
   weepe with bytterneſſe.
In fyne, both ritche and poore haue iuſt caufe
   giuen to wayle ;
The ritch in counſell lacke a frende, the poore
   their comfort fayle.
The troupe of maryed dames, whiche ſhall her
   vertues knowe,
Haue offered caufe in bytter teares ſome tyme
   for to beſtowe.
But ſith it is the goddes decree, to whom all fleſh
   muſt bende,
To take this ladie from the earth, and bringe her
   dayes to ende,
Who can withholde that they wyll haue? who
   dare their wyll withſtande?
To vayne it were for mortall men the caufe to take
   in hande.
Her vertues were ſo great, that they haue thought
   it meete
To take from hence vnto the heauens her chriſtall
   foule ſo fweete,
Which now inclofed is with aungelles rownde
   aboute.
Suche hoape we haue, no other caufe is giuen vs
   for to doubt.
Her corps ſhall ſhrowde in claye, the earth her
   right doth craue,
This ladie yeldes her parent too, her tombe, her
   cell and graue ;
From whence no kynge nor keyfar can, nor ruler
   bearynge fwaye,

For all their force and puiſſaunce, once ſtarte or
  go awaye.
All fleſhe ſhall haue an ende, as goddes do graunt
  and wyll,
And reape rewarde as they deſerue, hap good, or
  hap it yll.
But thoughe that death haue done his worſte, this
  dame to take awaye,
In ſpite of death her vertues ſhall endure and laſt
  for aye.
℃ Farewell, O ladye deare! the heauens haue
  choſen thee,—
Receyue this VALE; I haue done; thou getteſt no
  more of mee.

Poſt funera viuit virtus, quoth John Phillip.

Imprinted at London by Richarde Johnes.

༺᠁༻

℃ *A famous dittie of the joyful receauing of*
the Queens moſte excellent maieſtie by the worthy
citizens of London, the xij. day of Nouember,
1584, at her graces comming to Saint James.

To the tune of Wigmores Galliard.

HE twelfe day of Nouember laſt,
  Elizabeth, our noble queen,
To Londen-warde ſhe hied faſt,
  Which in the cuntry long had been.
The citizens went then apace,
On ſtately ſteeds, to meet her grace,
In veluet coats and chaines of golde,
Moſte gorgiouſly for to beholde.

❡ Each company in his degree
  Stood orderly in good aray,
To entertaine Her Maiefty,
  As fhe did paffe along the way.
And by each man did duly ftand
A wayter with a torch in hand,—
Becaufe it drue on toward night,—
Along the way her grace to light.

❡ The people flockéd there amain,
  The multitude was great to fee ;
Their joyful harts were glad, and fain
  To view her princely maiefty,
Who at the length came riding by,
Within her chariot openly ;   ·
Euen with a noble princely train
Of lords and ladies of great fame.

❡ Her maiefty was glad to fee
  Her fubiects in fo good a cafe,
Which then fell humbly on their knee,
  Defiring God to faue her grace.
And like a noble prince that day
For them in like forte did fhe pray ;
And curteoufly fhe anfwered ftill,
I thank you all for your good will.

❡ And bowing down on euery fide,
  Mofte louingly vnto them all,
A poor man at the length fhe fpied,
  Which down before her grace did fall.
And curteoufly fhe then did ftay,
To heer what he had then to fay ;
To whome he did prefent anon,
An humble fupplication.

Then plefantly fhe paffed on,
  Til fhe vnto Saint James came,
And alwaies, as fhe went along,
  The people cri'd with might and main,—
O Lord, preferue your noble grace,
And all your fecret foes deface!
God bleffe and keep our noble queen,
Whofe like on earth was neuer feen!

What traitors hart can be fo hard
  To hurt or harme that princely flower?
What wretch from grace is fo debard,
  That can againft her feem to lower,
Which is the onely ftar of light,
That doth amaze all princes fight,—
A mofte renowned virgin queen,
Whofe like on earth was neuer feen?

The daughter of a noble king,
  Defending of a royall race,
Whofe fame through all the world doth ring,
  Whofe vertues fhines in euery place;—
The diamond of delight and ioy,
Which guides her cuntry from anoy;
A mofte renowned virgin queen,
Whofe like on earth was neuer feen.

❡ The peerles pearle of princes all,
  So ful of pitty, peace, and loue,
Whofe mercy is not proued fmall,
  When foule offendors doo her mooue.
A phenix of mofte noble minde,
Vnto her fubiects good and kinde;
A mofte renowned virgin queen,
Whofe like on earth was neuer feen.

❦ The feruant of the mighty God,
  Which dooth preferue her day and night,
For whome we feel not of his rod,
  Although the pope hath doon his fpite.
The cheef maintainer of his Woord,
Wherein confifts our heauenly food ;—
O Lord, preferue our noble queen,
Whofe like on earth was neuer feen!

❦ And fuch as hollow-harted be,
  Partakers of the Romifh rout,
Which thinketh mifcheef fecretly,
  The Lord wil fuerly finde them out,
And giue them their deferuings due,
Which to her grace is found vntrue ;
But, Lord, preferue our noble queen,
Whofe like on earth was neuer feen !

❦ In many dangers hath fhe been,
  But God was euermore her guide ;
He wil not fee our gratious queen
  To fuffer harme through traitors pride ;
But euery one which fought her fall,
The Lord did ftil confound them all,
And fuch as thought her life to fpill
Themfelues mofte defperately did kil.

❦ And euery traitor in this land,
  Whofe wicked thoughts are yet vnknown,
The Lord confume them out of hand,
  Before they be more riper grown ;
Whofe harts are fet with one accord
Againft th' annointed of the Lord ;
But, God, preferue our noble queen,
Whofe like on earth was neuer feen !

  ❡ Lord, fend her long and happy daies,
    In England for to rule and raigne,
  Gods glory euermore to raife,
    True Juftice alwaies to maintain,—
  Which now, thefe fix and twenty yeers,
  So royally with vs appeers;—
  O Lord, preferue our noble queen,
  Whofe like on earth was neuer feen!

      Finis.   Richard Harrington.

❡ At London : printed by Edward Allde for
Yarath James, and are to be folde in Newgate
Market againft Chrift church gate.   1584.

A meruaylous ftraunge deformed Swyne.

HERE, good reader, fhalt thou beholde
a ftraunge and deformed fwyne,
farowed and brought foorth in Den-
marke, and there bought and brought
ouer by an Englifhman, which hath it at this
prefent; and is to be feen aliue, the proportion
wherof is wonderous ftraunge to beholde and
vew; the forepart therof from the fnoute beneath
the forefhoulders are in al pointes like vnto a
fwine, except the eares only, which refemble the
eares of a lion; the hinder parte (contrarie to
kinde) is proportioned in all pointes like vnto a
ram, hauing fofte wooll, both white and blacke,
mixed monge the hard heare, and fo groweth

from the fhoulders downewarde, all the body ouer ;
and it is a boare pyg, howbeit there doth nothing
appeare outwarde, but onely the pyfell vnder his
belly; but if a man lift to feele and gripe it in
the grindes, there ye may feele his coddes within
his belly; and the moft ftraungeft thinge of all
is the mifshapen and deformed feete, wheron grow
certayne tallents and very harde clawes, doubling
vnder his feete, euery claw fo byg as a mans
fynger, and blacke of colour, and the length of
euery of them are full x inches, very ftraunge and
wonderfull to beholde. It feedeth and eateth
diuers and fundrie thinges, as well haye and graffe
as breade and apples, with fuch other thinges as
fheepe and fwyne do feede on.

⁋ *An exhortacion or warnynge to all men, for*
amendment of lyfe.

COME neere, good Chriftians all,
  Beholde a monfter rare,
Whofe monftrous fhape, no doubt, fortels,
  Gods wrath we fhould beware.
His wondrous works we ought not iudge,
  As toyes and trifles vaine ;
Whither it be childe or brutifh beaft,
  Forwarnings they are playne.
As now this mingled brutifh beaft
  Gods creature is, we fee,
Although as ftraunge of fhape and forme
  As poffyblie may be;
For if you do way well ech poynt, *Wᵒ ᵐᶜ*
  His nature and his fhape,

I feare, refembles fome of thofe
    As on the fame do gape ;
For-why moft fwinifh are our liues,
    And monftrous, that is fure.
Though we refemble fimple fheepe,
    Or lambes that be moft pure,
But euery tree itfelfe will try,
    At laft by his owne fruite ;
Though on our backs we cary woll,
    Our confcience is pollute ;
Though fmilingly, with flattering face,
    We feeme Gods word to loue,
Contrary wife fom hate the fame,
    As well their deedes did prooue,
Who ment the ruine of our realme ;
    As traytours to our queene,
Som white-fafte lambs, haue fought to do,
    Nay, monftrous fwine, I weene.
I meane not here at large to fhowe
    Offences as they bee,
In whom they raigne, in hie or low,
    I name here no degree ;
But generally I fay to all,
    Repent, amend your life ;
The greedy rich, the needy poore,
    Yea, yong man, maide, and wife !
The proteftant, the papift eke,
    What fecte fo that ye be,
Gripe your own confcience, learne to do
    As God commaundeth ye ;
For all are finners, Dauid faith,—
    Yea, do the beft we may,
Vnprofitable feruaunts ftill we be,—
    We can it not denay.
Judge ye therfore how far amiffe
    All thofe their liues do frame,

That outwardly profeſſe Gods truth,
   And inward hate the ſame.
Judge ye againe that hate your prince,
   And ſeeke the realme to ſpoyle,
What monſtrous ſwine you proue at length,
   For all your couert coyle.
Experience late by Felton falſe,
   And Nortons two, I weene ;
Their treaſon known were wondred at,
   As they had monſters been ;
And ſurely I can iudge no leſſe
   But that they monſters were,
Quite changed from true ſubjeĉts ſhape,
   Their deedes did ſo appere.
Then let their deedes example be
   To vs that ſubieĉts are,
For treaſon ends by ſhamfull death,—
   Therfore by them beware.
I ſpeake not here of monſtrous pride
   In man, in mayde, and wife ;
Nor whoordom, which is daily vſde
   In England ranke and rife.
Of couetouſneſſe what ſhould I ſay,
   Or vſery daily don ?
It booteth not to ſpeake therof,
   So much therby is wonne.
But if they well do count their cardes,
   How God they do offend,
I wis their ſweete ill-gotten gaines
   Hath ſowre and bitter end.
From the which end deliuer vs, Lord,
   And graunt both hie and low
To become thy ſeruaunts iuſt and true,
   And then our end we know.
God grant our gracious ſouerain queen
   Long ouer vs may raigne ;

And this life paſt, with Chriſt our Lord
Heauens ioyes ſhe may attaine!

Finis, I. P.

Imprinted at London by William How, for
Richard Iohnes, and are to be folde at his
ſhop ioyning to the ſouth weſt doore of Paules
Churche.

Love deſerveth Love.

YOONGE man that on VENVS ſporte
doth raunge,
Taking delight his miſtreſeſſe to
chaunge,
In lewe of LOVE doth hope to be regarded,
And with a gentle looke to be rewarded.
He proffers ſeruice, vowing all he maye,
That, were ſhe deade, there neuer would be daie!
Saying then,—Phœbe, thow art more deuine,—
Shee borroweth Phœbus light, and Phœbus thine;
And one the top his eſtridge plumed helme
He beares her gloue, his foes to ouerwhelme;
And for reward he nothinge doth requier
But loues ſweet-water to aſſwage luſte' fier;
He ſeekes not for abundance out of meaſure,
But loue's reward is all his hop'te for treaſure.

T. W.

A *spell for Ione*.

TELL me, fweete girle, how fpellſt thou
   Ione;
   Tell me but that, is all I craue,—
I ſhall not neede to lye alone,
When ſuch a louely mate I haue.
That thou arte one who can denye,
   O one whoſe praiſe no tonge can tell?
And all will graunt that I am I,—
   O happy I, if right thou fpell;—
If I am I, and thou art one,
Tell me, fweete wench, how fpellſt thou Ione?

IONE.

Ile tell you, fir, and tell you true,
   For I am I and I am one,
So can I fpell Ione without you,
   And fpelling fo, can lye alone :
My I to one is conſonant,
   But as for yours, it is not fo ;
If then your I agrement want,
   I to your I muſt aunfwer no ;
Wherfor leaue of your fpelling plea,
And let your I be I per fe.

RES.

Your aunfwer makes me almoſt blind,
   To put out one and leaue one I ;
Unleſs herein fome hope I find,
   Therfor I muſt difpayre and dye ;

But I am you, when you doe fpeake ;—
O fpeak againe, and tell me fo !
My hart with forrow canot break
    To heare fo kinde a graunting, no ;
For this is all for which I fue,
That I may be turnd into you.

IONE.

Nay, if you turne and wind and prefs,
    And in the crofs-row haue fuch fkill,
I am put down, I muft confefs ;
    It bootes me not to crofs your will.
If you fpeak tru, fay I ftand to it,
    For you and I are now but one ;
And I will ly that you may doe it,—
    Now put together we fpell Ione ;
But how will Ione be fpeld, I wonder,
    When you and I fhall part afunder ?

A Paradox.

WHAT lyfe is beft to lead in citty or in
    towne ?
    In thone both witt and wealth, court
    getts vs great renown ;
The country keepes in health, bringes quietnes of
    mind,
Where wholfome ayre with exerfice and pretty
    fportes we find.
Wed, and thou haft a bed of follace and of ioye ;
Wed not, and haue a reft without anoy ;

The fetled loue is fafe, fwete is the loue at large ;
Thy children are thy comforters, no childrun are
　no charge ;
Youth lufty is and getts, age honnord is and wife ;
Then not to dye or be vnborne is beft, by my
　aduife.

* * * * *

Thefe verfes found I thus placed on a wall,
For want of ink, twas written with a coale,
By one who fince hath chaungd his ftat of lyf,
For liuing fingle now hath gott a wife.
So that, howere we men think ftraung to mary,
It is our cheif defyr, though long we tary ;
Witnefs this party, who thefe lines hath penned,
Which doutles then was of an other mind.
But graunt this tru, that here is fayd of menn,
Much more in maydes and widowes I thinke then ;
Yett left I fhould proue tedious with my rime,
Here will I end, wifhing you a good hufband in
　time.　　　　　　　　　　　　　I. G.

The Ficklenefs of Women.

Dust is lighter then a fether,
And the wind more light then ether ;
But a womans fickle minde
More light then feather, duft or wind.

o

An Epitaph on Edmund Sandford, written in gould.

Y fand ftill refts, though lyfe doth paffe
Fleete as the ford, parting my name ;
So parte remaines, though run my glafs,
For what was fand is ftill the fame.
Thus death dicaies not all my truft,
For fand I was, and now am duft.

❡ *The forme and ſhape of a monſtrous Child,
borne at Maydſtone in Kent, the xxiiij. of
October,* 1568.

As ye this ſhape abhorre
In body for to haue,
So flee ſuch vices farre
As might the ſoule depraue.

In Gods power all fleſh ſtands, '
As the clay in the potters hands,
To faſhion euen as he wyll,
In good ſhape or in yll.

T Maydſtone in Kent there was one
Marget Mere, daughter to Richard
Mere, of the fayd towne of Maydſtone,
who, being vnmaryed, played the
naughty packe, and was gotten with childe, being
deliuered of the fame childe the xxiiij. daye of
October laſt paſt, in the yeare of our Lord 1568,
at vij. of the clocke in the afternoone of the fame

day, being Sonday; which child, being a man-child,
had firſt the mouth flitted on the right fide, like
a libardes mouth, terrible to beholde, the left
arme lying vpon the breſt, faſt therto ioyned, hauing as it were ſtumps on the handes, the left leg
growing vpward toward the head, and the ryght
leg bending toward the left leg, the foote therof
growing into the buttocke of the ſayd left leg.
In the middeſt of the backe there was a broade
lump of fleſh, in faſhion lyke a roſe, in the myddeſt
whereof was a hole, which voyded like an iſſue.
Thys ſayd childe was borne alyue, and lyued xxiiij.
houres, and then departed this lyfe,—which may
be a terrour as well to all ſuch workers of filthynes
and iniquity, as to thoſe vngodly liuers who (if
in them any feare of God be) may mooue them
to repentance and amendement of lyfe, which
God for Chriſtes ſake graunt both to them and
vs. Amen! Witneſſes hereof were theſe :
William Plomer, John Squier, glaſier, John
Sadler, goldſmith, befides diuers other credible
perſons, both men and women.

A warnyng to England.

Tʜɪs monſtrous ſhape to thee, England,
    Playn ſhewes thy monſtrous vice,
If thou ech part wylt vnderſtand,
    And take thereby aduice.

For waying firſt the gaſpyng mouth,
    It doth full well declare
Vꟲhat rauine and oppreſſion both
    Is vſed wyth greedy care.

For, for the backe and gorging paunch,
    To lyue in wealth and eafe
Such toyl men take, that none may ftaunch
    Their greedy minde, nor pleafe.

For in fuch fort their mouthes they infect
    With lying othes and flaightes,
Blafpheming God, and prince reiect,
    As they were brutifh beaftes.

Their filthy talke and poyfoned fpeech
    Disfigures fo the mouth,
That fom wold think ther ftood the breech,
    Such filth it breatheth forth.

The hands which haue no fingers right,
    But ftumps fit for no vfe,
Doth well fet forth the idle plight
    Which we in thefe daies chufe.

For rich and poore, for age and youth,
    Eche one would labour flye ;
Few feekes to do the deedes of truth,
    To helpe others thereby.

The leg fo clyming to the head,
    What meaneth it but this,
That fome do feeke not to be lead,
    But for to leade amis ?

And as this makes it moft monftrous
    For foote to clyme to head,
So thofe fubiects be moft vicious
    That refufe to be lead.

The hinder part doth fhew vs playne
  Our clofe and hidden vice,
Which doth behind vs run amayne
  In vyle and fhameful wyfe.

Wherefore to ech in England now,
  Let this monfter them teach
To mend the monftrous life they fhow,
  Leaft endles death them reach.

⁋ Imprinted at London by John Awdeley, dwellyng in Little Britain ftreete without Alderfgate,
the xxiij. of December.

⚜

A mournfull Dittie on the death of certaine
Judges and Juftices of the Peace, and diuers
other Gentlemen, who died immediatly after
the Affifes holden at Lincolne laft paft.

To the tune of Fortune.

ECOUNTING griefes and dolors long
      tyme done,
    Or blazyng forth the danger none
      can fhon,
Might feeme a ftudy altogether vayne ;
Yet outwarde words oft eafeth inward payne.

Then patiently my woefull tale attend,
Where forrowe doth each feuerall peryod end,
And euery word a bitter figh doth found,
For thofe great plagues which we haue often found.

At Oxford firſt the iuſteſt judge of all
Our earthly judges firſt to count dyd call,
And ſecondly at Exceſter againe ;
And laſt of all did Lincolne witnes plaine

How ſore for ſinne the Lord offended was,
How ſore for ſinne his wrath from him did pas,
And how for ſinne the prudent of our land
Hath felt the force of his moſt heauie hand.

Come, Shute, I ſaie, make vp the number then,
Thou worthie judge among vnworthie men ;
Thy godly zeale and wiſedome plaine did ſhow,
Thou waſt too good for wretched men below.

Thy ſodaine death at Lincolne Sifes wrought,
Remaines a terror to each ſeuerall thought ;
Although with life thou didſt from thence depart,
Yet there did ſicknes ſlaie thy tender hart.

And like lament for Hollice may we make,
Whoſe life likewiſe moſt cruell death did take ;
A vertuous man and juſtice of the peace,
Whom Creſſius wealth cannot from graue releaſe.

Copartner with theſe breathles perſons here,
Lies maiſter Tyrwhite, bound vpon the beere ;
O fickle life, how brittle is thy ſtate,
And how vncertaine is thy finall date !

And Littlebury, by birth a good eſquier,
Whoſe ſeruice then the lawe did well requier,
The foreman of a jurie there was he,
Whom death areſted with a deadly fee.

The fkilfull clarke which to the peace pertaind,
That long in credit in the place remaind,
Welby, I faie, his name was called fo,
Which at that place receiude a deadly blo.

Nor could graue Cauthron fcape from cruel death,
Though likely long to harber vitall breath ;
His wit, his wifedome, and his fage aduice
With life was loft and turned to a trice.

Where fhould I finde meete wordes for to expreffe
Our inward woe, our griefe and heauines,
For Butlers death, a man of good degree,
And for the loffe of many more then hee.

Let this fuffice, that our eternall God
In fecret wifedome had prepard this rod
For our examples that remaine behind,
To cleere our eyes that Sathan fo did blind.

Thrice in this fort our judges haue bin flaine,
At three Affifes, as is proued plaine,
And warning thrice herein our eies haue feene,
But more then thrice haue our offences beene.

Some iudge of this, and fome doe iudge of that,
Some fpeak and prate, and faie they know not what;
Then learne of Chrift this leffon tolde to thee,
Judge not at all, leaft that thou iudged be.

The caufe hereof to God is onely knowen,
No caufe at all by any man was fhowen;
Yet without caufe God neuer wrought the fame,
As chiefeft caufe ourfelues our finnes may blame.

And like as men, by naturall defcent
From Adams loines, to wicked finne is bent,
So may I faie, the lawyer is not cleere
From vile corruption, while he liueth heere.

Then they, as we muft both with one accord,
Repent their finnes before the mightie Lord,
Leaft in his wrath a greater plague be fent
On flintie hearts that would not once relent.

Vprightly deale with euerie poore mans caufe,
Againft the truth wring not nor wreaft the lawes,
And haue a confcience in your common fees,
For God, thou knowft, all inward motions fees.

Let not your hearts with bribes polute your hands,
And by oppreffion do not inlarge your lands ;
For curfed gold fell not your foules away,
A practife found too common at this day.

Haue thou an eare vnto the wronged wight,
Defpife not him that fimple is in fight ;
Do right and iuftice vnto each degree,
Then in the end thou fhalt moft bleffed bee.

And for our queene of moft exceeding fame,
Let vs defire, in Jefus Chriftes name,
That God will ftill preferue her royall grace,
That fhe may runne a long and ioyfull race.

FINIS.

Imprinted at London by John Wolfe, for
William Wright.   1590.

❡ *A difcription of a monftrous Chylde, borne at Chychefter in Suffex, the xxiiii. daye of May. This being the very length, and bygnes of the fame.* MCCCCCLXII.

[Here is an engraving of the child, 6⅝ inches in height.]

HEN God for fynne to plage hath
        ment,
    Although he longe defarde,
    He tokens truly ftraunge hath fent
To make hys foes afearde ;

That they thereby might take remorce
    Of their yll lyfe mifpent,
And, more of loue then feare or force,
    Their formall faultes repent.

Before the earth was ouerflowen
    With waters huge throughout,
He fent them Noe, that holy one,
    Who dayly went about

To call them then to godly lyfe,
    At whome they laughte and fumde ;
He was contemde of man and wyfe,
    Tyll they were all confumde.

Loth did preache moft earneftly,
    But it did not preuayle ;
When fyre and brymftone verely
    Upon them doune did hayle.

Pharaoes heart had no remorce,
 Though wounders ftraunge he fawe,
But rather was therfore the worce,
 Without all feare or awe;

Untyll bothe he and his therfore,
 By iuftice fent of God,
In raginge feas were all forlore,
 And then he felt the rod.

Ten tymes truely were the Jewes
 In captiue brought and led;
Before eche tyme, our God did vfe
 Hys tokens ftrange, we red.

The yeare before Vafpatian came,
 The Jewes a heyfer dreft,—
Whiche beynge flayne, did calue a lame,—
 This fygne they fone did wreft,

As others doe, and ftyll haue done,
 In making it as vayne;
Or els good lucke, they faye, fhal come,
 As pleafe their foolifh brayne.

The heathen could forefe and faye
 That when fuche wounders were,
It did forefhew to them alwaye
 That fome yll hap drew nere.

The Scripture fayth, before the ende
 Of all thinges fhall appeare,
God will wounders ftraunge thinges fende,
 As fome is fene this yeare.

The felye infantes, voyde of fhape,
   The calues and pygges fo ftraunge,
With other mo of fuche mifhape,
   Declareth this worldes chaunge.

But here, lo! fee, aboue the reft,
   A monfter to beholde,
Procedinge from a Chriftian breft,
   To monftrous to be tolde!

No caruer can, nor paynter maye,
   The fame fo ougly make;
As doeth itfelf fhewe at this daye,
   A fight to make the quake!

But here thou hafte, by printing arte,
   A figne therof to fe;
Let eche man faye within his harte,—
   It preacheth now to me,

That I fhoulde feke to lyue hencefoorth |
   In godly lyfe alwaye,
For thefe be tokens now fent foorth
   To preache the later daye.

Alfo it doeth demonftrate playne
   The great abufe and vyce, |
That here in Englande now doeth raygne,
   That monftrous is the guyfe.

By readinge ftories we fhall fynde,
   In Scripture and elles-where,
That when fuche thinges came out of kynde, |
   Gods wrath it did declare.

But if we lightely weye the fame,
    And make but nyne dayes wonder,
The Lord our ftoutnes fone will tame,
    And fharpely bringe vs vnder.

Then ponder wel, be tymes long paft,
    The fequel of fuche fignes,
And call to God by prayer in haft
    From finne to chaunge oure myndes.

Repent, amende, both hygh and lowe,
    The woorde of God embrace,—
To lyue therto as we fhould doe
    God gyue vs all the grace!

Quod Jhon D.

¶ The father hereof is one Vyncent, a boutcher;
bothe he and hys wyfe being of honeft and quiet
conuerfation, they hauing had chyldren before
in natural proportion, and went with this her
full tyme.

¶ Imprynted at London by Leonard Afkel, for
Fraunces Godlyf, in the yeare of oure Lorde
1562.

❡ *A new balade entituled as foloweth:*

❡ To fuch as write in metres I write
Of fmall matters an exhortation,
By readyng of which men may delite
In fuch as be worthy commendation.
My verfe alfo it hath relation
To fuch as print, that they doe it well,—
The better they fhall their metres fell.

❡ And when we haue doen al that euer we can,
Let vs neuer feke prayfe at the mouth of man.

ORACE, that noble poet, did write
In his learned booke, the Arte of
Poetrie,
Notable thinges of which to refite ;
One is now to be noted fpeciallie
In thefe our dayes, and wot ye whie ?
For fome there be, take matters in hand
Chiefly in metre, to fhew their fancie,
As did in his dayes a certaine band.

❡ Read in his bookes, and then vnderftand,
They vexed his eares, they troubled his eyes,
With metres in number compared to the fand,
And lacked not fuch as wolde to the fkyes
So prayfe their workes—fuch was their guyfe,—
And alfo extoll their metres fo
With wordes freuolous and manifeft lyes,
That lyke vnto them there was no mo.

❡ But what faith HORACE, afore we go
Any further herein ? Becaufe they did vfe
To procure freendes, left that their fo
Shoulde paint them out, and fo accufe

Their doinges in verſe and their abuſe,
Which men to praiſe them were not ſo preſt,
As Horace agayne wolde ſtyll refuſe
To admit that number into his breſt.

❦ Suche coulde not dwell in his ſtudie or cheſt.
Lvcilivs, with other in Horace dayes,
Was one which he coulde not diſgeſt;
His verſe in wordes or ſence alwayes
For the moſt parte deſerued ſmall prayſe,
And why? becauſe he had more reſpeɛt
To couet the garland of lawrel or bayes,
For number rather then verſe ſeleɛt.

❦ For when by writing men doe deteɛt
Their wyſedome or els their follie in deede,
Yf it be fooliſh, they doe correɛt,
Or ought that can, and that with ſpeede,
As Horace did, the vnſkylfull breede
Of poets that wrote in his time, I ſay;
The workes of ſuch, as ye may read,
Continue not long, but fall away.

❦ Such ſpices and wares as come from the ſea,
They be good to vſe from towne to towne,—
To the pedler they be a right good ſtay
To put in his ſtuff, blacke, white or browne;—
Good for the maſter, and good for the clowne;
So make—as ye know—the matter cleane,
Good to take vp, and good to caſt downe;
When ye haue doen, ye know what I meane.

❦ Your balades of loue, not worth a beane,
A number there be, although not all;
Some be pithie, ſome weake, ſome leane,
Some doe runne as round as a ball;—

Some verſes haue ſuch a pleaſant fall,
That pleaſure it is for any man,
Whether his knowledge be great or ſmall, }
So that of a verſe ſome ſkyll he can.

℣ But ſome yf ye take in hand to ſkan,
They lacke their grace, they lacke good ſence ;
The printer ſhoulde, therfore, with his fan
Pourge chaff from corne, to avoyde offence ;
And not for lucre, vnder pretence
Of newes, to print what commeth to hand,
But that which is meete to bring in pence
Let him print, the matter well ſcand.

℣ Our Englyſhmen, ſome out of the land,
A forte of rebelles ſturdye and ſtoute,
With our pope, holy men, that ouerthwart band,
At Louaine, with open ſclander breath oute
What enuie can doe, to bryng in doubte
The godly workes, well written of late
Of learned men, and now go aboute
To ſtirre vp againſt vs warre and debate.

℣ Wherfore let vs not open a gate,
Eyther the printer, or they which write,
To ſuch as they be, knowyng their ſtate,—
Their ſclanderous pen doth cruelly byte.
Let them not ſay that thoſe which endyte '
Lacke knowledge in that the pen doth expreſſe ;
Let them not ſay that a rauenyng kyte
Is as good as a larke at a printers meſſe.

℣ But now, leſt ye thinke me to vſe exceſſe,
I wyll to an end myſelf prepare,   \
Wyſhyng all them that wyll adreſſe   \
Their pen to metres, let them not ſpare   \

To folow Chawcer, a man very rare,
Lidgate, Wager, Barclay and Bale,
   With many other that excellent are,
In thefe our dayes, extant to fale.

❡ Let writers not couet the bottom or dale,
   Yf they may come to the hyll or brinke ;
And, when they haue written their learned tale,
   The printer muft vfe good paper and inke,
   Or els the reader may fometime fhrinke,
When faulte by inke or paper is feene ;—
   And thus euery day, before we drinke,
Let vs pray God to faue our queene.   Amen.

❡ Finis.   By R. B.

❡ Imprinted at S. Katherins, befyde the Towre
   of London, by Alexander Lacie.

❡ *O maruelous tydynges, both wonders old and new,*
The Deuyll is endited, yf many mens wordes be tru.

N all chriftendom Chriftes godfpell now
      is rad
   Of man, woman and chyld; it maketh
      their harts glad,
Whiche with fhamefull fyns before were full fad ;—
   O wounders good tydynges, yf al fayinges be tru!

❡ It is rad fo oft, and with foch diligence,
That no text is wrefted thorow raifche negligence;

Playn declaracions help moche to the true fenfe.
We all haue caufe to reioyfe, yf thefe tydyngs
be tru.

Now after Chriftes rule all folk do lead theyr lyfe,
They abhor all chydyng, braulyng, fyghtyng,
and ftryfe;
Grete feruent charytie is betwyne man and wyfe,
No worfe wordes then honycomb, fweet hart
of gold moft tru.

℃ One neybur reforteth fryndly to another,
As though all were kynsfolk, lyke brother and
brother;
Greter loue was neuer betwyne chyld and mother.—
This world is no world, yf all tydynges be tru;

It is rather lyke heuyn, or pleafaunt paradyfe,
The folk be lyke angels, difcrete, fober, and wyfe;
If one fall through fraylty, he, repentyng more
then twyfe,
Ryfeth ftyll a new man, a good Chriftian and
tru.

℃ Folk faft, pray, and ferue God not hipocritically,
Only to be feen of men for folyfh vayn glory,
But from the very hart, the Lord God to gloryfy,
Defpyfyng fond fantafyes, as falfe thynges and
not tru.

℃ Euery body now, in fom trade of lyuyng,
Doth labour for his foode with trauell or fwetyng;
Som dyggyng, fom fpynnyng, fom wrytyng, fom
redyng,
Som geuyng good counfell, lyke honeft folk
and tru.

P

℃ They knowe that they muſt make a rekenyng
    to God
Of theyr diſpenſacion, they feere gretely Gods rod ;
The ryche do helpe the poore with roſt meat or
    with ſod,
    None lye ſtaruyng in ſtreets, yf all mens
    tonges be tru.

℃ Great ryche men be afrayd leaſt they dye
    ſodaynly,
Leaſt theyre goods (after them) be ſpent in foolery ;
Leaſt God wyll call them fooles, therfore liberally
    They ſpend moche in theyr lyfe vpon poore
    folk and tru.

℃ They be redy, alſo, ſomwhat to pryſons to ſend,
If any through frayltie chaunſe folyſhly to offend ;
But now priſons be empty; the world doth ſo
    amende,
    There be but iiij. ſcore and ten in Kynges Benche,
    it was tru.

℃ Of them that be in pryſon ſom be tyed with
    clogges,
Som gnaw broun cruſtes of bred, ſom burniſh
    boones like doggs ;
Som wyſh to fyll theyr gutts with catts, ratts,
    myſe, or froggs ;
    Specyally this deere yere, now, they ſay, they
    wyll be tru.

How many be in Ludgate and Neugate I can
    not tel,
But they that be abrode be afrayd, I truſt well,
And fall to wourk luſtely thorow theyr exampell,—
They abhorre Clinkerum, they ſay they wyll be
    tru.

❧ A man may goo now ouer Fynſbery fylde
Without ſweard and buckler, without ſpeare or
 ſhylde,
With an houndred poundes, as ſafe as with a nylde,
 In a myſty mornyng and by nyght, yf tales be
 tru.

❧ All England and Spayn, all Scotland and
 Germany,
All Fraunce and Ireland, all Denmark and
 Hungary,
Be purged ſo, I truſt, from vice and idolatry,
 That the Turk doth beghyn to thynk the
 Godſpele tru.

❧ The Saracens and Jewes, I truſt, do now conuert,
Moued with godlynes that is in Chriſtians harte;
They fere leaſt Chryſts ſcourge wyll make theyr
 bones to ſmart,—
 I truſt they receyue baptyme, and belyue the
 Godſpell is tru.

They hire it ſo diſcuſſed by calculacyon
That Doomeſday is at hand; yf mens ſpeculacion
In aſtronomye be tru, the worldes transformacyon
 Wyl be within x. yeres, ſtraunge newes yf it be tru.

❧ I—one of xl. yeres—thought to prouyde for
 age,
Houſe for one and twenty yere, or ſom fat
 perſonage,
Som prebend, deanery, or ſom vicarage,
 But now I pas not moche, yf aſtronomers be tru.

❧ Yea, whither aſtronomers be true eyther no,
Or that generall iugement be commyng to or fro,
This one thyng I kno ſure, that I ſhall hence go,
 I kno nor day nor ooure, nothyng is more tru.

❦ And douteles yf all men wolde be of my mynde,
We wold fom better way for to lyue here out fynde;
Men fhulde be fet awurk, onleffe they were ftark
    blynd,
    Yea, blynde fhuld do fomwhat to kepe them-
    felfe tru.

❦ Helthy folke lackyng wourk fhuld reforte to
    a place
With theyr tooles and inftrumentes, as fom vfe
    to fhew their face;
Then fet awourk, or fed, of mens fauour and grace,
    With fom comon purfe, to kepe themfelfs tru.

❦ So that it fhuld be a ftraunge thyng for to fee
Any theft or murder euer committed to be,
As—thankes be to God!—folk burne fo in
    charytie,
    That no knauery raigneth, yf all mens wordes
    be tru.

❦ The Deuyll hath ben a knaue, and hath kylde
    many men,
Yea, both foule and body, moe perchaunfe then ten;
Now he is endyted, as witneffeth my pen,
    His queft is empayneld, he is founde falfe, not
    tru.

Here folowe the names of the xij. men that goo vpon
the Deuyll.

❦ Gen. iii. 1 Paralip. xxj. Job i. ii. Sapien. ii.
Chrift in Math. xiij. and in Luke viij. Math. iiij.
Mar. i. Luke xxij. Joan xiij. and 1 Joan iij.
Paull to the Ephefians vj. 1 Pet. v. Jacob iiij.

❡ It wyl be hard to kyll fuche an immortall knaue,
He recoueryth fo oft, though a ftronge hoofte we
  haue ;
Call in Turkes and Saracens, that they alfo may
  be faue,—
  Through Gods help, we may breke Satans hed,
  it is tru.

❡ To breke Satans hed, of all wayes this is one,
With the buckler of fayth to refyft fuggeftion,
And ftrongly to belyue that Chriftes paffion,
  Chriftes wordes and myrakels all, be moft furely
  tru.

All Chriftian kyngs do now theyr wittes bende
Theyr letters in print to the Turkes for to fende,
With many New Teftamentes, theyr blynd lyfe to
  amend,
  For fere of hell fyre, I truft it wyl be tru.

❡ When Satan the Deuyll feeth fuch a great
  hooft,
Suche a fort of Chriftians, to diminifh his booft,
He muft nedes be compelld to graunt his great
  ftrenght loft,
  When his pate is broken, God graunte this may
  be tru.

❡ Then the golden world, I truft, wyll com agayn,
That folk may lyue eafyly without any great
  payn ;
Many egges for a peny at London I wolde fe fayn,
  Flefche and fifche better chepe, I truft it wyl be
  tru.

❡ All other thynges good chepe I truſt to ſe er I
   dye,
Coynes, meaſures, and weyghtes in good vnifor-
   mitie
Thorow all the world, I truſt to ſe ſchortely,
   Onles that diuerſitie doth more good, it be tru.

Jentyll reder, farewell! Thou knoeſt part of my
   mynde,
There lye in my harte many ſuch thynges be-
   hynde;
Whiche towards the brekyng of Satans hed I fynde,
   That all may be mery and wyſe in Chriſt: It
   is tru.

❡ Printed by Cornelis Woltrop, dwellyng
   at Saynt Antonies.

*As pleaſant a dittie as your hart can wiſh,
Shewing what vnkindnes befell by a kiſſe.*

M Y miſtris ſings none other ſong,
   But ſtil complains I do her wrong;
   Beleeue her not, it is not ſo,
     For I did but kiſſe her,
     For I did but kiſſe her,
     And ſo let her goe.

And now ſhe ſwears I did—but what?
Nay, nay, I muſt not tell you that;

And yet I will, it is fo fweet,
  As teehe taha,
  As teehe taha,
    When louers do meete.

But womens words they are heedles,
To tell you more it were needles;
I ran and caught her by the arme,
  And then I kift her,
  And then I kift her,
    Was this any harme?

Yet out, alas! fhees angry ftill,
Which fheweth but a womans will;
She bites the lippe, and cries, fie, fie!
  And kiffing fweetly,
  And kiffing fweetly,
    Away fhe doth fly.

Acteon for one fight did die,
So for one fillie kiffe muft I;
Vnwares fond loue did me betray,
  When I gaue her vantage,
  When I gaue her vantage,
    And fhe fled away.

She ftriued and wrangled ful fore with me,
And cryedft,—For fhame, let it be!
You doe me wrong to vfe me fo,—
  Therefore be quiet,
  Therefore be quiet,
    And now let me goe.

Yet ftill I held her by the hand,
Her words could not my will withftand;

She fround, fhe pouted, fhe lookt fower,
And ftill I held her,
And ftil I held her
 Within my power.

At laft fhe gan for anger cry,
And then my hart with griefe did die;
I could no longer her containe,
 But thus we parted,
 But thus we parted,
 Vnto my great paine.

And fince, when I with her do meete,
With words vnkind fhe doth me greet;
At me her wanton head fhe fhakes,
 And as a ftranger,
 And as a ftranger,
 My fauours fhe takes.

But yet her looks bewrayes content,
And cunningly her brawles are ment,—
As louers vfe to play and fport,
 When time and leafure,
 When time and leafure
 Is too-too fhort.   Finis.

At London : printed for T. P.

The true difcription of two monfterous children,
laufully begotten betwene George Steuens and
Margerie his wyfe, and borne in the parifh
of Swanburne in Buckynghamfhyre the iiij. of
Aprill, Anno Domini 1566; *the two children*
hauing both their belies faft ioyned together, and
imbracyng one another with their armes : which
children wer both alyue by the fpace of half an
hower, and wer baptized and named the one
John, and the other Joan.

READ how Affrique land was fraught,
   For their moft filthy life,
With monftrous fhapes confuzedly,
   That therin wer full rife.

❧ But England now purfues their vyle
   And deteftable path,
Embracyng eke all mifcheefs great,
   That moues Gods mightie wrath.

❧ As thefe vnnaturall fhapes and formes,
   Thus brought forth in our dayes,
Are tokens true and manifeft
   How God by dyuers wayes

Doth ftyrre vs to amendment of
   Our vyle and cankred lyfe,
Which to-to much abufed is
   In man, in chylde, and wyfe.

¶ We wallow fo in filthie fin,
    And naught at all regarde,
Nor wyll not feare the threats of God,
    Tyll we, for iuft rewarde,

Be ouerwhelmd with mifcheefs great,
    Which, ready bent for vs,
Full long ago decreed wer,
    As Scriptures doth difcus.

¶ Both tender babes and eke brute beaftes
    In fhape disfourmed bee;
Full manie wayes he plagues the earth,
    As dayly we may fee.

¶ Thus mightie Ioue, to pearce our harts,
    Thefe tokens ftraunge doth fend,
To call vs from our filthie lyfe,
  \ Our wicked wayes t'amend.

And thus, by thefe two children here,
    Forewarnes both man and wyfe,
How both eftates ought to bewayle
    Their vile and wretched lyfe.

¶ For fure we all may be agaft
    To fee thefe fhapes vnkynd,
And tremblyng feare may pearce our harts,
    Our God to haue in mynd.

For yf we printed in our breft,
    Thefe fignes and tokens ftraunge
Wold make vs from our finnes to fhrinke,
    Our liues anew to chaunge.

❧ But fome proude boaftyng Pharifie
   The parents wyll detect,
And iudge with heapes of vglie vice
   Their liues to be infect.

❧ No, no ; but leffons for vs all,
   Which dayly doe offend ;
Yea, more, perhaps, then hath the freends
   Whom God this birth did lend.

❧ For yf you wyll, with fingle eye,
   Note well and view the text,
And marke our Sauiours aunfwer eke
   That thereto is annext,

Where his difciples afked him,
   To know therein his mynd,
Yf greatter wer the parents finnes,
   Or his that was borne blynd.

❧ To whom Chrift aunfwered in a breef,
   That neither hee nor they
Deferued had that crooked fate,
   Although they fin each day ;

But to the end Gods glorie great,
   And miracles diuine,
Might on the earth apparaunt be,
   His workes for to define.

❧ Such lyke examples moued me,
   In thefe forgetfull dayes,
To rue our ftate, that vs among
   Vice beares fuch fwings and fwayes ;

℃ Wherein the goodneſſe great of God
  We way and ſet ſo light;
By ſuch examples callyng vs
  From ſin both day and night.

Where we doe runne at randon wyde,
  Ourſelues flatteryng ſtyll,
And blazyng others faults and crimes,
  Yet we ourſelues moſt yll.

℃ But if we doe conſider right,
  And in euen balaunce way
The ruine great of hartie loue
  Among vs at this day;

And well behyld, with inward eyes,
  Th' embracyng of theſe twinnes,—
That God by them vpbraides vs for
  Our falſe diſcemblyng ſinnes;

We would with Niniuie repent
  Our former paſſed yeares,
Bewaylyng eke our ſecret ſinnes
  In ſackecloth and in teares.

℃ Therfore in time amend your ſtate,
  And call to God for grace,—
Bewayle your former lyfe and ſinnes,
  While you haue time and ſpace.

℃ Finis, quod John Mellys Nor.

℃ Imprinted at London by Alexander Lacy, for
William Lewes, dwellyng in Cow Lane, aboue
Holborne Cundit, ouer againſt the ſigne of the
Plough.

A newe Ballade intytuled, Good Fellowes
muſt go learne to daunce.

OOD fellowes muſt go learne to daunce,
   The brydeall is full nere a ;
There is a brall come out of Fraunce,
   The tryxt ye harde this yeare a ;
For I muſt leape, and thou muſt hoppe,
   And we muſt turne all three a ;
The fourth muſt bounce it lyke a toppe,
   And ſo we ſhall agree a.
I praye thee, mynſtrell, make no ſtoppe,
   For we wyll merye be a.

The brydegrome would giue twentie pounde
   The mariage daye were paſte a ;
Ye knowe, whyles louers are vnbounde,
   The knotte is ſlyper faſte a ;—
A better man maye come in place,
   And take the bryde awaye a.
God ſend our Wilkin better grace,
   Our pretie Tom, doth ſaye a,—
God vycar, axe the banes apace,
   And haſte the mariage daye a.

A bande of belles, in bauderycke wyſe,
   Woulde decke vs in our kynde a ;
A ſhurte after the Moryce guyſe,
   To flounce it in the wynde a.
A wyffler for to make the waye,
   And Maye brought in withall a,
Is brauer then the ſunne, I ſaye,
   And paſſeth round or brall a ;

For we will trype fo tricke and gaye,
　　That we wyll paffe them all a.

Drawe to dauncinge, neyghboures all,
　　Good fellowfhyppe is beft a,
It fkylles not yf we take a fall,
　　In honoringe this fefte a.
The bryde wyll thanke vs for oure glee,
　　The worlde wyll vs beholde a;
O where fhall all this dauncinge bee,
　　In Kent or at Cotfolde a?
Oure Lorde doth knowe, then axe not mee,—
　　And fo my tale is tolde a.

Adewe, Sweete Harte.

X

DEWE, fweete harte, adewe!
　　Syth we muft parte!
　　To lofe the loue of you
　　　It greues my harte.
Once againe come kyffe me,
Syth I fo long muft mys thee;
[My w]illinge harte fhall wyfhe thee,
　　To eafe me of my fmarte.
And thoughe I nowe do leaue thee,
It wyll I not deceaue thee,
But come againe and wedde thee,
　　Euen for thy iuft defarte.

Syr Launcelotte comes againe, fyr,
　　So men do faye;
Tom Toffe wyll fayle to Spayne, fir,
　　By Tyborne awaye.

Subtoll finne wyll haue her ;
Thoughe wyttie Watte do craue her,
Yet cuttinge clowne fhall faue her,
   Vnleffe he lofe his praye.
And though ye be fo wyleye,
And fhe do loke fo hyleye,
At length fhe wyll begyle ye,
   And [ftriue] the beft ye maye.

L . . . . . is fo coye, fir,
   She . . . be folde,
W . . . . . s her ioye, fir,
   T . . . . tolde,
Ra . . . . wyll not blade it,
Jack . . . r wyll not fwade it,
The byllbowes are not made it,
   Therof ye maye be bolde.
Although ye now haue cought her,
Ye wyll repent hereafter,
For farder ye haue fought her
   Then I haue thought ye would.

Finis.

¶ Imprinted at London, in Flete ftrete at the
figne of the Faucon, by Wylliam Gryffith, and
are to be folde at his fhoppe in S. Dunftones
Churchyearde, 1569.

❧ *The braineles bleſſing of the Bull.*

The hornes, the heads, and all,
Light on their ſquint-eyed ſkonſes full,
That boweth their knees to Ball.

The cancred curſe, that wolde conſume this realme with wracke
and ruine,
Returne to Rome with fyre and fume, to bryng the pope in
tune !
If neither curſe nor bleſſyng bare may mend theſe parties
throwe,
I them bequeath—curſt as they are—to Plutoes kyngdome
nowe !

AS neuer worlde ſo farre from orders
rule,
That men durſt ſpeake ſuch ſawcie
words of kings,
Nor neuer pope ſo lyke an aſſe or mule,
Or dunghyll cocke, to crow and clap his winges.
Stand backe, good dogs, the bul he leapes and
flinges,
He bleates and bleathes as he a-baightyng we͏̈re,
And fomes at mouth, lyke boare with briſtled
heare ;
A beaſtlye ſound comes runnyng from his paunch,
He beates the ground with foote, with hip and
haunch,
As though hell gates ſhould open at his call,
And at his becke the heauens high ſhould fall.

❧ O Sathans ſonne ! O pope puft vp with pryde !
What makes thee clayme the clowdes where
God doth dwel,
When thou art knowne the glorious greedie guyde

That leades in pompe poore feelye foules to hell ?
The pumpe of fhip hath not fo fowle a fmell
As hath the fmoke and fume that flames from
　　thee;
O graceles grace, O rotten hollow tree !
The branches bud, but neuer bryng forth leaues;
Thy corne is dead when reaper lookes for fheaues;
Thy golde is glaffe, and gliftereth gay a whyle,
Tyll tromperie comes, and makes the worlde to
　　fmyle.

❡ Who bad thee bliffe ? O buzzarde blynd of
　　fight,
　　Buylt God his church vpon fuch clots of clay ?
Thou doeft blafpheme thereby the GOD of might,
　　And robbeft with craft his honour cleane away.
　　Curfe whome thou lift, he better thryues that day;
Bleffe whome thou wylt, and I dare gage my head,
For all thy charmes, he brynges a foole to bed.
Booke, bell and fyfe are bables fit for thofe
That gape for flyes where wafpes and hornets
　　blowes;
The pardonles boxe, wherein thy reliques lye,
Doth fmell lyke fox, or fwyne fhut vp in ftye.

❡ A pope was wont to be an odious name
　　Within our land, and fcrapt out of our fcroules;
And now the pope is growne fo farre paft fhame,
　　That he can walke with open face in Poules.
　　Go home, mad bull, to Rome, and pardon foules
That pyne away in purgatorie paynes,—
Go triumph there, where credit moft remaines.
Thy date is out in England long ago,
For Ridley gaue the bull fo great a blow,　│
He neuer durft apeach this land tyll now,—
In bullyng time, he met with Hardyngs cow.

Q

❡ A calfe or twayne hath here ben gotten fince,
 Whofe heades were folde of late in Butcher Row;
Come cheape calues heads, and bring in Peter pence!
 Though fome are bought, our butchers looke
 for mo,
For Walthams calues to Tiburne needes muft go
To fucke a bull and meete a butchers axe;
The fhambles full is ftuft with prettie knacks,
As goate and lambe, and fhepe of three fcore yeare.
We haue good hope calues heads wyll not be
 deare;—
If Hardyngs cow be bulled as fhee ought,
Calues heads enough for little wyll be bought.

❡ The pope doth nought but practize mifcheif
 ftyll,
And lets his bul runne ryot for his eafe;
But whiles his calues are drawne vp Holborne hyll,
 Both bull and cow are fafe beyond the feas.
 O that it might our holy father pleafe
To come himfelfe, and hang but halfe an hower
With fuch poore freendes as here maintaine his
 power!
I fay no more, for feare the babes awake
That holde with pope, and hang for Hardyngs fake;
Some knackes now lurkes that we fhal know ful
 playne,
When Hoballes oxe bulles Hardyngs cow agayne.

❡ I fcorne to write a vearce in any frame,
 To anfwer wordes that rayled haue fo much,
Yet baightyng oft may make a bull fo tame,
 That euery dog that comes may haue a twitch.
 I here proteft, if that my power were fuch,
By pen or fkyll to chaffe the bull at ftake,
I wolde be glad fome further fporte to make;

But fince I want the cunnyng and the arte
To baight the beaft, and play the maftiffs parte,
Let this fuffife to let you thinke in deede,
I hate the bull and all the Romifh breede.

❡ Finis.

❡ Imprinted at S. Katherins, befide the Tower
of London, ouer againft the Beare Daunce, by
Alexander Lacie.

A Ballad.

HAT lyfe is beft ?   The nedy is full of
woe and awe,
The welthy full of brawles and quarells
of the lawe ;
To be a maryed man how much art thou beguiled,
Seeking thy reft by carking ftill for houfhold,
wif, and child !
To till it is a toyle to grace a gredy gaine,
And fuch as gotten is with drudging and with paine.
A fhrewd wyfe bringes debate,—wiue not and
neuer thriue ;
Children are charge,—childlefs, the greateft lack
aliue ;
Youth witlefe is and frayle, age fickly and forlorne;
Then beft it is to dye betime, or neuer to be borne.

The crie of the poore for the death of the right

Honourable Earle of Huntington.

To the tune of the Earle of Bedford.

GOD, of thy mercie remember the
        poore,
And grant vs thy bleffings, thy plenty
        and ftore ;
For dead is LordHaftinges,—the more is our griefe;
And now vp to heauen we cry for reliefe.
    Then waile we, then weepe we, then mourne we
        ech one,
    The good Earle of Huntington from vs is gone.

To poore and to needie, to high and to low,
Lord Haftinges was friendly, all people doth know ;
His gates were ftill open the ftraunger to feede,
And comfort the fuccourles alwaies in neede.
    Then waile we, &c.

The hufbandles widdow he euer did cherrifh,
And fatherles infants he likewife would nourifh ;
To weake and to ficke, to lame and to blinde,
Our good Earle of Huntington euer was kinde.
    Then waile we, &c.

The naked he clothed with garments from cold,
And frankely beftowed his filuer and gold,—
His purfe was ftill open in giuing the poore,
That alwaies came flocking to Huntingtons doore.
    Then waile we, &c.

His tennants, that daylie repairde to his houfe,
Was fed with his bacon, his beefe and his foufe ;
Their rents were not raifed, their fines were but
    fmall,
And manie poore tennants paide nothing at all.
    Then waile we, &c.

Such landlordes in England we feldome fhall finde,
That to their poore tennants will beare the like
    minde,—
Lord Haftinges therefore is ioyfully crownde
With angels in heauen, where peace doth abound.
    Then waile we, &c.

His wifedome fo pleafed the queene of this land,
The fword of true juftice fhe put in his hand ;
Of Yorke he was Prefident made by her grace,
Her lawes to maintaine and rule in her place.
    Then waile we, &c.

Such mercifull pittie remainde in his breft,
That all men had juftice and none were opreft ;
His office in vertue fo godly he fpent,
That prince and his countrie his loffe may lament.
    Then waile we, &c.

And likewife Lord Haftings, S. Georges true
    knight,
Did weare the goold garter of England fo bright,—
The gift of a prince, King Edward firft gaue,—
A gem for a fouldier and counceller graue.
    Then waile we, &c.

His coyne was not whorded to flourifh in pride,
His kings and his jewels and chaines to prouide ;

But gaue it to fouldiers wounded in warres,
That pike and the bullet hath lamed with fcarres.
  Then waile we, &c.

He built vp no pallace nor purchafte no towne,
But gaue it to fchollers to get him renowne,
As Oxford and Cambridge can rightly declare
How many poore fchollers maintained are there.
  Then waile we, &c.

No groues he inclofed, nor felled no woodes,
No paftures he paled to doe himfelfe good;
To commons and countrie he liude a good friend,
And gaue to the needie what God did him fend.
  Then waile we, &c.

He likewife prouided, in time of great neede,
If England were forced with warres to proceede,
Both men and munition, with horfes of warre,
The proude foes of England at all times to fcarre.
  Then waile we, &c.

Our queene and our countrie hath caufe to com-
      plaine,
That death in his furie this noble hath flaine;
Yet England reioyce, we reioyce without feare,
Lord Haftinges hath left a moft noble heire.
  Then waile we, &c.

A thoufand poore widdowes for Huntingtons fake,
As manie poore children their praiers will make,
That God may long profper his heire left behinde,
And graunt him old Huntingtons true noble minde.
  Then waile we, &c.

Then pray we for countrie, for prince and for peares,
That God may indew them with moſt happie yeares;
Lord, bleſſe vs with vertue, with plentie and peace,
And manie more ſubiecẗs like him to increaſe!
   Then waile we, then weepe we, then mourne
     we ech one,
   Our good Earle of Huntington from vs is gone.

FINIS.

Printed at London for William Blackwall, and
are to be ſold at his ſhoppe, nere
Guild Hall gate. 1596.

⁂

*Joyfull Newes for true Subiecẗes, to God and the
Crowne,*
The Rebelles are cooled, their Bragges be put downe.

Come, humble ye downe,—come, humble ye downe,
Perforce now ſubmyt ye to the queen and the crowne.

L true Engliſh ſubiecẗs, both moſte and
   leſte,
   Geue thanks vnto God, with humble
   knees downe,
That it hath pleazde him, at our requeſt,
  To vanquiſh the rebels that troubled the
  crowne.
   Come, humble ye downe,—come, humble ye
   downe,
   Perforce now ſubmit ye to the quene and the
   crowne.

❡ The Weſtmerlande bull and man in the moone,
   The beare hath brought their brauerie downe ;
I dare ſaye for ſorowe they are redy to ſwoone,
   That euer they ymagynde to trouble the crowne.
      Come, humble ye downe, &c.

❡ And ſir John Shorne, as fame doth reporte,
   Is hangde vp ſo hye that he cannot come downe,
Becauſe he thought it ſo good a ſporte,
   To playe the traytour againſt the crowne.
      Come, humble ye downe, &c.

❡ And becauſe he ſhould not hange alone,
   To honor his prieſthoode of holy renowne,
Sir John Swingbreeche, his felow, a rebell well
      knowen,
   They ſay, is hangde with hym for troubling the
      crowne.   .
      Come, humble ye downe, &c.

❡ The reſt that are fled wyll ſoone be caught,
   Though yet they lye lurkyng in countrey and
      towne ;
And than they be truſde vp by and by ſtrayght,
   Except the quenes mercie that weareth the
      crowne.
      Come, humble ye downe, &c.

❡ But her Maieſtie of mercie is endued with ſtore;
   That knewe they full well that nowe are put
      downe,
Els would they not aventerd to rayſe this vprore.
   Now be they foorth commyng, as pleaſeth the
      crowne.
      Come, humble ye downe, &c.

❡ The reſt of the rebelles and traytours forſworne,
To ſee them trufde vp, I would gage my gowne,
And ſpecially the ſeᵭ of Syr John Shorne,
To teache them to trouble the realme and the
crowne.
Come, humble ye downe, &c.

❡ But that pertayneth no matter of mine ;
Yet for my good will on me do not frowne ;—
It muſt be as pleaſeth God to aſſigne
The hart of our quene that weareth the crowne.
Come, humble ye downe, &c.

❡ But, thankes bee to God ! their ſpyte is donne,
They haue ſpyt their venom, both knyght and
clowne ;
In deede, I muſt ſaye, verye fayre haue they
ſponne ;—
They had better haue kept them true to the
crowne.
Come, humble ye downe, &c.

❡ No doubt the deuill had them bewitcht,—
They lackt biſhop Boner, to cuniure him
downe ;
If he had liued till now, his eares would haue icht
For joye to heare how they trouble the crowne.
Com, humble ye downe, &c.

❡ And ſure he would haue written in haſte
To his holy father of hie renowne,
For helpe to ſpoyle, conſume and waſte,
All thoſe that deſpiſed his triple crowne.
Come, humble ye downe, &c.

And that was the meaning of thofe that began
  To roote out Chriftes doctrine, fuppreffe and
    put downe ;
They haue mift their purpofe, now fhift how they
    can,—
  God hath preuented them from troubling the
    crowne.
    Com, humble ye downe, &c.

❡ If they had preuayled, then had we been wo,
  Then had ben olde wayling in countrie and
    towne ;
Then fhould many a woman her hufband forgoe,
  All longe of the rebelles that troubled the
    crowne.
    Come, humble ye downe, &c.

❡ Then had ben many a fatherleffe childe,
  That fhoulde haue gon begging vp and
    downe ;
Yea, many a chafte damfell fhould haue ben defilde
  By thofe popifh prieftes that troubled the
    crowne.
    Come, humble ye downe, &c.

Yea, many a good preacher fhould haue loft his
    lyfe,
  Many a lorde and lady of noble renowne ;
Yea, many an infant and many a wyfe,
  By thofe cruell rebelles that troubled the
    crowne.
    Come, humble ye downe, &c.

❡ To fpoyle common wealth it was the next waye,
  Example by other realmes of renowne,—

How warre and rebellyon bred their decaye,
And all for matters perteynynge the crowne.
Come, humble ye downe, &c.

⁋ But prayfed be God, they haue not theyr will!
The hurt they ment other to them doth
redowne,
In daunger both life and goods to fpill,—
Thefe fruicts do they reape for troubling the
crowne.
Com,. humble ye downe, &c.

God faue the queenes maieftie and confound hir
foes,
Els turne their hartes quite vpfidowne
To become true fubiectes, as well as thofe
That faythfully and truely haue ferued the
crowne!
Come, humble ye downe, &c.

⁋ God graunt euery one, after his vocation,
To remember the accompt he muft laye downe;
And that we maye all, in this Englyfh nation,
Be true to God, the queene and the crowne!
Come, humble ye down,—come, humble ye
downe,
God graunt Queene Elizabeth longe to
weare the crowne!

FINIS.   W. Kyrkh.

⁋ Imprinted at London, in Fleet ftreete, by
Wyllyam How for Richard Johnes.

❡ *A dittie in the worthie praiſe of an high and mightie Prince.*

HEN heapes of heauie hap had fild
  my harte right full,
  And ſorrow ſet forth penſiuenes, my
  ioyes away to pull,
I raunged then the woods, I romde the fields
  aboute,—
A thouſand ſighes I ſet at large, to ſeeke their
  paſſage out;
And walkyng in a dompe, or rather in diſpaire,
I caſt my weeping eye aſide, I ſaw a fielde full
  faire;
And lokyng vpwarde than I ſpied a mount
  therein,
Which Flora had, euen for her life, deſt as you
  haue not ſeen;
Then could I not but thinke the ſame ſome ſacred
  place,
Where god or goddes ſuch did dwell as might
  releue my caſe.
I ſat me downe, for whie? Death could but ſtop
  my breath,
And to a man ſo ſorrowfull what ſweter is then
  death?
No ſooner was I ſet, but ſlepe approcht mine eye,
Wherein the nymphes of Helicon appeared by
  and by,—
And ſtraight thoſe ſiſters nine, the ground of
  muſicks arte,
My thought did ſtriue who might preuaile to eaſe
  my heauie harte.

The cunning they fhewed there, the fubtile notes
    they foung,
As were awreft clene from my hart, my thought
    the cares they wrong.
Celeftiall were the notes which then, amazde, I
    hearde,—
Their ditties eke were wonderfull, note ye whome
    they preferde.
As for thy bloud, quod they, right noble, we
    confeffe,—
Thy pettigree, to long for vs, the heralds can
    expreffe ;
But, happie, happie Duke, the fecond chylde of
    Fame,
Which, next vnto the higheft, fhe doth fo
    recoumpt the fame !
And happie Thomas ones, twife happie Norffolke
    toe,
Thrife happie men that leade your liues where
    Howard hath to doe,—
Which Howards happie daies they praied God to
    encreafe
Three times the fpace of Natures courfe, like
    Neftor liue in peace !
What age hath feen his like, fo free of purfe and
    toung ?
Where liues a iufter juftice now, though rare in
    one fo young ?
What plaint can there be tolde to his moft godlie
    eare,
But that he kepes the other ftyll, the blamed foule
    to heare ?
In mekenes he more meke then is the mekeft doue,
Yet is his fecret wifedome fuch he knoweth whome
    to loue ;

In freendſhip he ſurmounts Giſippus and his Tite,
All nobles may well note his race, and thereby take
    their lighte ;—
In peace a Salomon, in warre ſo ſtoute a prince
As raigned not tyll Heċtor came, nor liued neuer
    ſince,—
Then Sceuola more firme, which, for his cuntries
    turne,
His hand from arme before his foes in fierie flame
    did burne ;
He in the prideof peace delights in marciall ſhowe,—
Doe marke his turnoys vpon horſe, note well his
    vſe of bowe ;
Nay, marke him yet that ſhall note well his payne-
    fulnes,
No ſugred ſlepe can make him freend to ſluggiſh
    Idlenes.
What that becomes a prince in his good grace
    doth want?
In peace a courtier for the courte, a ſecond Mars
    in camp.
Thus ſtyll they ſoung, whoſe notes were cauſe of
    my releefe,
And I be-wrapped in a traunce had cleane forgot
    my greefe ;
And triple were my ioyes, ones cauſe my paynes
    were paſt,
And twiſe agayne, becauſe that prince amongſt vs
    here is plaſt,
I clapt my handes for ioye,—alas ! I wakt withall,
And then my muſes and their ſonges, my ioyes,
    were gone and all.
And then retournd my greefe,—I felt a further
    care,
Becauſe to ſhew what I had ſeen did paſſe my
    power ſo farre ;

And that a man vnlearnd, of arte that hath no
    ſkyll,
Should haue a charge ſo great as this, and could
    doe it ſo yll.
Yet thus I gan to wright I knew right well that he,
Which due deſert did thus commend, ſhould ſhade
    the want in me ;
To whome I pray the Lorde to ſend like yeares
    as Noye,
In happie health and quiet ſtate, to his and all our
    ioye.

❡ Finis, Ber. Gar.

❡ Imprinted at London, without Alderſgate, in
    Little Britaine, by Alexander Lacy.

❡ *A newe Ballade, intituled, Agaynſt Rebel-*
lious and falſe rumours. To the newe tune of
the Blacke Almaine vpon Sciſſillia.

HAT rumores now are raiſed of late,
    Within this Engliſh lande,
    Which is not much for to be prayſed,
    The caſe ſo harde doth ſtand.
For euery one doth talke,
There tongues contrary walke,
And femes to meddell of this and that,
There babling tongues ſo large doth chatte,
As fooliſhe fancye moues them ſaye,
So out there fooliſh talke they braye ;

And euery one doth befie him ftill
About the thing he hath no fkill.

❡ Some of his neighbors doth inquire
   What newes abrode there is,—
If that he any thinge doth here,
   Of thofe that dyd amiffe.
Some longeth to here tell
Of thofe that dyd rebell,
And whether they be fled or take,—
Thus ftill inquirie they do make ;
Some fayth to Scotland they be goe,
And other fayth it is not fo ;—
The rumerous deuell is now abrode,
Which makes them fo to laye on lode.

❡ Some fayth this yeare there fhal be hapte
   Much trouble in the lande ;
Of prophefies they carpe and clappe,
   As they that haue them fkande.
Doth tell them fo abrode,
And thus they laye on lode,
And filles the peoples eares with lyes ;
Thus rumor ftill abrode he flyes,
Which makes them now in fuch a rore,
As all true hartes may well deplore.
And praye to God if that he pleafe
Thefe foolifh rumores once maye ceafe.

❡ And let vs nowe applye our tyme
   In prayer to the Lorde,
That he may ceafe this furious cryme,
   That now is blowne abrode.
And euery one to ftaye
His tongue, and nothing faye

But of the thinges he hath in hand,
And fee his befynes well be fcand,
And not to meddle of princes actes,
What they will do, nor of their factes.
If occupied well we thus abyde,
The Lorde for vs will well prouide.

❡ For furely plagues we do defarue
   Moſt horrable and great,
Becaufe from God we ſtill do fwarue,
   And dayly doth him frette.
And ſtill prouoke his ieare,
Which glous as hotte as fyare ;
His bow is now all redye bent,
Therfore in tyme let vs repent,
Leaſt he for finne do vs depriue,
For warned folkes, they faye, may liue,
And warning take by other men,
Which we before our eyes haue fene.

❡ We haue hard in Fraunce the rumur there,
   That hath bene many a daye,—
There countrey fpoyled in ruth and feare,
   Vnto there cleane decaye,
With loffe of many a man,
Since firſt that ſturre began,
And many a noble hath bene flayne,
A duke, and eake a prince certayne,
Which weare the chiefe ſtayes of that land,
Wherfore in hazarde now they ſtande;
For where the chiefe are taken awaye,
The reſt muſt nedes runne to decaye.

❡ In what eſtate doth fouldiers ſtand,
   Great ruth it is to here ;

R

That there is wrought the tirants hand,
    We nede not to declare.
Experiaunce well may ſhowe
What numbers here doth flowe
Of Flemminges fled from tirantes hand,
Which dayly commeth to this land;
Whoſe harts in wrath full long hath boyld,
And eake there countrye cleane diſpoyld;
Which thing may warne vs well, I ſaye,
Leaſt that we feele the lyke decaye.

℀ The Lorde hath ſuffered vs full longe,
    And ſpared hath his rodde,—
What peace hath bene vs now among
    Aleuen yeares, prayſed be God !
And round about vs hath
Bene warre and cruell fayth,—
And all to cauſe vs to repent,—
For we deſarue worſſe punniſhment
Then any of theſe landes haue done ;
I feare we ſhall be plagued right ſone ;
Thy judgement ſure our God hath had,
To plague the good ſtill for the bad.

℀ Wherefore let vs with one accorde
    Fall all to faſt and praye,
And pardon craue now of the Lorde,
    To kepe vs from decaye ;
And leaue this murmoring ſpight,
Which God doth not delight ;
The Scripture playnely doth declare
The Iſralites they plagued weare,
Becauſe the murmered at there God,—
Therin we do deſarue lyke rod.

With hartes deuoute now let vs praye,
To kepe this realme from all decaye.

Finis, quod Thomas Bette.

❦ Imprinted at London, in Fleteftreat, at the
figne of the Faucon, by Wylliam Gryffith, and
are to be fold at his fhoppe in Sainɛt Dunftones
Churchyarde, 1570.

*The true Difcripcion of a Childe with Ruffes,
borne in the parifh of Micheham, in the countie
of Surrey, in the yeere of our Lord* MDLXVI.

HIS prefent yeere of our Lord MDLXVJ.
the vij. day of June, one Helene
Jermin, the wife of John Jermin,
hufbandman, dwelling in the parifhe
of Micheham, was deliuered of a woman-childe,
named Chriftian, beeing after this maner and
fourme following : that is to fay, the face
comly and of a cheerful countenaunce ; the
armes and hands, leggs and feet, of right fhape,
and the body, with all other members therunto
apperteining, wel proporcioned in due fourme and
order, fauing that it is as it were wunderfully
clothed with fuche a flefhy fkin as the like at
no time hath ben feene. For it hath the faid
flefhy fkin behinde like vnto a neckerchef
growing from the veines of the back vp vnto
the neck, as it were with many ruffes fet one

after another, and beeing as it were fomthing
gathered, euery ruf about an inche brode, hauing
here growing on the edges of the fame, and
fo with ruffes comming ouer the fhoulders
and couering fome part of the armes, proceding
vp vnto the nape of the neck behinde, and almofte
round about the neck, like as many womens gownes
be,—not cloce togither before, but that the throte
beeing (with a faire white fkin) bare betweene
bothe the fides of the ruffes, the faid ruffes about
the neck beeing double, and as it were thick gathered, muche like vnto the ruffes that many do
vfe to weare about their necks.

❡ This childe beforfaid (the day of the date
vnder written) was to be feene in Glene Alley, in
Suthwark, beeing aliue and x. weeks olde and iiij.
dayes, not vnlikly to liue long.

❡ *An admonition vnto the Reader.*

THIS picture, preft in paper white,
    Our natures dooth declare,
Whofe fourme fo ftraunge by natures fpite
    May lerne vs to beware.

❡ By natures fpite,—what doo I faye?
    Dooth nature rule the rofte?
Nay, God it is, fay wel I may,
    By whom nature is toft.

❡ The face ful faire, the members all
    In order ftand and place;
But yet too muche by natures thrall
    Dooth woork a great difgrace.

❡ This ruffeling world, in ruffes al rolde,
 Dooth God deteſt and hate ;
As we may lerne the tale wel tolde
 Of children borne of late.

❡ What meanes this childe, by natures woork
 Thus ruffed for to be ?
But by thefe ruffes our natures ſpurk
 We might beholde and fee.

❡ Her ſquares our ſquaring dooth fet out,
 This here our heres dooth checke ;
This monſtroufe monſter, out of dout,
 Agreeth in eche refpect.

❡ Our filthy liues in pigges are ſhewd ;
 Our pride this childe dooth bere ;
Our ragges and ruffes, that are fo lewd,
 Beholde her fleſhe and here.

❡ Our beaſtes and cattel plagued are,
 All monſtroufe in their ſhape ;
And eke this childe dooth wel declare
 The pride we vfe of late.

❡ Our curled here her here dooth preche,
 Our ruffes and gifes gaie,
Our ſtraunge attire wherto we reche,
 Our fleſhe that plefe we may.

❡ The poet telleth how Daphenes was
 Transformd into a tree ;
And Io to a cow did paſſe,—
 A ſtraunge thing for to fee.

❡ But poets tales may paſſe and go
   As trifels and vntrueth,
When ruffes of flesſhe, as I doo trowe,
   Shall moue vs vnto ruthe.

❡ Deformed are the things we were,
   Deformed is our hart;
The Lord is wroth with all this geere,—
   Repent for fere of ſmarte!

❡ Pray we the Lord our hartes to turn,
   Whileſt we haue time and ſpace,
Leſt that our ſoules in hel doo burn,
   For voiding of his grace.

❡ And thou, O England, whoſe womankinde
   In ruffes doo walke to oft,
Parſwade them ſtil to bere in minde
   This childe with ruffes ſo ſoft.

❡ In fourme as they, in nature ſo,
   A maid ſhe is indeed;—
God graunt vs grace, howeuer we go,
   For to repent with ſpeed!

FINIS, quod H. B.

❡ Imprinted at London by John Allde and
   Richarde Johnes, and are to be ſolde at the long
   ſhop adioining vnto S. Mildreds churche, in the
   Pultrie, and at the litle ſhop adioining to the
   North-weſt doore of Paules churche, anno
   domini M. D. lxvi. the xx. of Auguſt.

x

❡ *Other thus it is, or thus it ſhoulde bee.*

HE golden world is now come agayne,
God is knowen, beleued, loued and
obeyed;
True doctryne is taught and falſe ex-
yled cleane,
Sinne is mortified, all vice is decayed;
Peace doeth take place, all warres be delayed;
Youth is brought vp in learnyng vertuouſlye;
Commonwealth doeth flouriſh, pouertie hath
ayde;—
Other thus it is, or thus it ſhoulde be.

❡ Kynges and princes doe Gods lawes aduaunce,
Juſtice and equitie alſo they doe maintayne;
They loue peace, they hate war and variaunce,
Vice they ſuppreſſe, and vertue cauſe to raigne;
To get learning and knowledge they take great
payne;
They make good lawes, and ſee them kepte iuſtlie;
To defend their cuntries great trauel they
ſuſtaine;—
Other thus it is, or thus it ſhoulde bee.

❡ Maieſtrates and officers, each one in their degree,
Geue good enſample of obedience and liuyng;
For the commonwealth alſo they take great ſtudie,
They execute iuſtice iuſtlie in euery kynd of
thyng;
To the poore pouertie they be good and louyng,
The wylfull they reſtrayne from their iniquitie;

To the humble and good they be gentle and
   benigne ;—
Other thus it is, or thus it ſhoulde bee.

❡ Biſhops and miniſters doe themſelues apply
   Sincerelie to preach Gods holie law and goſpell,
Accordyng to their doctrine they liue vertuouſly,
   In hoſpitalitie and almes deed they greatly excell;
    They geue good example for other to doe well,
They be chaſte and ſobre, and full of humilitie,
   They ſtudie the Scriptures, all vice they doe
     expell ;—
Other thus it is, or thus it ſhoulde bee.

❡ Judges that ſit in iudgement, matters for to
   heare,
   Be ſo vncorrupte that no bribes they wyll take,
Tyll they heare both parties they ſtop the one eare,
   By the lawe deliberately the caſes they debate,
   By euidence and witneſſes the truth they out
    beate,
Falſehod they fetter, but right they doe ſet free,
   Juſt iudgement they geue, none can entreate;—
Other thus it is, or thus it ſhoulde bee.

❡ Juſtices and gentlemen peace doe maintayne,
   The queenes lawes and ſtatutes they ſee executed,
Contention and variaunce they doe ſubdue cleane,
   The oppreſſour they puniſh, the naughty is
    rebuked ;
   The ſturdy they correcte, the poore be refreſhed,
They lyue on their landes rented reaſonablie,
   Matters before them be iuſtly and ſoone ended ;—
Other thus it is, or thus it ſhoulde bee.

⁋ Mayours and bayliffes, and all other officers
   Of cities, boroughes, and of townes corporate,
They ftudie fuch decrees and fuch godly orders,
   That the people be wel ruled; great paine they
      take
For the commonweale; tumult and debate
They deftroy; but they encreace godly vnitie,
   They caufe plentie by prudence, dearth they
      abate;—
   Other thus it is, or thus it fhoulde bee.

⁋ All lawyers doe perfwade their clients to agree
   Rather then at the lawe to fpend out their money;
Yf they wyl not, they fearch their cafe profoundlie,
   And therein they proceed without fraude or
      delay;
   They bryng it to iudgement, or to fome godly
      ftay;
Yf they promife their clientes, they performe
   iuftly;
   They take reafonable fees for their paynes
      alway;—
   Other thus it is, or thus it fhoulde bee.

⁋ The commons feare God and obey the queene,
 ′ They come to heare Gods wurd and together
      pray;
Difobedience in no cafe is now no more feene,
   Contention they hate, they loue peace alway.
   Euery one is content to liue as he may,—
The rich helpe the poore, yea, and that gladly;
   The poore be content and for them doe pray;—
   Other thus it is, or thus it fhoulde bee.

⁋ Parents doe bryng vp their children very godly,
   Children obey their elders and folow their aduice;

Hufbandes loue their wiues, and they them hartely;
 Women be fober and gentle, neither proude nor
   nice ;
Seruants be faithful, they need no warning twice;
To vertue and learning youth geueth all their
   ftudie ;
 Yf any fall in decay, he is holpen agayne to
   arice ;—
   Other thus it is, or thus it fhoulde bee.

❡ All fubiects faithfully pray for their queene,
 That God may endue her royall hart alway
With faith, feare, and loue, before him to be feene,
 And for her honorable counfell they humbly
   pray,
 That good lawes and ftatutes fet furth they
   may,
To the wealth of the realme and communaltie ;
 That the queene may rule wel, and they truly
   obey ;—
   Amen.   God graunt that fo it may bee !

❡ Finis.

❡ Imprinted at London without Alderfgate in
 Little Brittaine, by Alexander Lacy.

A Ditty delightfull of mother Watkins ale,
A warning wel wayed, though counted a tale.

HERE was a maid this other day,
And fhe would needs go forth to play;
And as fhe walked fhe fithd and faid,
I am afraid to die a mayd.
With that, behard a lad
What talke this maiden had,
Whereof he was full glad,
     And did not fpare
To fay, faire mayd, I pray,
Whether goe you to play?
Good fir, then did fhe fay,
     What do you care?
For I will, without faile,
Mayden, giue you Watkins ale;
Watkins ale, good fir, quoth fhe,
What is that I pray you tel me?
Tis fweeter farre then fuger fine,
And pleafanter than mufkadine;

And if you pleafe, faire mayd, to ftay
A little while, with me to play,
     I will giue you the fame,
     Watkins ale cald by name,—
     Or els I were to blame,
          In truth, faire mayd.
     Good fir, quoth fhe againe,
     Yf you will take the paine,
     I will it not refraine,
          Nor be difmayd.

He toke this mayden then afide,
And led her where fhe was not fpyde,
And told her many a prety tale,
And gaue her well of Watkins ale.

Good fir, quoth fhe, in fmiling fort,
What doe you call this prety fport?
Or what is this you do to me?
Tis called Watkins ale, quoth he,
 Wherein, faire mayd, you may
 Report another day,
 When you go forth to play,
  How you did fpeed.
Indeed, good fir, quoth fhe,
It is a prety glee,
And well it pleafeth me,
 No doubt indeed.
Thus they fported and they playd,
This yong man and this prety mayd,
Vnder a banke whereas they lay,
Not long agoe this other day.

When he had done to her his will,
They talkt, but what it fhall not fkill;
At laft, quoth fhe, fauing your tale,
Giue me fome more of Watkins ale,
 Or elfe I will not ftay,
 For I muft needs away,—
 My mother bad me play,—
  The time is paft;
 Therfore, good fir, quoth fhe,
If you haue done with me.
 Nay, foft, faire maid, quoth he,
  Againe at laft

Let vs talke a little while.
With that the mayd began to fmile,
And faide, good fir, full well J know,
Your ale, I fee, runs very low.

This yong man then, being fo blamd,
Did blufh as one being afhamde;
He tooke her by the midle fmall,
And gaue her more of Watkins ale;
   And faide, faire maid, I pray,
   When you goe forth to play,
   Remember what I fay,
      Walke not alone.
   Good fir, quoth fhe againe,
   I thanke you for your paine,
   For feare of further ftaine,
      I will be gone.
Farewell, mayden, then quoth he;
Adue, good fir, againe quoth fhe.
Thus they parted at laft,
Till thrice three months were gone and paft.

This mayden then fell very ficke,
Her maydenhead began to kicke,
Her colour waxed wan and pale
With taking much of Watkins ale.
   I wifh all maydens coy,
   That heare this prety toy,
   Wherein moft women ioy,
      How they doe fport;
   For furely Watkins ale,
   And if it be not ftale,
   Will turne them to fome bale,
      As hath report.

New ale will make their bellies bowne,
As trial by this fame is knowne ;
This prouerbe hath bin taught in fchools,—
It is no iefting with edge tooles.

Thrife fcarcely changed hath the moon
Since firft this pretty tricke was done,
Which being harde of one by chance,
He made thereof a country dance ;
 And, as I heard the tale,
 He cald it Watkins ale,
 Which neuer will be ftale,
  I doe beleeue ;
 This dance is now in prime,
 And chiefly vfde this time,
 And lately put in rime.
  Let no man greeue
To heare this merry iefting tale,
The which is called Watkins ale;
It is not long fince it was made,—
The fineft flower will fooneft fade.

Good maydes and wiues, I pardon craue,
And lack not that which you would haue ;
To blufh it is a womans grace,
And well becometh a maidens face,
 For women will refufe
 The thing that they would chufe,
 Caufe men fhould them excufe
  Of thinking ill ;
 Cat will after kind,
 All winkers are not blind,—
 Faire maydes, you know my mind,
  Say what you will.

When you drinke ale beware the toaſt,
For therein lay the danger moſt.
If any heere offended be,
Then blame the author, blame not me.

FINIS.

A prettie newe Ballad, intytuled :

The Crowe ſits vpon the wall,
Pleaſe one and pleaſe all.

To the tune of, Pleaſe one and pleaſe all.

PLEASE one and pleaſe all,
Be they great, be they ſmall,
Be they little, be they lowe,—
So pypeth the crowe,
Sitting vpon a wall,—
Pleaſe one and pleaſe all,
Pleaſe one and pleaſe all.

Be they white, be they black,
Haue they a ſmock on their back,
Or a kircher on their head,
Whether they ſpin ſilke or thred,
Whatſoeuer they them call,—
Pleaſe one and pleaſe all,
Pleaſe one and pleaſe all.

Be they fluttifh, be they gay,
Loue they worke, or loue they play,
Whatfoeuer be theyr cheere,
Drinke they ale, or drinke they beere,
Whether it be ftrong or fmall,—
Pleafe one and pleafe all,
Pleafe one and pleafe all.

Be they fower, be they fweete,
Be they fhrewifh, be they meeke,
Weare they filke or cloth fo good,
Veluet bonnet or French hood,
Vppon their head a cap or call,—
Pleafe one and pleafe all,
Pleafe one and pleafe all.

Be they halt, be they lame,
Be fhe lady, be fhe dame,
If that fhe doo weare a pinne,
Keepe fhe tauerne or keepe fhe inne,
Either bulke, bouth, or ftall,—
Pleafe one and pleafe all,
Pleafe one and pleafe all.

The goodwife I doo meane,
Be fhee fat or be fhe leane,
Whatfoeuer that fhe be,
This the crowe tolde me,
Sitting vppon a wall,—
Pleafe one and pleafe all,
Pleafe one and pleafe all.

If the goodwife fpeake aloft,
See that you then fpeake foft;
Whether it be good or ill,
Let her doo what fhe will;

And, to keepe yourfelfe from thrall,
Pleafe one and pleafe all,
Pleafe one and pleafe all.

If the goodwife be difpleafed,
All the whole houfe is difeafed,
And therefore, by my will,
To pleafe her learne the fkill,
Leaft that fhe fhould alwaies brall,—
Pleafe one and pleafe all,
Pleafe one and pleafe all.

If that you bid her doo ought,
If that fhe doo it not,
And though that you be her goodman,
You yourfelfe muft doo it than,
Be it in kitchin or in hall,—
Pleafe one and pleafe all,
Pleafe one and pleafe all.

Let her haue her owne will,
Thus the crowe pypeth ftill,
Whatfoeuer fhe command
See that you doo it out of hand,
Whenfoeuer fhe dooth call,—
Pleafe one and pleafe all,
Pleafe one and pleafe all.

Be they wanton, be they wilde,
Be they gentle, be they milde,
Be fhee white, be fhe browne,
Dooth fhe fkould or dooth fhe frowne,
Let her doo what fhe fhall,—
Pleafe one and pleafe all,
Pleafe one and pleafe all.

S

Be fhe coy, be fhe proud,
Speake fhe foft or fpeake fhe loud,
Be fhe fimple, be fhe flaunt,
Dooth fhe trip or dooth fhe taunt,—
The crowe fits vpon the wall,—
Pleafe one and pleafe all,
Pleafe one and pleafe all.

Is fhe hufwife, is fhe none,
Dooth fhe drudge, dooth fhe grone,
Is fhe nimble, is fhe quicke,
Is fhe fhort, is fhe thicke,
Let her be what fhe fhall,—
Pleafe one and pleafe all,
Pleafe one and pleafe all.

Be they ritch, be they poore,
Is fhe honeft, is fhe whore,
Weare fhe cloth or veluet braue,
Dooth fhe beg or dooth fhe craue,·
Weare fhe hat or filken call,—
Pleafe one and pleafe all,
Pleafe one and pleafe all.   .

Be fhe cruell, be fhe curft,
Come fhe laft, come fhe firft,
Be they young, be they olde,
Doo they fmile, doo they fkould,
Though they doo nought at all,—
Pleafe one and pleafe all,
Pleafe one and pleafe all.

Though it be fome crowes guife
Oftentimes to tell lyes,
Yet this crowes words dooth try
That her tale is no lye,

For thus it is and euer ſhall,—
Pleaſe one and pleaſe all,
Pleaſe one and pleaſe all.

Pleaſe one and pleaſe all,
Be they great, be they ſmall,
Be they little, be they lowe,—
So pipeth the crowe,
Sitting vpon a wall,—
Pleaſe one and pleaſe all,
Pleaſe one and pleaſe all.

Finis.   R. T.

Imprinted at London for Henry Kyrkham,
dwelling at the little north doore of Paules,
at the ſigne of the Blacke Boy.

An Epitaph on the death of the Right honor-
able and vertuous Lord Henry Wrifley, the
Noble Earle of Southampton, who lieth interred
at Touchfeelde in the countie of Hamfhyre, the
30 day of Nouember, 1581, and in the 24 yeare
of our moft drad and foueraigne Ladie Elizabeth,
by the grace of God, of England, Fraunce and
Ireland Queene, &c.

OU noble peeres, refraine your courtly
        fportes awhyle,
    Caft on your wailefull weedes of woe,
        Dame Pleafure doo exile.
Beholde a platforme playne of death, fit for the
        graue,
Who late inioyed a lyuing foule, as you this
        feafon haue ;
His birth right noble was, honour befet him
        rounde,
But Death amidft his luftie yeeres hath fhrind
        him in the ground.
When time is come, he waightes, according Gods
        decree,
To conquer lyfe, refpecting not the mightieft in
        degree ;
Intreatie cannot ferue, Death feekes no golden
        gift,
For from his reache no potentate to flye can
        make the fhift.

The glaſſe runne forth at large, the howre fully
    ſpent,
To ſhare lifes thred a-ſunder hee by mightie
    Joue is ſent.
The Daunce of Death no king nor kayſer but
    muſt trace,
The duke, the earle, the lord and knight to him
    muſt yeeld a place;
The aged olde, the midle ſort, the luſtie youth
    in prime,
To liue on earth cannot inioy the certentie of
    time.
For as time hath no ſtaie, but fleeteth euerie
    howre,
So is the lyfe of mortall men compared to a
    flowre,
Whoſe beautie knowne to daie, to-morrow fadeth
    quight,
And vaniſheth, as though therof man neuer had
    the ſight.
So fickle is our ſtate, we fading flowres bee,
To-daie aliue, to-morrow dead, according Gods
    decree.
Of lyfe no charters giuen to any worldly
    wight,
Oh, who can ſay that he ſhall liue from morne
    vnto the night!
He that at fyrſt gaue lyfe, of lyfe will beare the
    ſway,
And when him lykes, as pleaſeth him, will take
    this lyfe away.
Sith he workes all in all, and rules as ſeemes him
    beſt,
Lets learne that earth we are, and earth to claime
    her owne is preſt;

The perfeꝗ proofe wherof apparently is ſeene
By this good earle, whoſe luſty yeeres did floriſh
    faire and greene ;
But in a moment chaunged and withered lyke
    the haie,
Bereft of lyfe and honor great, and coutched
    cloſe in claie.
Yet though he ſenceleſſe lye, Southamtons Earle
    by name,
Yet Death in him lyes dead, no doubt, by meanes
    of noble fame ;
For whilſt on earth he liu'de to vertue he was
    bent,
And after wiſdomes lore to hunt he gaue his
    frank conſent ;
In juſtice was his ioye, and iuſtly he did deale,
As they can tell that for his aide had cauſe for
    to appeale ;
The widow poore oppreſt he carefully did
    ſhield,
And to the orphane in his right did dayly comfort
    yeeld ;
The needie poore he fed with mutton, bread, and
    beeffe,
His hand was neuer ſlack to giue the comfortleſſe
    releefe ;
The naked back to cloth he euer ready was,
No needy poore without reward from this earles
    gates could pas ;
His houſe-keeping right good, there plentie bare
    the ſway,
No honeſt man forbidden was within his houſe
    to ſtaie ;
His faith brought foorth ſweete fruite the Lord
    God to delight,

And made him, as a feruant good, accepted in his
    fight;
Vnto his tennauntes poore this earle was euer
    kinde,
. To work their weale he carefully did alwaies
    yeeld his minde;
Inhaunfing of his rentes did ne enlarge his ftore,
He alwaies had a care to help and aide his farmers
    pore;
His feruauntes weale to worke no time he did
    forbeare,
To doo them good that wel deferu'd his zeale
    did ftill appeare;
On God his hart was fet, in Chrift his hope did
    reft,
And of the mightie Lord of hoaftes this noble
    earle was bleft;
To Prince he was moft iuft, to countrie alwaies
    true,
The fruites of loue and loyaltie in him all ftates
    might view;
In wedlock hee obferued the vow that he had
    made,
In breach of troth through lewd luft he ne would
    feeme to wade.
Thrice happy thou, of God and man belou'de,
That euer foughtft to make a peace where difcorde
    ftriffe had mou'd;
Though thou from vs be gone, and taken hence
    by death,
Among the fonnes of mortall men thy prayfe
    fhall liue on earth;
For as thy lyfe was iuft, fo godly was thy ende,
Not on this world, but on fweet Chrift, thou
    alwaies didft depend;

And as in health his name thou reuerently didſt
    praiſe,
So in his feare in ſickneſſe thou didſt ſpend thy
    lotted daies ;
This world thou heldſt as vaine, thy lyfe thou
    thoughteſt no loſſe,
In hope of heauen and heauenly bliſſe thou
    deemſt al things but dros ;
Thus houering ſtill in hope, to heauen thou tookſt
    thy flyght,
Wherewith thy Chriſt, the juelle of ioy, thy hart
    is pight ;
And he in extreeme paine, when anguiſh did
    abounde,
To giue thee comfort from aboue was euer ready
    found.
Amidſt his mercie he, though iuſtice wrought thy
    ſmart,
Euen lyke a louing ſauiour did alwaies take thy part ;
When Sathan, ſinne, and death about thee round
    were ſet,
To pray for thee moſt earneſtly he neuer did
    forget ;
And like a ſouldier iuſt by faith thou foughtſt
    the feelde,
And armſt thyſelf gainſt all thy foes, to whom
    thou woldſt not yeeld,
But ſo didſt keepe the fort that all thy foes did
    flye,
And lyke a lambe in Jeſus Chriſt preparedſt
    thyſelfe to die.
Of court thou takeſt thy leaue, thy prince thou
    bidſt farewell,
For whoſe eſtate thou praydſt to God her enemies
    to quell.

The noble peeres eche one with hart thou bidſt
  adue,
And praiedſt that they to glad her hart may
  loyaltie enſue.
Of all thy louing friendes thou takeſt a fynall
  leaue,
And vnto God moſt conſtantly for comfort thou
  doeſt cleaue.
Thy noble children thou right louingly doeſt
  bleſſe,
To ſeruants all thou giueſt adue, they may thee
  not poſſeſſe,
From them thou doeſt prepare thy paſſage ſtraight
  to make,
And vnto Chriſt with cheareful voice thy ſoule
  thou doeſt betake,
Who, with outſtretched armes, receiues it to his
  grace,
And with his ſaintes in glorie great appointes the
  happye place.
Thy freendes thy loſſe lament, thy children waile
  and weepe
To ſee their father and their freend in clay in-
  cloſed deepe.
Thy ſeruants ſtreme foorth teares, they wring
  their wofull handes
To ſee that all to ſoone of lyfe death hath de-
  folued the bandes.
His tennants all doo mourne, their ſmoking ſobs
  abounde,
And to the ſkies the needie poore their pitious
  plaints refounde ;
Their foſter freend from them by death they ſay
  is hent,
Whoſe want in court and towne eche-where both
  old and yong lament.

But teares are fpent in vaine; though they fuppofe
  him dead,
He liues in heauen where Jefus Chrift with glory
  crownes his head.
And thus, right noble earle, thy laft adue receiue,
To thine auaile behinde thee thou good name
  and fame doeft· leaue,
Which fo fhall conquer Death that Death in thee
  fhall die,
And moue the fonnes of mortall men to heaue
  thy praife to fkie.

Omnis caro fenum, quod John Phillip.

A Ballad reioyfinge the fodaine fall,
Of Rebels that thought to deuower vs all.

EIOYCE with me, ye Chriftians all,
    To God geue laude and prayfe,
  The rebels ftoute haue now the fall,
    Their force and ftrength decayes.

Which hoped, through their traitrous traine,
    Their prince and natiue foyle
To put by their deuifes vaine
    Vnto a deadly foile.

And with their armies ftoute in feilde
    Againft their prince did rife,
And thought by force of fpeare and fheilde
    To win their enterprife.

It was the Erle of Weftmerland
   That thought himfelfe fo fure,
By the aide of his rebellious bande,
   His countrie to deuoure.

The Erle eke of Northumberland
   His traitorous parte did take,
With other rebels of this lande,
   For Aue Maries fake.

Saying they fought for no debate,
   Nor nothing els did meane,
But would this realme weare in the ftate
   That it before hath ben.

What is that ftate, I would faine know,
   That they would haue againe ?
The popifh maffe it is, I trowe,
   With her abufes vaine,—

As by their doings may apeare,
   In comming through ech towne ;
The Bibles they did rent and teare,
   Like traytours to the crowne.

And traytours vnto God, likewife,
   By right we may them call,
That do his lawes and worde defpife,
   Their country, queene and all.

The lawes that fhe eftablifhed
   According to Gods word,
They feeke to haue abolifhed
   By force of warre and fword,

Forgetting cleane their loyaltie
    That to their prince they owe,
Their faith, and eke fidelitie,
    That they to hir fhould fhow.

And rather feeke to helpe the Pope
    His honour loft to winne,
In whom they put their faith and hope
    To pardon al their finne ;

That if they fhould their natiue land,
    Their queene and God denie,
They fhould haue pardon at his hand
    For their iniquitie.

Therfore with thofe that loue the Pope
    They did their ftrength employ,
And therby fteadfaftly did hope
    Gods flocke cleane to deftroy.

And then fet vp within this land,
    In euery churche and towne,
Their idols on roodeloftes to ftand,
    Like gods of greate renowne.

Their aulters and tradicions olde,
    With painted ftocke and ftone,
Pardons and maffes to be folde,
    With Keryeleyfon.

Friers fhoulde weare their olde graye gownes
    And maides to fhrift fhould com,
Then prieftes fhould finge with fhauen crownes,
    Dominus vobifcum.

All thefe and fuch-like vaneties
    Should then beare all the fway,
And Gods word through fuch fantafies
    Should cleane be layd away.

But like as God did them defpife
    Which were in Moyfes dayes,
That did a calfe of gold deuife
    As God, to giue him prayfe;

And for the fame idolatry,
    In one day with the fword
Did thre and twenty thoufand dye,
    That did negleﬆ his worde.

The children eke of Ifraell,
    In Ezechias time,
He made among their foes to dwell,
    That did committe that crime.

But when that Ezechias praied
    To God to helpe his owne,
The Lorde forthwith did fend them aide,
    Their foes weare ouerthrowne.

A hundred thoufande eightie fiue,
    By Gods aungelles weare flaine,
And none of them were left aliue
    That toke his name in vaine.

Senacherib alfo, the kinge
    Then of the Affirians,
As he his God was honouring,
    Was flaine by his two fonnes.

Like as he did thofe rebels ftill,
  Which did his flocke purfewe,
From time to time, of his free will,
  By force of warre fubdewe.

As Hollifernus and the reft
  He put them ftill to flight,
That had his little flocke oppreft
  In prefence of his fighte.

So hath he now thefe rebels all,
  Through their vngodly trade,
Caft downe into the pit to fall
  That they for others made.

To whom ftill daily let vs praye,
  Our noble queene to fende
A profperous raigne, both night and day,
  From her foes to defende

Her and her counfaile, realme and all,
  During her noble life,
And that ill hap may them befall
  That feeke for warre and ftrife.

Finis.

Imprinted at London, in Fleete ftreete, by William
  How, for Henry Kirkham, and are to be
  folde at his fhop at the middle north doore of
  Paules Churche.

Notes.

AGE 1, line 2. *As Donſtable waye.* " As plain as Dunſtable road. It is applied to things plain and ſimple, without welt or guard to adorn them, as alſo to matters eaſie and obvious to be found, without any difficulty or direction," Bedfordſhire Proverbs in Fuller's Worthies. Howell gives the proverb in a ſlightly different form,— " as plain as Dunſtable high-way." The author of the Cobler of Canterburie, 1608, ſpeaks of the " clownes plaine Dunſtable dogrell."

Page 1, line 4. *Syr Thomas Plomtrie. Sir* is here the title of a prieſt, anſwering to the Latin *dominus.* This clergyman took a conſpicuous part in the rebellion, and was amongſt thoſe executed at Durham early in the year 1570. " The 4. and 5. of January did ſuffer at Durham to the number of three ſcore and ſix, conſtables and other, among whom an alderman of the towne named Struthar, and a prieſt called Parſon Plomtree, were the moſt notable," Stow's Annales, ed. 1615, p. 664.

Page 2, line 13. *Northumberland.* The Earl fell into the hands of outlaws on the Borders, and was treated with great indignity. He was ſubſequently betrayed, and confined in the caſtle of Loch Leven. See Sir C. Sharp's Memorials, 1841, p. 323. Weſtmoreland made his eſcape to Flanders, and ſpent the remainder of his life on the Continent, dying, at a very advanced age, in November, 1601. He concealed himſelf in Scotland for a time immediately after the rebellion, and Elderton, in another ballad, preferved in the library of the Society of Antiquaries, fays of the two earls,—

And to Saint Androwe be they gone,
With very harde fhyfte, to make theare moane,
And fom of theare ladies lefte behinde.

Page 2, line 16. *No more is not Norton.* Several members of this family were concerned in the rebellion, but the perfon here alluded to was Richard Norton, of Norton Conyers, generally called " old Norton," a very confpicuous leader in the movement. On the flight of the rebels, a fpy, named Conftable, endeavoured to perfuade him to put himfelf under his protection in England until a pardon could be obtained; but he wifely declined. He fled into Flanders, and received a penfion from the King of Spain. The period of his death is uncertain. There is a portrait of him ftill preferved at Grantley Hall. " The countenance," obferves Sir C. Sharp, " is florid; the hair grey, but the flight beard on the chin and upper lip is of a fandy colour; his eyes are fmall and grey; the contour is pleafing, and the general expreffion is grave, but not ftern,—vigilant, wary, and contemplative," Sharp's Memorials, p. 277.

Page 2, line 24. *Gentyll John Shorne.* This was the name of a Kentifh faint, whofe fhrine was much vifited by pilgrims in the early part of the fixteenth century. Latimer, in one of his fermons, fays he prefers not to " fpeak of the popifh pilgrimage, which we were wont to ufe in times paft, in running hither and thither to Mafter John Shorne or to our Lady of Walfingham." The bones of Shorne were originally depofited at Canterbury, where his fhrine remained, but it would appear from MS. Afhmole 1125, f. 107, that they were removed in 1478, probably to Windfor, where there was a chapel confecrated to him. The name of John Shorne afterwards became to be ufed as a generic term for a Roman Catholic prieft.

Page 6, line 4. *Aftonyed.* " Troubled in minde, *aftonied*, made fore afeard," Baret's Alvearie, 1580.

Page 5, line 7. · *By Thomas Colwell.* " Receved
of Thomas Colwell, for his lycenfe for the pryntinge
of a ballett intituled a newe wel a daye, as playne, m^r.
papefte, as Dunftable waye, iiij.*d.*," Regifters of the
Stationers' Company, 1569-70. A tune called *Well-
a-day* is frequently mentioned. See Chappell's Popular
Mufic, p. 175.

Page 5, line 11. *The Black Almayne.* A tune often
referred to, for inftance in a Handeful of Pleafant
Delites, 1584, in Collier's Old Ballads, p. 53, &c.
The tune itfelf is unknown.

Page 6, line 1. *I-wys.* Certainly; truly. This
old Anglo-Saxon adverb was now beginning to be
corrupted into the pronoun and verb, *I wis,* I know.

Page 8, line 25. *The upper end of Fleet lane.*
Moft of the pieces which iffued from the prefs of
Richard Jones are dated from St. Paul's. This was
one of his early publications, mentioning a refidence
not heretofore noticed. He was living at St. Paul's in
the following year, 1573.

Page 9, line 2. *Gar.* Literally, make. The late
Mr. Bright poffeffed an early MS. mifcellany, in which
there was a copy of this ballad, fubfcribed,—" Fynis,
quod Jhon Heywood." This ballad was licenfed to
Alde, as a ballad " agaynfte detrection," in 1561-2.

Page 9, line 8. *And all thofe.* So in the original,
but it appears from the MS. copy that *and* is an error
for *on.*

Page 10, line 5. *Skaine.* A kind of fcimitar.
Hall, in his Chronicle, 1548, fpeaks of " a band of
Iryfhmen armed in mayle with dartes and *fkaynes,*
after the manner of their countrey." Palfgrave, however, in 1530, explains *fkeyne,* " a knyfe," a word
frequently fynonymous with dagger.

Page 10, line 22. *Bothe.* All, Bright MS.

Page 11, line 31. *Heere.* Cleere, MS. Bright. In
the next page, line 2, for *it is,* we here, MS. ibid.

Page 12, line 17. *Me to enfue.* Meete to efchewe,
MS. Bright.

Page 12, line 29. *Wo by.* Wo be, MS. Bright.

T

This and the previous ſtanza are tranſpoſed in the MS. In the next page, line 8, the manuſcript reads :—

> To make them glowe,
> As grace by grace may ſtay.

Page 13, line 1. *To ſleke.* "I ſlecke, I quenche a fyre; whan you ſlecke a hoote fyre with water, it maketh a noyſe lyke thunder," Palſgrave, 1530.

Page 14, line 3. *New luſty gallant.* The favourite tune of the Luſty Gallant is frequently alluded to, but Mr. Chappell conſiders that the preſent ballad was intended for another air, becauſe there are ſeven lines in each ſtanza. See his Popular Muſic of the Olden Time, vol. i. p. 91. Breton, in his Workes of a Young Wyt, 1577, mentions a dance tune called the Old Luſty Gallant. An early notice of the tune occurs in MS. Aſhmole 48, f. 112.

The preſent ballad was printed in the year 1569, as appears from the following entry in the books of the Stationers' Company,—"Receved of Thomas Colwell for his lycenſe for pryntinge of a ballett intituled the prayſe of my lady marques, iiij.*d.*" *Marques*, marchioneſs. Shakeſpeare makes Henry the Eighth ſpeak of the "lady marquis Dorſet," act v. ſc. 2. In the original ballad there are five woodcuts, in a line at the top of the ſheet. The fourth, which repreſents a ſage holding up the forefinger of the left hand, is alſo found, with the addition of three ſtars, in the title-page of Larke's Boke of Wiſdome, 1565.

Page 16, line 9. *Finis quod W. Elderton.* Drayton, in his Elegies, ſpeaking of his beginning to read the Claſſics as a boy, ſays,—

> I ſcorn'd your ballet then, though it were done
> And had for *Finis,* William Elderton.

Page 16, line 14. *The Priſoners' Petition.* This title is not in the original, which is printed on a ſlip of paper meaſuring 5 by 3½ inches, and appears to be a

hand-bill fent round to the wealthy inhabitants of the City.
Page 16, line 19. *The hole of Wood-ftreet Counter.*
There is no doubt that the beft portion of Wood-ftreet Counter was very far from being an agreeable place of refidence, but *the hole*, as it was called, was the very worft part of the prifon.

Put. Well, wee cannot impute it to any lacke of good-will in your worfhip,—-you did but as another would haue done ; twas our hard fortunes to miffe the purchafe, but if ere wee clutch him againe, the Counter fhall charme him.

Rauen. The *hole* fhall rotte him.

> *The Puritaine, or the Widdow of Watling-*
> *ftreete,* ed. 1607, fig. F.

> Next from the ftocks, *the Hole*, and Little-eafe,
> Sad places, which kind nature do difpleafe.
> *The Walks of Hogsdon*, 4to. 1657.

On the eaft fide of this ftreet (Wood Street) is one of the prifon houfes pertayning to the fhiriffes of London, and is called the Compter in Wood-ftreet, which was prepared to be a prifon houfe in the yere 1555, and, on the Eue of S. Michaell the Archangell, the prifoners that lay in the Compter in Bred-ftreete were remoued to this Compter in Wood-ftreete.— *Stow's Survay of London*, ed. 1603, p. 298.

Page 17, line 14. *Ballad of Patient Griffell.* This is the earlieft copy known of a ballad which was frequently reprinted. There are numerous variations in the later editions, few, however, of which are of much importance. The ftory was introduced to Englifh readers by Chaucer, who derived the incidents from Boccaccio ; and in the fixteenth century it was extremely popular in this country, becoming the fubject of plays, chap-books, and ballads. See notices of thefe collected in the Shakefpeare Society's reprint of the comedy of Patient Griffil, 1841. The prefent ballad forms the larger portion of a little chap-book of the feventeenth century entitled, " The Pleafant and

Sweet Hiftory of Patient Griffell, fhewing how fhe, from a poore mans daughter, came to be a great lady in France, being a patterne to all vertuous women. Tranflated out of Italian. London: Printed by E. P. for John Wright, dwelling in Giltfpur Street at the figne of the Bible," n.d. The poem is here introduced by the following epifode,—" In the countrey of Salufa, which lyeth neere Italy and France, there lived a noble and wealthy prince named Gualter, Marqueffe and Lord of Salufa, a man of fuch vertues that the world did ring of; beloved of his fubjects for his good parts, that, before his dayes nor fince, was very few the like for his continuall care of his fubjects good, and they, in their dutifulneffe, fought to out-ftrip him in love. From his youth his onely exercife was hunting, wherein he tooke fuch delight, that nothing was more pleafing unto him; withall the fubjects loyalty to this worthy prince, in their carefulneffe that fuch excellent vertues fhould not faile for want of iffue, intreated him by humble petition to marry, that from his loynes their children might enjoy the like happineffe. This fpeech thus fpoke to the prince drave fuch love and affection into his mind, that moft gracioufly he made them anfwer that when it fhould pleafe God that hee fhould fee one that he could love, hee moft willingly would fulfill their good and honeft requeft. Withall this anfwer gave them fuch content, that they earneftly prayed to fee that day."

Page 17, line 15. *The Brides Good-morrow.* The ballad of the Bride's Good-Morrow, " to a pleafant new tune," is in the Roxburghe Collection, i. 15, " Printed by the Affignes of Thomas Symcocke," but the ballad itfelf is older than the period of that printer. It commences thus,—

> The night is paffed, and joyfull day appeareth,
>   Moft cleare on every fide;
> With pleafant mufick we therefore falute you,—
>   Good morrow, Miftris Bride.

The exclamation, " Good morrow, Miftrefs Bride," is found, obferves Mr. Collier, " as a quotation, in more

than one play of the time of Shakefpeare, with other
allufions to this ballad." The tune itfelf has not been
found under this title. Did Shakefpeare have the
ballad in his recollection when he makes Petruchio
fay,—

> But what a fool am I, to chat with you,
> When I fhould bid good-morrow to my bride,
> And feal the title with a lovely kifs?

Page 19, line 16. *Malift.* Maliced; envied.
Page 21, line 6. *Alone.* " All alone," 'chap-
book ed.
Page 21, line 21. *Biffe and pureft pall.* Bifs and
pall were filk and cloth of expenfive and fine textures.
They are frequently mentioned in the old Englifh
romances as figns of the wealth of their poffeffors.
" That grete cite that was clothed with *biffe* and pur-
pur, and overgyld with gold and prefious ftonys,"
Wimbleton's Sermon, 1388. " And on hym were
the purpull palle," MS. Afhmole 61.
Page 22, line 25. *All and fome.* That is, every-
body—

> We are betrayd, and y-nome,
> Horfe and harnefs, lords, *all and fome.*
> *The Romance of Richard Coer de Lion,* 2284.

Page 23, line 2. *Brauery.* That is, rich apparel.
" Lionello he haftes him home, and futes him in his
braverye," Tarlton's Newes out of Purgatorie, 1590.
Page 23, line 4. *As he.* " At his," later verfion.
And, in the next line, "I will afk of thee." The
chap-book verfion, at the conclufion of the ballad,
adds the following,—" The lords and gentlemen, being aftonifhed, looked one upon another, and feeing
no remedy, but that the noble Marqueffe had an
unremoveable love upon her, befought her to pardon
them of their envy towards her, and to take them into
her favour, which fhe, with a modeft behaviour, promifed to doe. The noble Marqueffe, feeing all in
peace, ordained a great and fumptuous feaft, where
patient Griffel fate miftreffe of the feaft; the Mar-

queffe on her right hand, on her left her aged father, old Janicola; her two children betweene them both, the lords and gentlemen doing them fervice. This feaft continued fourteene dayes, to the comfort of the commons. When this folemne feaft was ended, the Marqueffe, to fhew his love to his Griffell, made her father one of his counfel, and governour of his palace, where for many yeeres he lived in the love of the whole court. The noble Marqueffe and his faire Griffell lived almoft thirty yeeres, faw their children's children, and then dyed, beloved and bewayled of their fubjects."

Page 24, line 1. *Ballade of a Lover.* This ballad was originally printed by Colwell in 1563, as appears from the Regifters of the Stationers' Company,— " receved of Thomas Colwell for his lycenfe for pryntinge of a ballett intituled the lover extollynge hys ladyes, iiij.*d.*" In the original, the firft eight lines are fet to mufic. " The tune," obferves Mr. Chappell, " is worthlefs as mufic, and, I fufpect, very incorrectly printed. It feems a mere claptrap jumble to take in the countryman."

Page 24, line 3. *Damon aud Pithias.* " This," obferves Mr. Chappell, " is probably a tune from the very old drama of Damon and Pithias."

Page 25, line 6. *Woulde.* " Wolude," original.

Page 27, line 1. *A monftrous childe.* It is a curious fact that the woodcut of this child, and of fome other monfters defcribed in the prefent collection, fhould be copied by hand on the margins of the regifter-book of Wills in the Prerogative Court of Canterbury for the year 1562, headed by the following note, here copied exactly as it ftands in the original,—*Prodigiæ quædam contra folitum naturæ curfum nata et in lucem ædit: anno Domini* 1562. In addition to thofe found in thefe broadfides may be mentioned drawings of a caterpillar and of a dog with a band round its neck. " Item, ther was (a) pyge brothe to London in May with ij alff bodys, behyng with viij fette, that mony pepull dyd fe ytt; and after cam a fyne and token of a monftorous chyld that was borne be-fyd Colcheſter at a town callyd (*blank*)," Machyn's Diary, 1562, ed. J. G. Nichols, p. 281.

Page 27, line 16. *Braſt.* Burſt. "Braſt in the middes, or in ſundre," Huloet's Dictionarie, 1572.

Page 28, line 4. *Beholde a calfe.* "In Aprell was browth to London a pyde calff with a great ruffe about ys neke, a token of grett ruff that bowth men and women," Machyn's Diary, 1562, ed. J. G. Nichols, p. 280.

Page 28, line 24. *Linne.* Ceaſe. "He never *linns*, he gives it not over, he is alwaies doing," Terence in Engliſh, 1614.

Page 29, line 6. *A ſcape.* So Shakeſpeare, in King John, ſpeaks of a "ſcape of nature."

Page 30, line 16. *Lady, Lady.* A favourite burden to a ſong, as in that of the Conſtancy of Suſanna, quoted by Shakeſpeare in Twelfth Night. Compare a ſong in the old interlude of the Trial of Treaſure, 1567,—

> Thou paſſeſt Venus far away,
> Lady, lady;
> Love thee I will both night and day,
> My dere lady!

Page 31, line 2. • *Forked cap.* The mitre.

Page 31, line 12. *And famiſhed him till lyfe was donne.* The author does not here follow the ordinary popular belief of the time, which was afterwards adopted by Shakeſpeare. According to Stow, who quotes an in-edited MS. by Sir John Forteſcue as his authority, the king "was impriſoned in Pomfrait Caſtle, where xv. dayes and nightes they vexed him with continuall hunger, thirſt and cold, and finally bereft him of his life with ſuch a kind of death as never before that time was knowen in England." The Percies, in the manifeſto which they iſſued againſt Henry the Fourth the day before the battle of Shrewſbury, expreſsly charge him with the reſponſibility of this crime.

Page 32, line 7. *Trentalles.* "Trentals or trigin-tals were a number of maſſes, to the tale of thirty, ſaid on the fame account, according to a certain order inftituted by Saint Gregory," Ayliffe's Parergon.

Page 33, line 1. *The Pope in his fury.* This ballad was licenfed to Kirkham, or Kyrham, as it is written in the regifter, in 1570-1, " his lycenfe for pryntinge of a ballett, the Pope in greate fury doth." So the words of the entry conclude.

Page 33, line 2. *To a letter the which to Rome is late come.* This perhaps refers and is a fuppofed reply to another ballad, by Stephen Peele, now in the Miller Collection, " to the Tune of Row well ye Mariners," which is headed,—

> A Letter to Rome, to declare to the Pope,
> John Felton, his freend, is hang'd in a rope ;
> And farther, aright his Grace to enforme,
> He dyed a Papift, and feemed not to turne.

The fame day (4 Auguft, 1571) was arraigned at Guildhal of London Iohn Felton, for hanging a bull at the gate of the Bifhop of London's palace, and alfo two young men for coyning and clipping of coine, who all were found guilty of high treafon, and had judgement to be drawne, hanged and quartered.—*Stowe's Annales*, ed. 1615, p. 666. The eight of Auguft, John Felton was drawne from Newgate into Paules Church-yeard, and there hanged on a gallowes new fet up that morning before the Bifhoppes palace gate, and being cut downe aliue, he was bowelled and quartered.—*Ibid.*, p. 667.

Page 34, line 2. *To-to.* Exceedingly. " *Too-too*, ufed abfolutely for very well or good," Ray's Englifh Words, ed. 1674, p. 49.

Page 34, line 14. *Senceyng.* That is, incenfing. " And whan thei comen there, thei taken enfenfe and other aromatyk thinges of noble fmelle, and *fenfen* the ydole, as we wolde don here Goddes precyoufe body," Maundevile's Travels, p. 174, ed. 1839.

Page 34, line 16. *Mell.* That is, to meddle with. " Hence, ye profane ; *mell* not with holy things," Hall's Satires.

Page 35, line 21. *The Nortons' bones.* Two of

this family, Thomas and his nephew Chriſtopher Norton, were executed for their implication in the Northern rebellion, at Tyburn, in May, 1570. Their heads were ſet upon London Bridge, and their quarters upon the various gates. There was a little poem by Sampſon Davie on them printed the ſame year. " Receved of Wylliam Pekerynge for his lycenſe for pryntinge of the ende and confeſſion of Thomas Norton and Chriſtofer Norton, rebelles in Yorkeſhyre, which dyed the xxvij. of Maye, 1570," Stationers' Regiſters.

Page 36, line 7. *Frump.* That is, mock. "*Mocquer*, to mock, flowt, frump, ſcoffe, deride," Cotgrave. " To frump, *illudo*," Coles.

Page 36, line 20. *Queen Elizabeth.* Theſe lines under a portrait form together a ſingularly curious broadſide. In the State Paper Office is an undated draft of a proclamation, in the handwriting of Cecil, prohibiting all " payntors, pryntors, and gravors " from drawing Queen Elizabeth's picture, until " ſome conning perſon mete therefor ſhall make a naturall repreſentation of Her Majeſty's perſon, favour, or grace," as a pattern for other perſons to copy. This proclamation was moſt likely never publiſhed, as it is not mentioned in Humfrey Diſon's liſt of the proclamations of Queen Elizabeth. The " pycture of quene Elyzabeth " was entered to Gyles Godhed on the books of the Stationers' Company, 1562-3.

Page 37, line 11. *Ane new Ballet.* The date of this ballad fixes it to the period of the author's eſcape from Paris at the time of the St. Bartholomew maſſacre.

Page 37, line 15. *Tykit.* Tied, bound ?

Page 37, line 16. *At Baſtianes brydell.* The alluſion here is to Queen Mary's leaving Darnley, on the night of his murder, to attend a ball at Holyrood, on the occaſion of the marriage of one of her attendants named Baſtian. The intention of the author of the ballad is obviouſly to eſtabliſh a parallel between the murder of Darnley and the maſſacre at Paris.

Page 37, line 19. *Wyte of this cummer.* That is, blame of this trouble or vexation. "Delivir us fra all dangears and perrellis of fire and wattir, of fyirflauchtis and thundir, of hungar and derth, feditioun and battel, of pleyis and *cummar*, feiknes and peftilence," Hamiltoun's Catechifme, ap. Jamiefon.

Page 37, line 22. *Conuoyit.* By artful contrivance, deceitfully.

Page 38, line 4. *Farlie.* Wonder.

Page 38, line 6. *Ganzelon.* Ganelon, the celebrated traitor of the romances of Charlemagne, the perfon who was bribed into betraying the French army to the King of the Saracens. He was executed at Aix-la-Chapelle by order of Charlemagne.

Page 38, line 12. *Be doand ane quhyle.* Go on for a time.

Page 38, line 14. *Ding.* To overcome.

Page 38, line 18. *Wapis.* That is, cafts or throws. So, in Ramfay's poems,—

> Get Johnny's hand in haly band,
> Syne *wap* ye'r wealth together.

Page 38, line 21. *The feryne.* That is, the fyren. *Ouirfylit*, circumvented.

Page 38, line 24. *Volatill.* Bird. "Make we man to oure ymage and likneffe, and be he fovereyn to the fifchis of the fee, and to the *volatils* of hevene," Bible, MS. Bodl. "Volatile, wyld fowle," Prompt. Parv.

Page 39, line 6. *Burreo.* Executioner. Bourreau, Fr.

Page 39, line 8. *Sane.* That is, the river Seine. *Huking*, confidering, regarding.

Page 39, line 13. *Thy faces was four.* Thy fauce was four, taftelefs, or infipid.

Page 40, line 8. *Tythance.* Tidings.

Page 41, line 3. *Graith.* Accoutrements.

Page 41, line 9. *Calk.* That is, chalk (to mark with). Mark their doors with chalk.

Page 41, line 18. *Go fay.* So in the original.

Can thefe words be erroneoufly printed for *affay?*
In the next line *thie* in the original, clearly a mifprint for *this.*

Page 42, line 1. *The Bryber Gehefie.* "Receved
of Thomas Colwell, for his lycenfe for pryntinge of a
ballett intituled of bryber Jehefye, taken out of the
vth chapter of the iiijth Bokes of Kynges, iiij.*d*," Stationers' Regifters, 1566-7. The reference, in the
modern tranflations of the Bible, is to the Second
Book of Kings.

Page 42, line 3. *To the tune of Kynge Salomon.* It
appears, from the Newe Enterlude of Vice, conteyninge
the Hiftorye of Horeftes, 1567, that this is the fame
tune as "Lady, lady." The ftage-direction is,—
"Enter Egiftus and Clytemneftra, finginge this fonge
to the tune of King Salomon;" and then follows the
fong, commencing,—

> And was it not a worthy fight
> Of Venus childe, Kinge Priames fonne,
> To fteale from Grece a ladye bryght,
> For whom the wares of Troye begon,
> Naught fearinge daunger that might faull,
> Lady, ladie!
> From Grece to Troye he went withall,
> My deare lady!

It appears, from the regifters of the Stationers' Company, that Tyfdale had a licenfe in 1561-2 for printing
"a new ballett after the tune of Kynge Salomon."

Page 45, line 6. *The fhape of ii monfters.* This
broadfide is probably that mentioned in the following
entry in the Stationers' Regifters, 1561-2,—"Receved
of John Alde for his lycenfe for pryntinge of a
picture of a monfterus pygge, iiij.*d.*" It is alfo
alluded to in another ballad. See p. 64. There are
engravings of two "monftrous pigs" in the original
broadfide, but only one is defcribed in the text.

Page 49, line 3. *Feinzeit.* That is, feigned. The
word *cruellus*, in the next line, is invented for the fake
of the rhyme. This ballad evidently belongs to the
earlier part of the year 1581, before James Earl of

Morton was brought to trial, and executed on the following day.

Page 49, line 17. *Dowkand.* That is, diving.

Page 50, line 8. *Volt.* Face; countenance.

Page 50, line 9. *Ingyne.* Capacity; ability.

Page 51, line 8. *Potteris.* "Porteris," original. The claffical allufions in this ballad are too trite to require annotation.

Page 51, line 13. *Landwart.* That is, country. It is hardly neceffary to fay that *pleuch*, here and in other places, ftands for *plough*.

Page 51, line 19. *Ane tit.* A quick pull; a hafty turn of the wheel.

Page 51, line 26. *Subumbragit.* Overfhadowed.

Page 52, line 3. *Git.* The laft letter of this word in the original appears, on clofe examination, to be an imperfect *f*, not a *t*. Read *gif*, if.

Page 52, line 11. *Litils.* So in the original, but probably a mifprint for *litill*.

Page 52, line 16. *Law.* To lower or humble.

Page 52, line 29. *Danter.* Conqueror; fubduer. Under the firm government of Morton, the Border diftricts, which had become the fcene of great lawleffnefs, were reduced into order. "He was very wyfe, and a guid juftitiar in adminiftration. His fyve yeirs war eftimed to be als happie and peaceable as euer Scotland faw. The name of a Papift durft nocht be hard of; ther was na theiff nor oppreffour that durft kythe."—Melvill's Diary, 1577.

Page 53, line 21. *Franke.* So in the original, but it may poffibly be an error for *fracke*, active, diligent. So in a poem cited by Jamiefon,—

> He wald not lat the Papifts caufe ga bak,
> Gif it were juft, bot wald be for him *frak*.

Page 54, line 10. *Pleit.* Maintained; debated.

Page 54, line 13. *Eith.* That is, eafy.

Page 54, line 21. *Dowie.* Dull; melancholy.

Page 55, line 9. *Eluottis.* So in the original. It may be right, and a mere fpecimen of cacography, but more probably a mifprint for *Elyottis*.

Page 55, line 12. *Labeis.* Jamiefon has, "*Lebbie*, the lap or fore-fkirt of a man's coat, S. B. Loth."

Page 55, line 25. *Glaikrie.* Idle wantonnefs.

Page 56, line 3. *Detreitis.* So in the original, obvioufly intended for *decreitis.* In the previous line, *decore*, that is, decorate.

Page 56, line 7. *Sempill.* Can it be that the author is here quibbling upon his own name?

Page 56, line 10. *Robert Lekprewicke.* This printer was at Edinburgh from about the year 1561 until 1570. In 1571, he is found at Stirling, and in 1572 at St. Andrew's. See p. 41. In 1573, he had returned to Edinburgh.

Page 56, line 12. *The Plagues of Northomberland.* " Receved of Thomas Colwell, for his lycenfe for pryntinge of a ballett intituled, Plaiges of Northumberlande, iiij.*d*," Regifters of the Stationers' Company, 1569-70. At the top of this broadfide is a row of five woodcuts.

Page 56, line 13. *Appelles.* This tune is referred to in Googe's Eglogs, 1563, in the Handeful of Pleafant Delites, 1584, and in the Crown Garland of Golden Rofes, 1659. A " ballett intituled Kynge Pollicrate, to the tune of Apelles," was entered to Colwell in the Stationers' Regifters, 1565-6.

Page 56, line 14. *When that the Moone, in Northomberland.* The Silver Crefcent is a well-known creft or badge of the Northumberland family. It was probably brought home from fome of the Crufades againft the Saracens. In an ancient pedigree in verfe, finely illuminated on a roll of vellum, and written in the reign of Henry VII, we have this fabulous account given of its original. The author begins with accounting for the name of Gernon or Algernon, often borne by the Percies; who, he fays, were

> Gernons fyrft named Brutys bloude of Troy :
> Which valliantly fyghtynge in the land of Persè
> At pointe terrible ayance the mifcreants on nyght,
> An hevynly myftery was fchewyd hym, old bookys reherfe ;
> In hys fcheld did fchyne a *Mone* veryfying her lyght,

Which to all the oofte yave a perfytte fyght,
To vaynquys his enemys, and to deth them perfue :
And therefore the Persès the Creffant doth renew.

From a Note by Bifhop Percy.

Page 56, line 24. *With horfe and armes.* "I have
certaine advertyfement that all reteyners and hufehold
fervants appertening the Erle of Weftmorland, with
the mofte part of all others his tennants, beyng
furnifhed with armour and weapon, of his lordfhip of
Raby, in their warlike apparel, repared to Branfepeth
yefterday and this nyght paft, and all the reft of his
tennants ar by his lordfhip's officers commandyt to fet
forthe upon one hour's warning," Letter of Sir George
Bowes to the Duke of Suffex, 7 November, 1569.

Page 57, line 1. *Pyght.* That is, placed, fixed.
Redyght, to reftore, (Lat.)

Page 57, line 27. *Bellinge.* That is, bellowing.
" Bellynge of nete," Prompt. Parv. " Becking,
belling, ducking, yelling, was their whole religio,"
Anfwere to a Romifh Rime, 1602.

Page 60, line 4. *In Somer time.* This is the fame
tune which is mentioned in a ballad in the Pepys'
Collection, " The Rimer's New Trimming, to the
tune of *In Sommer time*," which commences as
follows,—

A rimer of late in a barber's fhop
Sate by for a trimming to take his lot ;
Being minded with mirth, until his turn came
To drive away time he thus began.

Page 61, line 20. *Fat.* A vat or brewing-tub.
" Fatte, a veffel, *quevue*," Palfgrave, 1530. " A vate
or fat, *labrum*," Rider's Dictionarie, ed. 1617.

Page 63, line 17. *A monfterous Chylde.* In 1564-5,
there was entered on the books of the Stationers'
Company,—" Receved of William Greffeth, for his
lycenfe for pryntinge of a pycture of a chylde borne in
the Ile of Wyghte, with a clufter of grapes about ys
navell, iiij.*d.*" Notwithftanding the variation in this
defcription, there can be little doubt that this entry

refers to the broadfide printed in the text. If fo, the ingenious compiler of the narrative altered the charac- ter of the "clufter" between the date of entry and the period of iffue.

Page 65, line 23. *Vnparfett.* An unufual form of the word. Huloet has, " unperfecte, *imperfectus*," ed. 1572; and *unparfited*, for *unperfected*, occurs in Surrey's Songs and Sonnets, 1557. In the next line, the word *porte*, by a fingular licenfe, appears to be ufed for *report*.

Page 66, line 3. *Confortor.* A genuine old form of the word, derived from the Anglo-Norman.

Page 66, line 12. *The Marchants Daughter.* This is the earlieft copy of this ballad known to exift. William Blackwall, its printer, dwelt " over againft Guildhall Gate," but very few productions from his prefs are known to exift. See another fpecimen at p. 231. He is alluded to by the author of the Declaration of the true Caufes, 1592, as the printer "of obfcure and trifling matters." This ballad was extremely popular. The fiddler in Fletcher's Monfieur Thomas, 1639, mentions it as one of the fongs he is beft verfed in. A later copy, a few of the ftanzas being omitted, is preferved in the Roxburghe collection.

Page 66, line 13. *Briftow.* The ufual old way of fpelling the name of the town of Briftol.

Page 66, line 14. *The Maydens Joy.* This tune is referred to in Anthony Wood's collection of ballads at Oxford, in Old Ballads, 1729, vol. iii. p. 201, &c.

Page 67, line 12. *Fine.* "Then," ed. Roxburghe.
Page 67, line 18. *Wafte.* "Waile," ed. Roxburghe.
Page 68, line 7. *She.* " He," in the original.
Page 68, line 8. *Though naked.* Even as lately as the fixteenth century, the ufe of night linen was far from being univerfal. "To bed he goes, and Jemy ever ufed to lye naked, as is the ufe of a number, amongft which number fhe knew Jemy was one," Armin's Neft of Ninnies, 1608. Hence arofe the ex- preffion, *naked bed*, of which Shakefpeare has made fuch a pretty ufe,—

Who fees his true love in her naked bed,
   Teaching the fheets a whiter hue than white.

Page 71, line 23. *Joyfull.* " Mortall," ed. Roxburghe.

Page 72, line 7. *Trauell.* " Triall," ed. Roxburghe.

Page 72, line 14. *Al her iorneys.* " Her forrow,"
ed. Roxburghe.

Page 72, line 20. *On her perills.* " Of her
forrowes," ed. Roxburghe. The next ftanza is omitted in this later copy.

Page 73, line 10. *Euer.* This fhould be *evermore,*
as required by the rhyme, and as it ftands in the Roxburghe copy.

Page 73, line 18. *Eyes.* " Eys" in the original.

Page 73, line 24. *Such grieuous.* The fpace for
the word following thefe is alfo left blank in the original.
" Such grievous *doome,*" ed. Roxburghe. In the next
line, *ladies* is a mifprint in the original for *laddes.*

Page 74, line 28. *And of a paffing pure life.* " And
paffing pure of life," ed. Roxburghe.

Page 75, line 18. *Feareful.* " Freareful" in the
original.

Page 78, line 8. *To the tune of Labandalafhotte.*
This tune is the fame as " I waile in woe, I plunge in
pain." See the Handeful of Pleafant Delites, 1584,
and Ritfon's Ancient Songs, p. 151. The tune is referred to for " A fong of King Edgar, fhewing how he
was deceived of his Love." That ballad commences,—

Whenas King Edgar did govern this land,
   Adown, adown, down, down, down ;
And in the ftrength of his years he did ftand,
   Call him down-a, &c.

Mrs. Quickly fings this burden in the Merry Wives
of Windfor, act i. fc. 4, and Ophelia fang one of her
fnatches to the tune of Labandalafhotte. " You muft
fing, *Down-a-down, an you call him a-down-a,*" Hamlet,
act iv. fc. 5. " *Filibuftacchina,* the burden of a countrie fong, as we fay, hay doune a doune douna,"

Florio's Worlde of Wordes, 1598, p. 131. The fame
tune is clearly referred to in the Ballad againſt Slander
and Detraction, p. 9 ; and Rhodes, in his Anſwere to
a Romiſh Rime, 4to. 1602, ſays,—" I found it ſet to
no certaine tune, but becauſe it goeth moſt neere to the
olde tune of *Labandalaſhot*, therefore I have made that
all may be ſung to that tune, if neede be."
     Page 79, line 5.   *Marketſted.*   A market-place.
"And their beſt archers plac'd the market-ſted about,"
Drayton's Polyolbion.
     Page 79, line 30.   *Ance.*   That is, once, in the
ſenſe of, once for all.   "Once, twenty-four ducattes
he coſt me," Gaſcoigne's Suppoſes.
     Page 80, line 22.   *Nicholas Colman of Norwich.*   A
new name in the hiſtory of Engliſh publiſhing.   The
ballads were printed for him in London.
     Page 81, line 1.   *A proper newe ſonet.*   It is pro-
bably this ballad, not the preceding one, which is
thus entered in the Stationers' Regiſters for 1586,—
"Nicholas Colman, receved of him for printinge a
ballad of the lamentation of Beckles, a market towne
of Suffolke, on St. Andrewes day laſte paſte, beinge
burnt with fier, to the number of lxxx. houſe, and
loſſe of xx. m. *li.*"   Contributions in aid of the
ſufferers from this fire were raiſed throughout the
counties of Norfolk and Suffolk.   Blomefield mentions a ſum of money as having been collected in the
pariſh of Harpham "for the burning of Beccles."
In the book of the Mayor's Court at Norwich is
this entry,—" William Fleming, preacher of Beccles,
raiſed in Court of Mr. Mayor, £30 . 10 . 8, which
was collected in this city towards the re-edifying of
Beccles Church, which was lately burnt," Suckling's
Suffolk, vol. i. p. 12.
     Page 81, line 8.   *To Wilſon's Tune.*   This tune
does not appear to be known.   In the library of the
Society of Antiquaries is, A proper newe Ballad declaring
the ſubſtaunce of all the late pretended Treaſons againſt
the Queenes Majeſtie, 1586, *To Wilſon's new Tune.*
     Page 83, line 11.   *The church and temple by this*
U

fyre. "The roof, feats, and woodwork of the church were confumed, though the walls and the ftonework of the windows efcaped deftruction. The lower part of the fteeple remains blackened with fmoke in a very remarkable degree to the prefent day," Suckling's Hiftory and Antiquities of the County of Suffolk, vol. i. p. 12. The parifh regifters were, probably, deftroyed, the prefent books commencing in the year 1586.

Page 85, line 1. *Franklins Farewell.* James Franklin was the apothecary whofe poverty or whofe will confented to furnifh the poifons, according to order, in the Overbury murders. See his Trial in Cobbett's State Trials, vol. ii. col. 947. According to his own account, he bought the poifons at the entreaty of the Countefs and Mrs. Turner, protefting his ignorance of what they intended to do with them. See further particulars in Amos's Great Oyer of Poifoning, 1846. In the library of the Society of Antiquaries is a broadfide, entitled,—" James Franklin, a Kentifhman of Maidftone, his owne Arraignment, Confeffion, Condemnation, and Judgment of Himfelfe, whilft hee lay Prifoner in the Kings Bench for the Poifoning of Sir Thomas Overbury. He was executed the 9 of December, 1615."

Page 88, line 1. *The xxv. orders of Fooles.* "Receved of Henry Kyrham, for his lycenfe for the pryntinge of a ballett, intituled the xx. orders of fooles, iiij.*d*," Regifters of the Stationers' Company, 1569-70.

Page 88, line 4. *A quarterne.* That is, a quarter (of a hundred). Maundevile fpeaks of the moon being in " the feconde quarteroun," Travels, p. 301.

Page 88, line 19. *Or els a fox-tayle.* One of the diftinguifhing badges of a fool. " I fhall prove him fuch a noddy before I leave him, that all the world will deeme him worthy to weare in his forehead a coxcombe for his foolifhnefs, and on his back a fox tayle for his badge," The Pope's Funerall, 1605.

Page 89, line 17. *Wood.* That is, mad. " Phœbus

grows ftark *wood* for love and fancie to Daphne,"
Countefs of Pembroke's Ivy-Church, 1591. "The
name Woden fignifies fierce or furious; and in like
fenfe we ftill retain it, faying, when one is in a great
rage, that he is *wood,* or taketh on as if he were *wood,*"
Verftegan's Reftitution of Decayed Intelligence, 1605.
" Woode or madde, *fureux,*" Palfgrave.
Page 91, line 1. *Foole.* "Feele" in the original.
Page 92, line 23. *Apayd.* Satisfied; pleafed. "In
herte I wolde be wele apayede," MS. Lincoln. "I
am well apayed, *je fuis bien content,*" Palfgrave, 1530.
Page 95, line 12. *Or els to Lolers tower toft.* "At
eyther corner of this weft end (of St. Paul's) is alfo
of auncient building a ftrong tower of ftone, made
for bell towers, the one of them, to wit, next to the
pallace is at this prefent to the vfe of the fame
pallace; the other, towardes the fouth, is called the
Lowlardes Tower, and hath beene ufed as the
Bifhoppes prifon, for fuch as were deteƈted for
opinions in religion contrary to the faith of the
church," Stow's Survay of London, ed. 1603, p.
372.
Page 95, line 16. *To fwage.* "I fwage, I abate
the fwellyng of a thyng" Palfgrave, 1530. "Swage,
or to mitigate or appeafe, *complacare,*" Huloet's Dictionarie, 1572.

> But wicked wrath had fome fo farre enraged,
> As by no meanes their malice could be fwaged.
> *Gafcoigne's Works,* 4to. 1587.

Page 96, line 9. *A forayne.* That is, a foreigner.
(Fr.)
Page 96, line 29. *Threape.* That is, obftinately
maintained. "I threpe a mater upon one, I beare
one in hande that he hath doone or faide a thing
amyffe; this terme is alfo farre northren; he wolde
threpe upon me that I have his penne," Palfgrave,
1530.
Page 98, line 1. *A Ballad.* This is probably the
earlieft, as it undoubtedly is the moft curious, of
the Englifh verfions of a notion which fubfequently

became familiar as the Five Alls. As late as the reign
of George the Third, there was iffued a fatirical print
by Kay in five compartments, the firft of which repre-
fented a clergyman in his defk, with the infcription,
" I pray for all ;" the fecond a barrifter, " I plead for
all ;" the third a farmer, " I maintain all ;" the fourth
a foldier, " I fight for all ;" the fifth his Satanic ma-
jefty, " I take all." There are feveral old epigrams,
each line ending with the word *all.* See copies of two
in Larwood and Hotten's Hiftory of Signboards, p.
452. Inns called the *Four Alls* are ftill well-known ;
but the fign appears to be gradually going out of
fafhion.

Page 101, line 1. *A godly Ballad.* This ballad is
printed on the back of a wafte fheet of an old alma-
nac, one fide only having been printed of the latter,
which was a Prognoftication for the year then following, 1567. Each month is illuftrated by a fmall woodcut.

" Receved of John Alde for his lycenfe for pryntinge of a ballett intituled declarynge by the Scriptures
the plages that have infued of whoredom, iiij.*d,*" Stationers' Regifters, 1566-7.

Page 101, line 5. *Left in.* " Left if" in the original. Perhaps the correct reading may be, *left in.*

Page 101, line 15. *The woorm.* That is, the ferpent. The ufe of the word in this fenfe is very common in early Englifh.

Page 101, line 21. *The harmes.* " Thy harmes" in
the original.

Page 105, line 8. *Tantara.* This odd word was
ufually employed to fignify the noife made by a drum.
So, in the old ballad of the Winning of Cales,—

> Long the proud Spaniards had vaunted to conquer us,
>   Threatning our country with fyer and fword ;
> Often preparing their navy moft fumptuous
>   With as great plenty as Spain could afford.
>   Dub a dub, dub a dub, thus ftrike their drums :
>   *Tantara, tantara,* the Englifhman comes.

It was alfo, however, the name of a tune. A fong

called Gibſon's Tantara is given in the Handeful of
Pleaſant Delites, 1584. In the Miller collection is a
ballad, dated 1590, "to the tune of the new Tantara."
The uncouth orthography uſed by the writer of this
ballad, and the alluſion to Bewdley ale, indicate a provincial origin. Such words as *bloſe*, blows, *Rafe*,
Ralph, *ſincke*, cinque, *goſe*, goes, hardly require expla-
nation.

Page 106, line 2. *Upon the molde*. Upon the ground
or earth. This was a favourite expreſſion in the old
Engliſh romances. "Moold or ſoyle of erthe, *ſolum*,"
Prompt. Parv.

Page 106, line 14. *Plaie*. "Plate" in the original.

Page 106, line 28. *To baſte*. That is, to beat.
"To baſt, beat, *fuſte cædere*," Coles. *Baſtian*, a
cudgel. "*Baculus*, a baſton, a ſtaffe," Nomenclator,
1585. *Bumbde*, ſtruck, beat. The verb *to bum*, to
beat, is ſtill in uſe in the North. *Vnguentum Bakaline*,
ointment for the back.

Page 107, line 19. *He ſpurres his cutte*. That is,
his horſe. "Am I their cutt? muſt Jack march with
bag and baggage," Play of Sir Thomas More. "But
maſter, 'pray ye, let me ride upon Cut," Sir John
Oldcaſtle.

> He's buy me a white cut forth for to ride,
> And ile goe ſeeke him throw the world that is ſo wide.
> *The Two Noble Kinſmen*, 1634, p. 42.

Page 108, line 8. *Her life*. "His life" in the
original.

Page 110, line 17. *Bedſtaffe*. A wooden pin in the
ſide of the bedſtead for holding in the bed-clothes.
"Hoſteſſe, lend vs another bedſtaffe here quickly,"
Every Man in his Humour, ed. 1601, ſig. C. 4.

Page 111, line 12. *Did laugh a-good*. In good
earneſt. "The world laughed *a-good* at theſe jeſts,"
Armin's Neſt of Ninnies, 1608. "This mery aunſwer
made them all laughe a-good," North's Plutarch.

Page 112, line 1. *Deſcription of a monſtrous pig*.
"Receved of Garrad Dewes, for his lycenſe for

pryntinge of a pyⒸure of a monſterus pygge at Hamſted,"
Regiſters of the Company of Stationers, 1562. There
are two views of the pig in the original broadſide.

Page 112, line 19. *Flean.* That is, flayed.

Page 113, line 15. *The tune of Lightie Loue.* This
tune, which is conſtantly alluded to by our early
writers, and twice by Shakeſpeare, will be found in
Chappell's Popular Muſic of the Olden Time, p. 224.
The words of the original ſong have not been diſcovered. " Hee'l dance the morris twenty mile an
houre, and gallops to the tune of *Light a' love*," Two
Noble Kinſmen, 1634, p. 77. The earlieſt notice of
the tune yet met with occurs in ProⒸor's Gorgious
Gallery of Gallant Inventions, 1578, in which " the
louer exhorteth his lady to be conſtant, to the tune of,
Attend thee, go play thee." It commences,—-

> Not light of loue, lady,
> Though fancy doo prick thee.

Page 114, line 1. *Nicyngs and ticings.* Pretty
follies and allurements. *Tyſing* for *enticing* occurs in
Aminta, 1628.

Page 114, line 6. *Shouer.* Perhaps for *ſhiver*,
tremble.

Page 114, line 10. *Gloſe.* Diſſimulation; falſehood.

> Tell me, Gobrias, doſt thou ſimplie thinke
> That this diſcourſe is naught but naked truth,
> Or elſe ſome forged or diſſembled *gloſe*.
> *The Warres of Cyrus, King of Perſia,* 1594.

Page 114, line 15. *And you twincke.* "Twynkyne
wythe the eye, *conniveo*," Prompt. Parv.

> Some turne the whites up, ſome looke to the foote;
> Some winke, ſome twinke, ſome blinke, &c.
> *Lane's Tom Tel-Troths Meſſage,* 1600.

Page 115, line 18. *Bearyng your louers in hande.*
To bear in hand, that is, to perſuade to a falſe
concluſion. " I beare in hande, I threp upon a man
that he hath done a dede or make hym byleve ſo,"
Palſgrave, 1530.

Page 118, line 1. *Sapartons Alarum.* There was licenfed to Colwell, in 1569-70, " a ballett intituled my gentle John Saperton," who may be the fame perfon with the author of the prefent ballad.

Page 119, line 14. *What thoe?* What then? This expreffion alfo occurs in Shakefpeare. See Henry the Fifth, act ii. fc. 1.

Page 120, line 5. *The barded horfe.* The horfe equipped with military trappings or ornaments. "Their horfes were barded for feare of arrowe fhotte," Palfgrave, 1530. " At all alarmes he was the firft man armed, and that at all points, and his horfe ever barded," Comine's Hiftory, 1596. The word is fometimes written *barbed.* ▪

Page 120, line 30. *Vnder the Lotterie houfe.* The Lottery Houfe was fituated for many years near the weftern gate of St. Paul's Cathedral. It is defcribed by Stow as " an houfe of timber and boord." See his Annales, ed. 1615, p. 719.

Page 122, line 13. *A let.* That is, a hindrance. " Let, *impedimentum*," Huloet's Dictionarie, 1572. " Let, impediment, hinderaunce," Baret's Alvearie, 1580.

Page 122, line 27. *Stroy.* That is, deftroy. " Some they ftroye and fome they brenne," MS. Cantab. " Stroyed in difhonour," Antony and Cleopatra, act iii. fc. 9.

> Diffolving all her circles and her knots,
> And *ftroying* all her figures and her lots.
> *Harington's Orlando Furiofo,* 1591.

P. 123, line 19. *The Groome-porters lawes at Mawe.* The Groom-porter was an officer of the royal houfe-hold, whofe chief bufinefs it was to provide cards and dice, and to decide all difputes refpecting games of chance. Mawe was a favourite old game at cards, and is frequently alluded to. Braithwait obferves that " in games at cards, the maw requires a quicke conceit or prefent pregnancy," which implies that it was a game of unufual difficulty. All the games at cards played by our anceftors were, however, more difficult

whence the heavy steed that carries armor was called a bard?

and complicated than thofe in vogue at the prefent day.

Page 123, line 27. *Vied cardes.* Cards which have been betted upon. So, in Hall's Satires,—

> More than who *vies* his pence to fee fome tricke
> Of ftrange Morocco's dumb arithmeticke.

Page 125, line 12. *Sodome and Gomorra.* Kyrkham had a licenfe, in 1570-1, " for pryntinge of a ballett of Sodom and Gomore."

Page 127, line 21. *Shryked.* " I fhrike, I kry out, as one dothe that is fodaynly afrayde, *je me efcrie*," Palfgrave, 1530.

Page 129, line 18. *A mery balade.* Alexander Lacy, the printer of this ballad, appears to have either died or retired from bufinefs about the year 1571.

Page 130, line 7. *Neither mocke nor mow.* " I mowe with the mouthe, I mocke one; he ufeth fo moche to mocke and mowe, that he disfygureth his face," Palfgrave, 1530. *Loute*, in the next line, has a fimilar meaning, perhaps to contemn. " Lowted and forfaken of theym by whom in tyme he myght have bene ayded and relieved," Hall's Chronicle. This is alfo probably the meaning of the term in a paffage in the Firft Part of Henry the Sixth, act iv. fc. 3.

Page 130, line 19. *Houfe-kepers.* Perfons who keep at home. Shakefpeare ufes the term in the fame fenfe in the play of Coriolanus.

Page 131, line 2. *To hyll.* That is, to cover. " You muft hyll you wel nowe anyghtes, the wether is colde," Palfgrave, 1530.

Page 131, line 8. *Sad.* That is, ferious. The ufe of the term in this fenfe was very common.

Page 132, line 26. *The iob.* The peck or ftroke. " Jobbyn wythe the bylle, byllen or jobbyn as bryddys," Prompt. Parv.

Page 133, line 1. *The Othe of euerie Freeman.* A woodcut of the City arms is at the top of this broad-fide. Hugh Singleton, the printer, appears to have ftarted in bufinefs about the year 1562. He died in 1592 or 1593. A later copy of this oath is given in Stow's Survey of London, ed. 1633, p. 689.

Page 133, line 7. *Obeyfant.* Submiffive. " That were obeiffant to his hefte," Gower.

Page 134, line 10. *Neybourhed, loue, &c.* " Receved of Rychard Lante for his lycenfe for pryntinge of a ballett intituled, how neyghborhed, love, and tru dealinge ys gonne, iiij*d.*," Regifters of the Stationers' Company, 1561.

Page 136, line 16. *Percialneffe.* Partiality.

Page 138, line 14. *Philofophers learnynges.* There is a row of five woodcuts at the top of this fheet. The firft one is alfo introduced by Colwell into Larke's Boke of Wifdome, ed. 1565, fig. B. i. Colwell had a licenfe " for pryntinge of a ballett intituled the philofifor lernynges" in 1568-9.

Page 138, line 17. *Que paffa.* A dance, properly called *Qui paffa*, but fometimes fpelt *quipafcie* or *kypafcie.* There is a fong " to the tune of Kypafcie" in the Handeful of Pleafant Delites, 1584.

Page 139, line 5. *Surance.* Warrant; fecurity; affurance. " Now give fome furance that thou art Revenge," Titus Andronicus, act v. fc. 2.

Page 140, line 3. *Corzye.* Diftrefs; inconvenience. " To have a great hurt or domage, which we call a corfey to the herte," Eliote's Dictionarie, 1559.

Page 140, line 10. *Exuperate.* Surmount. (Lat.)

Page 141, line 11. *It is olde fyr John.* The title of *fir* was formerly the defignation of a Bachelor of Arts, and, in confequence, the Englifh clergy were diftinguifhed by this title affixed to their Chriftian names. Hence Shakefpeare introduces Sir Hugh, Sir Topas, &c. " Within the limits of myne own memory, all readers in chapels were called *firs,*" Machell's MSS., temp. Car. II.

Page 141, line 18. *A graye.* A badger. " Grey, beeft, *taxus,*" Prompt. Parv. " Graye, a beeft, *taxe,*" Palfgrave, 1530. " Graye, bagger, brocke, a beaft," Huloet's Dictionarie, 1572.

Page 142, line 24. *The fwap of the fwalowe.* The

flang expreffions in this and fome other of thefe ballads can only be conjecturally explained. Can this
mean, the blow of the drunkard?
Page 143, line 8. *To bewite.* To hinder.
Page 143, line 11. *Mome.* A blockhead. "*Ca-
parrone*, a pugge, an ape, a munkie, a babuine, a gull,
a ninnie, a mome, a fot," Florio's Worlde of Wordes,
1598. "She will make a mome of thee, if fhee get the
upper hand once," Withals' Dictionarie, ed. 1608,
p. 460.

> And pluck up thy hart, thou faint-harted *mome ;*
> As long as I lyve, thou fhalt take no harme.
> *The Conflict of Confcience, by N. Woodes,* 1581.

> And yet, to fpeake the veritie, I roame not farre from home ;
> My yeeres be not expyred yet that bound me for a *mome.*
> *The Caftell of Courtefie, by James Yates,* 1582.

Page 143, line 12. *Talle.* Valiant ; warlike. "He
is as tall a man as any in Illyria," Twelfth Night.
Page 145, line 1. *Marueilous ftraunge Fifhe.* This
is one of the earlieft broadfides relating to "ftrange
fifhes" known to exift, and is a modeft account
in comparifon with that given by Stowe of a fifh taken
near Ramfgate in 1574, one of the eyes of which,
"being taken out of his head, was more then fix
horfes in a cart could draw ; a man ftoode upright
in the place from whence the eye was taken ;" Annales, ed. 1615, p. 677. The fondnefs of the public
for exaggerated accounts of fuch things is pleafantly
ridiculed by Shakefpeare,—"Here's another ballad, Of
a fifh, that appeared upon the coaft, on Wednefday the
fourfcore of April, forty thoufand fathom above water,
and fung this ballad againft the hard hearts of maids."
I am not acquainted with any very early ballad refpecting a fifh, but in the Miller collection is a broadfide,
"The Difcription of a rare or rather moft monftrous
fifhe, taken on the Eaft Coft of Holland the xvii. of
Nouember, anno 1566," at the conclufion of which
are fome verfes commencing thus,—

As thou this formed fifhe doeft fee
I-chaunged from his ftate,
So many men in eche degree
From kynd degenerate;
To monfters men are turned now,
Difguifed in their raye,
For in theyr fonde inuentions new
They kepe no meane ne ftaye.

Page 145, line 14. *Scooles.* Shoals. " Into the town of Rochell, they fay, God hath fent a *fkull* of fifh for their relief," MS. Harl. 388.

Page 146, line 15. *Daye fertayne.* The comma here fhould be placed after the word *daye.* In the 15th line of this page the laft word in the line is, in the original, mifprinted *ferteintaintie.*

Page 146, line 17. *The Kinges Head in new Fifh-ftreat.* A celebrated tavern for the "faft" men of the time of Elizabeth, noted for its wines. "Ha' your diet-drinke ever in bottles ready, which muft come from the Kings-head," Ben Jonfon's Magnetick Lady, ed. 1640, p. 37. "The King's-head in New Fifh-ftreet, where royfters do range," Newes from Bartholomew Fayre.

Page 147, line 12. *The fantafies.* This poem and the three following are printed together in double columns on one page of a large broadfide. This firft one is alfo found amongft the "Songes and Sonnettes of Uncertain Auctours," in Tottel's Mifcellany, 1557, there ·headed, "Of the mutabilitie of the world." Lacy, in 1565-6, had a licenfe "for prynting of a ballett intituled a fonge of Appelles, with another dytty;" and Griffith, in the fame year, "for prynting of a ballett intituled of Apelles and Pygmalyne, to the tune of the fyrft Apelles." Lacy, however, alfoin the fame year, had a licenfe "for pryntinge of a ballett intituled the Fantifes of a trubbled mans hed;" fo that the firft poem in the prefent broadfide may have been iffued feparately.

Page 147, line 17. *A fea of wofull forrowes.* "Or to take arms againft a fea of troubles," Hamlet.

Page 148, line 10. *And is.* "As is," ed. 1557.

Page 148, line 17. *Payne.* " Gaine," ed. 1557, which has alſo *runne* for *rome* in the next line but one.

Page 149, line 12. *Of euyll tounges.* This is alſo printed in Tottel's Miſcellany, 1557, the preſent copy giving the name of the author, which was unknown to the compiler of that work.

Page 150, line 5. *Ye make great hatred.* In ed. 1557 this ſtanza commences thus,—

> Ye make great warre, where peace hath been of long;
> Ye bring rich realmes to ruine and decay.

Page 151, line 24. *Coucht.* Laid ; placed. This term was ſpecially applied to artiſtic work.

> Alle of palle werke fyne,
> *Cowchide* with newyne.—*MS. Lincoln.*

Page 152, line 2. *A worlde it was to ſee.* That is, it was worth a world to ſee, it was wonderful to ſee. " It is a worlde to ſe him lowte and knele," Palſgrave, 1530. " It is a worlde to ſee what a wit wickedneſſe hath," Racſter's Booke of the Seven Planets, 1598.

> It is a worlde to ſee eache feate diſplaying wiſe,
> Of Venus nimphes, of curtizans, whom folly doth diſguiſe.
> *Grange's Golden Aphroditis,* 1577.

> But, Lord, it is a world to ſee how fooliſh fickle youth
> Accompts the ſchoole a purgatorie, a place of paine and ruth.
> *The Chariot of Chaſtitie, by James Yates,* 1582.

Page 154, line 7. *Roiſters.* Rioters.

> If he not reeke what ruffian *roiſters* take his part,
> He weeldes unwiſely then the mace of Mars in hand.
> *Mirrour for Magiſtrates,* ap. Nares.

Page 154, line 12. *Crake.* " I crake, I boſte, *je me vante ;* whan he is well whyttelled, he wyll crake goodly of his manhode," Palſgrave, 1530. " Cracke or to bragge foolyſhely, *exultare,*" Huloet's Dictionarie, 1572.

Page 154, line 29. *Gage.* A pledge or pawn. " He

that taketh a gage for a furetie of payment," Baret's Alvearie, 1580.

Page 156, line 2. *Holborne Hill.* Holborn Hill was always the road through which criminals, taken from Newgate to be hung at Tyburn, were conducted. There are innumerable references to this in our old writers.

Page 156, line 17. *Capichini.* So in the original. "Behold yet a new fwarm of locufts, the order of the Capuchins, and of thofe fhamelefs companions which attribute unto themfelves the name of the companie of Jefus, which are within thefe forty years crawled out of the bottomlefs pit," Sermon publifhed in 1587.

Page 157, line 3. *Lies.* "Lie" in the original.

Page 157, line 8. *The faire Widow of Watling ftreet.* This ballad has no connection with the play fo called. It was entered in the Stationers' Regifters by Richard Jones in Auguft, 1597, as "two ballads, being the firft and fecond partes of the Widowe of Watling Street." No copy printed by Jones is known to exift, the prefent, iffued by Pavier, being the earlieft edition yet difcovered. There is a later copy in the Roxburghe collection "printed for Fr. Cowles."

Page 157, line 12. *To the tune of Bragandary.* In Anthony Wood's collection of ballads at Oxford is one entitled, "A Defcription of a ftrange and miraculous fifh caft upon the fands in the meads, in the hundred of Worwell in the county Palatine of Chefter or Chefheire; to the tune of Bragandary."

Page 158, line 25. *For-why.* Becaufe.

Page 162, line 6. *Fauor.* Countenance. "He was a youth of fine favour and fhape," Bacon's Hiftory of Henry the Seventh.

Page 162, line 20. *A fort.* A company. "What care I for waking a forte of clubbifh loutes," Enterlude of Jacob and Efau, 1568. "A fort of country fellows," Tale of a Tub. "Ye fhall be flain, all the fort of you," Pfalms.

Page 162, line 23. *Witneffes.* "Witneffe" in the original, and fo alfo in the Roxburghe copy.

Page 163, line 9. *And how it fell.* " And how it befell, they two mark'd it well," Roxburghe ed.
Page 163, line 19. *As the scuse.* " An excuse," ed. Roxburghe. This is simply a modernization. *Scuse* for *excuse* occurs in Shakespeare.
Page 163, line 23. *You masters.* " My masters," Roxburghe ed.
Page 164, line 6. *Quod the widdow.* " Quoth the young man," Roxburghe ed.
Page 164, line 11. *He.* " She" in the original, corrected in the Roxburghe copy.
Page 164, line 18. *To speake so.* The word *so*, wanting in the original, is supplied by conjecture. The Roxburghe copy reads *ill.*
Page 165, line 4. *Stamberd.* Stammered. " Stamber, or to stutte, *titubo*," Huloet's Dictionarie, 1572. " Playes on thoughts, as girls with beads, when their masse they stamber," Armin's Nest of Ninnies, 1608.
Page 165, line 15. *To loose, at the least.* These two lines are thus given in the Roxburghe edition,—

> For forfeit even all the goods he possest,
> To loose both his eares, and banisht so rest.

Page 166, line 15. *Almightie God I pray.* This and the next article are printed on one broadside page. The initial letters of the lines in the present poem read, when placed together,—" *Tempvs edax rervm*, Time bryngethe al thynges to an ende, qvod Christopher Wilson."
Page 167, line 6. *Xpe.* Christe.
Page 169, line 15. *Reduce.* Bring back (Lat.) " The mornynge, forsakyng the golden bed of Titan, reduced the desyred day," History of Lucres and Eurialus, 1560.
Page 173, line 17. *Trone.* " Trone or seate royall, *thronus*; trone-sitter, or he that sytteth in Maiestye, *altitronus*," Huloet's Dictionarie, 1572.
Page 174, line 15. *Pepper is blacke.* There was a dance-tune so called. " When his wench or friskin was footing it aloft on the greene, with foote out and

foote in, and as bufie as might be at Rogero, Bafilino, Turkelony, all the flowers of the broom, *Pepper is black*," &c., Nafh's Have With You to Saffron-Walden, 1596. The tune is found in the Dancing Mafter, 1650. See it in Chappell's Popular Mufic, p. 121.

Page 175, line 15. *Baggage.* Refufe. " Scum off the green baggage from it, and it will be a water," Lupton's Thoufand Notable Things.

Page 178, line 8. *An Epitaph.* The name of the Lord Mayor was Avenon, not Avenet, as here given. The death of this eftimable lady in July was, fingularly enough, followed by the widower's marriage on October 22nd in the fame year. " 1570, Oct. 22, was married Sir Alexander Avenon, Lord Mayor, and miftrefs Blunden, widow, by a licenfe, within his own houfe," Regifter of Allhallows, Bread Street, ap. Malcolm, ii. 12. The epitaph upon this lady is recorded in Stow's Survay of London, ed. 1618, p. 496. His firft wife, the lady commemorated in the ballad, was Elizabeth, daughter of John Slow of King's Norton. See a pedigree in MS. Harl. 1096.

Page 178, line 18. *Fine.* End. This word is now only ufed in the expreffion, *in fine*.

Page 179, line 10. *Schortchyng.* The *r* is probably inferted by miftake in this word, which feems to be merely a form of *fcotching*.

Page 179, line 14. *Could not want.* That is, could not do without. " I myffe, I wante a thyng that I feke for," Palfgrave, 1530. " *De cela je ne puis paffer*, I can by no meanes want it, I cannot bee without it," Cotgrave.

And he is one that cannot wanted be,
But ftill God keepe him farre enough from me.
Workes of Taylor, the Water-Poet, 1630, ii. 134.

Page 181, line 18. *Keyfar.* An old term for an emperor, confidered by fome to be a corruption of Cæfar. " Es there any kyde knyghte, kayfere or other," Morte Arthure, MS. Lincoln. " Mighty kings and kefars into thraldom brought," Spenfer.

" To be kaifer or kyng of the kyngdom of Juda,"
Piers Ploughman.
Page 182, line 10. *A famous dittie.* " The 12. of
Nouember the queenes maieftie, returning after her
progreffe, came to her manor of S. James, where the
citizens of London, to the number of 200, the graueft
fort in coats of veluet and chaines of gould, on horfe-
back, and 1000 of the companies on foote, hauing with
them 1000 men with torches ready there to giue light
on euery fide, for that the night drew on, receiued and
welcomed her."—*Stow's Annales*, p. 700.
Page 182, line 14. *Wigmores Galliard.* This tune
is given in Chappell's Popular Mufic of the Olden
Time, p. 242, from William Ballet's MS. Lute-Book.
It is frequently alluded to by our early writers.
" This will make my mafter leap out of the bed for
joy, and dance Wigmore's Galliard in his fhirt about
his chamber," Middleton's Five Gallants.
Page 186, line 13. *A meruaylous ftraunge deformed
Swyne.* This and other marvels of the time are
thus alluded to in a letter from Bifhop Jewell to
H. Bullinger, written in Auguft, 1562,—" Incredibilis
fuit hoc anno toto apud nos cœli atque aeris
intemperies. Nec fol, nec luna, nec hyems, nec ver,
nec æftas, nec autumnus, fatisfecit officium fuum. Ita
effatim et pene fine intermiffione pluvit, quafi facere jam
aliud cœlum non queat. Ex hac contagione nata funt
monftra : infantes fœdum in modum deformatis
corporibus, alii prorfus fine capitibus, alii capitibus
alienis ; alii trunci fine brachiis, fine tibiis, fine
cruribus ; alii offibus folis cohærentes, prorfus fine
ullis carnibus, quales fere imagines mortis pingi folent.
Similia alia complura nata funt e porcis, ex equabus, e
vaccis, e gallinis. Meffis hoc tempore apud nos
anguftius quidem provenit, ita tamen ut non poffimus
multum conqueri."
Page 187, line 8. *Tallents.* Talons. This form
of the word was very common, and the occafion of
many a quibble. " Are you the kite, Beaufort?
Where's your talents?" Firft Part of the Contention,
1600.

Page 188, line 17. *White-faſte.* That is, white-faced.

Page 190, line 8. *Love deſerveth Love.* This, and the four pieces which follow, are not printed, but accompany the ballads in contemporary manuſcript.

Page 190, line 19. *He beares her gloue.* The glove of a lady, worn in a helmet as a favour, was conſidered a very honourable token, and much of the wearer's ſucceſs was ſuppoſed to be derived from the virtue of the lady. See Nares, in v.

Page 191, line 2. *Tell me, ſweete girle.* There is another MS. of this ballad in MS. Aſhmole 781, beginning, "Tell mee, ſweete *harte*," fol. 145.

Page 192, line 9. *Croſs-row.* The alphabet, ſaid to be ſo called from the croſs prefixed to it in the early horn-book.

> Thine eies taught me the alphabet of love,
> To kon my croſs-rowe ere I learn'd to ſpell.
> *Drayton's Idea.*

Page 194, line 8. *A monſtrous Child.* "Receved of John Sampſon, for his lycenſe for the pryntinge of a monſterus chylde which was bornne at Maydeſtone, iiij.*d*," Regiſters of the Stationers' Company, 1568-9. This entry is not inconſiſtent with the imprint, Sampſon frequently ſtyling himſelf Awdeley, which was, in faēt, his *alias.* The original is embelliſhed with two hideous wood-engravings, ſhowing the front and back of the child.

Page 194, line 22. *Played the naughty packe.* "A whore, queane, punke, drab, flurt, ſtrumpet, harlot, cockatrice, *naughty pack*, light huſwife, common hackney," Cotgrave.

Page 195, line 3. *Libardes.* "Libarde, *leopardus*," Huloet's Diētionarie, 1572. "Hee is a moſt excellent turner, and wil turne you waſſel-bowles and poſſet-cuppes, carv'd with libberdes faces and lyons heades, with ſpoutes in their mouthes to let out the poſſet-ale moſt artificially," Sir Gyles Gooſecappe, 1606.

x

Page 197, line 16. *To the tune of Fortune.* This favourite old tune is given in Queen Elizabeth's Virginal Book, and in various other muſical compilations. See a long account of it in Chappell's Popular Muſic, p. 162.

Page 198, line 9. *Shute.* Robert Shute was a Juſtice of the Queen's Bench from the year 1586 until his death in 1590. See Foſs's Judges of England, vol. v. p. 541.

Page 201, line 1. *A diſcription of a monſtrous Chylde.* "The iiij day of June ther was a chyld browth to the cowrte in a boxe, of a ſtrange fegur, with a longe ſtrynge commyng from the navyll,—browth from Chechefter," Machyn's Diary, 1562, ed. J. G. Nichols, p. 284. Francis Godliff had a licenſe, in 1562, for "the pyꬓure of a monſtrus chylde which was bourne at Chechefter." See Herbert's Ames, p. 1325.

Page 202, line 11. *Our.* The original has *it*, and the alteration may be unneceſſary. When it was made, it was not recolleꬓed that *it* occaſionally ſtands for *yet*. "And *it*, God knowes what may befall," Marriage of Wit and Wiſdome, 1579.

Page 202, line 15. *A lame.* A lamb. "Lam or loom, yonge ſcheep, *agnus*," Prompt. Parv. "*Agnus*, a lame ; *agna*, a new lame," Nominale MS.

Page 203, line 2. *The calues and pygges ſo ſtraunge.* "This yeare (1562) in England were manie monſtruous births. In March, a mare brought foorth a foale with one bodie and two heads, and, as it were, a long taile growing out betweene the two heads. Alſo a ſow farrowed a pig with foure legs like to the armes of a manchild with armes and fingers, &c. In Aprill, a ſow farrowed a pig with two bodies, eight feet, and but one head. Manie calves and lambs were monſtruous, ſome with collars of ſkin growing about their necks like to the double ruffes of ſhirts and neckerchers then uſed. The foure and twentith of Maie, a manchild was borne at Chichefter in Suffex, the head, armes and legs whereof were like to an anatomie, the breaſt and bellie monſtruous big, from the navill as it

were a long ſtring hanging; about the necke a great
collar of fleſh and ſkin growing like the ruffe of a ſhirt
or neckercher comming up above the eares, pleited
and folded, &c." Holinſhed's Chronicles, ed. 1587,
vol. 3, p. 1195. Cf. Stow's Annales, ed. 1615,
p. 647.

Page 206, line 7. *Diſgeſt.* A common form of
digeſt. " I have ſet you downe one or two examples
to try how ye can *diſgeſt* the maner of the deviſe,"
Puttenham.

Page 206, line 27. *Take.* "Toke" in the original.

Page 207, line 28. *Meſſe.* Entertainment. The
term is generally applied to a party of four. "And
you are the fourth, to make up the meſſe," Wapull's
Tyde Taryeth no Man, 1576. "The meſſe of
conſtables were ſhrunke to three," Taylor's Workes,
fol. Lond. 1630.

Page 208, line 2. *Lidgate, Wager, Barclay and
Bale.* There was a William Wager, the author of
the comedy called, The Longer thou Liueſt the more
Foole thou Art, n. d. Another comedy by him, entitled, 'Tis Good ſleeping in a Whole Skin, was amongſt
the number of plays deſtroyed by Warburton's ſervant,
and Winſtanley aſcribes the play of the Trial of
Chivalry to the ſame writer. The perſon alluded to
in the text may, however, be Lewis Wager, the
author of "A new Enterlude, never before this tyme
imprinted, entreating of the Life and Repentaunce
of Marie Magdalene," 1567. The other writers
alluded to in the text are too well known to require
a note.

Page 211, line 1. *Fynſbery fylde.* Open fields
outſide Moorgate. They were uſed for archery meet-
ings, and, at a period later than the probable date of
this ballad, they were the favourite reſort of the
citizens for walking. It would appear, from the
ſatirical remarks of the writer, that Finſbury Fields
were, at this early period, infeſted with thieves. There
is a long and intereſting account of the hiſtory of this
ſpot in Stow's Survey of London, ed. 1633, p. 475.

Page 211, line 3. *A nylde.* A needle. "Like pricking neelds, or points of fwords," Lucan's Pharfalia by Sir A. Gorges, 1614.

Page 211, line 20. *I pas not moche.* I care not much. "To paffe (care), *moror;* I pafs not for it, *quid mea;* I paffe not for his help, *ejus operam nihil moror,*" Coles.

Page 214, line 9. *Cornelis Woltrop.* No printer of this name is mentioned by Ames or Herbert.

Page 214, line 11. *As pleafant a dittie.* This popular ballad is printed in Robert Jones's Firft Booke of Songs and Ayres, 1601, with the mufic. In Marfton's Dutch Courtezan, 1605, Francifchina, who is the Dutch courtezan, fings in broken Englifh,—

> Mine mettre fing non oder fong,
> But ftill complaine me doe her wrong,
> For me did but kiffe her,
> For me did but kis her,
> And fo let her go!

That its popularity extended to Holland is proved by the Dutch words to the tune printed in Starter's Boertigheden, 4to. Amft. 1634. It is alfo quoted more than once by Shirley.

Page 214, line 14. *I do.* "I did," ed. Jones, 1601; and in the next line, *was* for *is.*

Page 215, line 2. *As teehe.* This jocular term was ufed to fignify the noife made in laughing. "Ye tee-heeing pixy," Exmoor Scolding.

Page 215, line 10. *Was this any harme.* "This was no harme," ed. Jones, 1601. In the next line, that printed copy reads,—"But fhee, alas, is angrie ftill;" and, after this ftanza, there is only the following one, correfponding to the laft verfe in our copy,—

> Yet fure her lookes bewraies content,
> And cunningly her brales are meant;
> As louers vfe to play and fport,
> When time and leifure is too-too fhort.

Page 219, line 17. *In a breef.* We now fay, in brief. The form of the phrafe, as it occurs in the text, is very unufual.

Page 220, line 5. *At randon.* A common old form, and the more correct, (Fr.)

> Oh yes, it may, thou haft no eyes to fee,
> But hatefully *at randon* doeft thou hit.
> *Venus and Adonis,* ed. 1593, fig. F. 4, v°.

Page 221, line 1. *Good Fellowes.* This and the next ballad are on one broadfide page. There appears to have been an earlier edition, for Griffith had a licenfe, in 1567-8, "for the pryntinge of a ballett intituled, Good felowes mufte go learne to daunce, &c."

Page 221, line 5. *A brall.* "*Branfle,* a brawle, or daunce, wherein many men and women, holding by the hands, fometimes in a ring, and otherwhiles at length, moue all together," Cotgrave's Dictionarie, ed. 1611.

Page 221, line 6. *The tryxt.* That is, the neateft. "Tricke, gallaunt and trymme, *cultus, eligans;* tricke, gallaunt or trimme wench," Huloet's Dictionarie, ed. 1572.

Page 221, line 16. *Slyper fafte.* Faftened in a flippery manner. "Slypper, *gliffant,*" Palfgrave, 1530.

Page 221, line 23. *In bauderycke wyfe.* That is, in the manner of a belt. It appears to have been a technical term applied to bells. "Payd to goodman Godden, for makinge the buckelle to the baldrike, and truffinge up the belle, ij.*s.* viij.*d*," MS. Accounts, Stratford-on-Avon, 1592.

Page 221, line 25. *A fhurte after the Moryce guyfe.* Alluding, perhaps, to the ftreamers worn by Morris-dancers on their fleeves, which fluttered in the wind, fpecimens of which are feen in the celebrated Tollett window.

Page 221, line 27. *A wyffler.* Wiflers were perfons who went before a leading perfonage in a proceffion to clear the way. They were furnifhed with wands, and formerly were an effential part of every proceffion of any magnitude. "Paffing the gate, wifflers, fuch officers as were appointed by the mayor to make me way through the throng of the people which preft fo mightily upon me, with great labour I got thorow that narrow preaze into the open market-place," Kemp's Nine Daies Wonder, 1600.

Page 222, line 5. *It fkylles not.* It matters not. "It fkills not greatly who impugns our doom," Second Part of Henry the Sixth, act iii. fc. 1.

Page 222, line 10. *Or at Cotfolde.* The allufion to dancing on the Cotfwold hills may here probably refer to the fhepherds' feftivals in that locality alluded to by Drayton. The Cotfwold games were not inftituted until a later period.

Page 223, line 2. *Wyttie Watte.* Wat was an old name for a hare, and hence ufed for a wily perfon. The more ufual expreffion was Wily Wat. *Cuttinge,* fwaggering. "Wherefore have I fuch a companie of cutting knaves to waite upon me?" Hiftorie of Friar Bacon.

Page 223, line 6. *Hyleye.* That is, highly.

Page 223, line 15. *The byllbowes are not made it.* That is, not made yet. The bilboes were a fpecies of ftocks ufed for the punifhment of failors. "The pore feloe was put into the *bilboes,* he being the firft upon whom any punyfhment was fhewd," MS. Journal of a Sea Voyage, temp. Eliz.

Page 224, line 1. *The braineles bleffing of the Bull.* Lacy had a licenfe in 1570 "for pryntinge of a ballett intituled the brayneles bleffynge of the bull."

"The 25. of May in the morning was found hanging at the Bifhop of Londons palace gate, in Paules Church-yard, a Bull which lately had beene fent from Rome containing diuerfe horrible treafons againft the Queenes maiefty, for the which one Iohn Felton was fhortly after apprehended, and committed to the Tower of London."—*Stow's Annales,* ed. 1615, p. 666.

This ballad is equalled in fiercenefs, and is well illuftrated, by an exceedingly curious contemporary tract entitled, "A Difclofing of the great Bull, and certain calues that he hath gotten, and fpecially the

Monfter Bull that roared at my Lord Byfhops gate,"
n.d.

Page 224, line 14. *Bleathes.* Bellows? This
word may poffibly be connected with the provincial
term *blether*, to make a great noife. " The felfe fame
monfter Bull is he that lately roared out at the Bifhops
Palace gate, in the greateft citie of England, horrible
blafphemies agaynft God, and villanous difhonors
agaynft the nobleft queene in the world, Elizabeth,
the lawfull Queene of England ; he ftamped and
fcraped on the ground, flong duft of fpitefull fpeches
and vaine curfes about him, pufhed with his hornes
at her noble counfellors and true fubieftes, and for pure
anger all to berayed the place where he ftoode," A
Difclofing of the great Bull, n. d.

Page 225, line 10. *Clots.* " Clodde or to clotte
lande, *occo*," Huloet's Dictionarie, ed. 1572. " No
clot in clay," Legen. Cathol., p. 2.

Page 225, line 14. *Gage my head.* A common
jocular form of a wager. So Biron exclaims,—

> I'll lay my head to any good man's hat,
> Thefe oaths and laws will prove an idle fcorn. .

Page 225, line 16. *Syfe.* " Syfe, waxe candell,
bougee," Palfgrave, 1530. In the folemn form of
excommunication, the bell was tolled, the book of
offices for the purpofe ufed, and three candles
extinguifhed, with certain ceremonies. See further in
Nares, in v. *Bell, Book, and Candle.*

Page 225, line 30. *Hardyngs cow.* " Since he
(the bull) came ouer fo lately difguifed, he hath light
upon certaine ranke kyen, who I thinke by their long
forbearing are become the luftier, that is, treafon,
fuperftition, rebellion and fuch other, and with them
he hath fo beftirred him that, by the helpe of maifter
Doctor Harding, Sanders, and other, fome there, fome
here, iolly cowkeepers and herdemen of Popifh clergie,
which fent and brought him ouer, and brake open for
him the feuerall hedges and fenfes of true religion,
obedience, allegeance, fayth, and honeftie, he hath be-

gotten a marueilous number of calues in fewe yeares,"
A Difclofing of the great Bull, n. d.
   Page 226, line 2.   *Butcher Row.*   There was
a place fo called near the Strand, " from the butchers'
fhambles on the fouth fide," Strype, iv. 118, ap.
Cunningham.
   Page 226, line 5.   *Walthams calues.*   In allufion
to the old proverb about Waltham's calf, which ran
nine miles to fuck a bull.   " Some running and
gadding calues, wifer than Walthams calfe that ranne
nine miles to fucke a bull, for thefe runne aboue nine
hundred miles," A Difclofing of the great Bull, n. d.
   Page 226, line 26.   *A twitch.*   A touch.   So we
have *twiche-box*, a touch-box, in the play of Damon and
Pithias.
   Page 227, line 10.   *What lyfe is beft.*   This is in
manufcript and figned by the initials I. G. in a
monogram.   It is fimilar in charaçter and evidently by
the fame writer as the poem already printed at p. 192,
but it is on a feparate paper, and apparently another
effay.
   Page 228, line 1.   *The crie of the poore.*   Henry,
the third Earl of Huntingdon, married Catherine,
daughter to John Dudley, Duke of Northumberland,
and dying at York in December, 1595, in the fixty-
firft year of his age, was buried at Afhby-de-la-Zouch
with great folemnity.   The expenfes of his funeral
amounted to nearly £1400.   The corpfe was embalmed
at an expenfe of £28 ; liveries to fixty poor men, £60;
in alms to the poor of divers parifhes, £26 13s. 4d.   The
wood-engraving which illuftrates the original-ballad was
probably intended for fome other fimilar fcene, and may
have been previoufly ufed for another purpofe.   Certain
it is, at leaft, that the Earl died inteftate, adminiftration
to his effeçts having been granted in June, 1596, to
his brother George, who fucceeded to the title.   See
the Adminiftrations in the Court of Probate, London,
3 June, 1596.   The Earl, whofe death is here la-
mented by one to whom he had probably been a kind
patron, was diftinguifhed by his piety and goodnefs.

There are letters of his to the Bifhop of Chefter, ftill
extant, in which he fpeaks of his ftrenuous endeavours
to obtain good preachers for the people.

Page 229, line 2. *Soufe.* " I fouce meate, I laye
it in fome tarte thynge, as they do brawne or fuche
lyke," Palfgrave, 1530.

Page 229, line 13. *Of Yorke he was Prefident made
by her grace.* " Henry Earle of Huntingdon was made
Prefident of the Councell in the North. This Prefi-
dentfhip, which is now full of honour, hath from a
poore beginning grown up in fhort time to this great-
neffe," Camden's Annales of 1574, ed. 1635, p. 179.

Page 232, line 1. *The Weftmerlande bull.* So, in
the ballad of the Rifing in the North,—

> Lord Weftmorland his ancyent raifde,
> The Dun Bull he rays'd on hye.

" The fupporters of the Nevilles, Earls of Weftmoreland, were Two Bulls Argent, ducally collar'd Gold,
armed Or, &c. In another ballad his banner is thus
defcribed,—

> Sett me up my faire dun bull,
> With gilden hornes, hee beares all foe hye."
> *Note by Bifhop Percy.*

Page 232, line 13. *Sir John Swingbreeche.* The
Proteftants of this time were fond of giving jocular
names to priefts. So, in a contemporary manufcript,
we have the names of Sir John Lack-Latin, Sir John
Mumble-Matins, and Sir John Smell-fmoke.

Page 232, line 17. *Though yet they lye lurkyng.*
" What a fond and folifhe ende thefe rebells have
made of their traiterous rebellion. They alwais fled
afore us after we cam firft within xij. myles of them,
and we folowed after them as faft as we might, without reft; neverthelefs you fee how they bee efcaped,
which they might eafily do in this waft and defolat
country," Sadler to Cecil, State Papers.

Page 232, line 21. *But her Maieftie of mercie is endued with ftore.* So, in a rare poem, An Aunfwere to
the Proclamation of the Rebels in the North, 1569,—

If lenity may make men rife,
  Or meekneffe gender yre,
If cold may caufe the coles to burne,
  Or water kindell fire;
If adamant may thruft away
  The iron or the fteel,
Or fhining fun the naked man
  May caufe the colde to feele;
Then may our Queene Elizabeth
  Be thought to be the caufe,
Why thefe rebels do go about
  The breaking of hir lawes.

Page 234, line 7. *Olde.* A common augmentative. "On Sunday at maffe, there was olde ringing of bels," Tarlton's Newes out of Purgatorie, 1590. "We fhall have old fwearing," Merchant of Venice, act iv. fc. 2.

Page 234, line 21. *Next.* Nigheft; neareft. "Home, home, the next way," Winter's Tale, act iii. fc. 3.

Page 235, line 10. *Vpfidowne.* Upfide-down.

Thus es this worlde torned upfodowne,
Tyll many mans dampnacyowne.—*Hampole.*

"Tornyng upfodowne, *fubuercion,*" Palfgrave, 1530.

Page 236, line 1. *A dittie.* This ballad in honour of Thomas Howard, the fourth Duke of Norfolk, was probably written about the year 1561, when the Duke was ftill young, but yet had diftinguifhed himfelf as a fuccefsful commander, two facts which are mentioned by the writer.

Page 237, line 6. *Thy pettigree.* "Petygrewe, *genealogie,*" Palfgrave, 1530. "Petigrewe, petigree, or geneologie, *ftemma,*" Huloet's Dictionarie, 1572.

Page 238, line 1. *Gifippus and his Tite.* An allufion to the well-known ftory of Titus and Gifippus, related in the Decameron, x. 8. In 1562 appeared a poem by Edward Lewicke entitled, "The moft wonderfull and pleafaunt Hiftory of Titus and Gifippus, whereby is fully declared the figure of perfect frendfhyp."

Page 238, line 8. *Turnoys.* "*Torno*, a turne, a twirle," Florio's Worlde of Wordes, 1598.

Page 239, line 5. *As Noye.* "A Noye" in the original, *Noye* being of courſe an old form of *Noah*.

Page 239, line 10. *A newe Ballade.* The alluſion to the uncertain fate of the rebels fixes the date of the compoſition of this ballad to the earlier part of the year 1570.

Page 241, line 11. *leare.* That is, ire.

Page 242, line 14. *Aleuen.* Eleven. "Aleuen widdowes and nine maides," Merchant of Venice, ed. 1623.

Page 242, line 20. *Plagued.* "Plagud" in the original.

Page 242, line 24. *And.* "Ond" in the original.

Page 243, line 8. *The true Diſcripcion.* There was a ballad at a later period on a ſimilar odd birth, which was licenſed in 1586-7, as "a newe ballad inti- tuled Stowp gallant, concerning a child borne with great ruffes." In the original copy of the broadſide here printed, each ſide of the leaf is filled with exactly the ſame matter. There are two hideous woodcuts repreſenting the front and back of the child.

Page 245, line 7. *Spurk.* That is, ſpirt.

Page 251, line 1. *Mother Watkins ale.* This ballad is mentioned in a letter with the ſignature of T. N. to his good friend A. M. [Anthony Munday], prefixed to the latter's tranſlation of "Gerileon of England," 1592,—"I ſhould hardly be perſwaded, that anie pro- feſſor of ſo excellent a ſcience (as printing) would be ſo impudent to print ſuch ribauldrie as *Watkin's Ale*, the Carman's Whiſtle, and ſundrie ſuch other." The tune is preſerved in Queen Elizabeth's Virginal Book in the Fitzwilliam Muſeum, Cambridge. See the muſic in Chappell's Popular Muſic of the Olden Time, p. 137. It has been ſtated in print that the muſic, without the words, has been diſcovered among the papers of Dr. Pepuſch. This ſtatement, however, is a ſilly and miſchievous fabrication.

Page 251, line 4. *Needs.* "Nœds" in the ori- ginal. *Sithd*, in the next line, ſighed.

Page 251, line 7. *Behard.* Beheard, i. e., heard.
Page 251, line 20. *Muſkadine.* A kind of ſweet wine, frequently alluded to by our early writers. Cotgrave, in v. *Muſcadet,* ſpeaks of "a cyder which, made of a verie ſmall and ſweet apple, reſembles muſcadine in colour, taſt, and ſmell."

Page 254, line 1. *Bowne.* That is, ſwell. The term is ſtill in uſe in the provinces. Palſgrave has *bowlne,* 1530.

Page 254, line 29. *Cat will after kind.* A common old proverbial ſaying, immortalized by Touchſtone,—

> If the cat will after kind,
> So, be ſure, will Roſalind.

"Cat after kinde, ſaith the proverbe, ſwete milke wil lap," Enterlude of Jacob and Eſau, 1568.

"What is hatcht by a hen will ſcrape like a hen, and cat after kinde will either hunt or ſcratch, and you are an ill bird ſo fowly to defile your neſt."— *Florio's Second Frutes,* 1591.

"An evill bird layeth an ill egge, the cat will after her kinde, and ill tree cannot bring foorth good fruit, the young cub groweth craftie like the damme."—*Arraignment of Lewd, Idle, Froward, and Unconſtant Women,* 1617, p. 44.

Page 255, line 7. *The Crowe ſits vpon the wall.* Entered on the Regiſters of the Stationers' Company in 1591-2, "xviij. die Januarii, 1591, Henry Kirkham entred for his copie under Mr. Watkin's hande a ballad intituled the Crowe ſhee ſittes vpon the wall; pleaſe one and pleaſe all." This ballad is of great intereſt, being the only copy known of the one referred to by Malvolio,—"But what of that, if it pleaſe the eye of one, it is with me as the very true ſonnet is,—Pleaſe one, and pleaſe all."

Page 255, line 19. *Their.* This word is here, and alſo in line 12 of the next page, miſprinted *her* in the original copy of the ballad. *Kircher,* kerchief.

Page 256, line 19. *Bulke.* A ſort of board or ledge outſide a houſe upon which articles were expoſed for fale. "*Balcone*, a bulke, a ftall of a fhop," Florio's Worlde of Wordes, 1598.

Page 258, line 3. *Be fhe flaunt*. That is, be fhe fine or fafhionable. Shakefpeare ufes the fubftantive *flaunts*, fineries, in the Winter's Tale, act iv. fc. 3. "The one a flaunting fellow, ufeth to wear a fcarlet cloak over a crimfon fattin fuit," Gee's Foot out of the Snare, 1624.

Page 260, line 2. *Lord Henry Wrifley*. The fecond Earl, born 30 November, 1546. See Efc. 4 Edw. VI., ii. 78. He was a devoted adherent of Mary Queen of Scots, an attachment which occafioned his being imprifoned in the Tower in 1572. Camden affigns the date of his death to the year 1583. See his Annales, ed. 1635, p. 255. This, however, is undoubtedly an error, for he died at the early age of thirty-five, on October 4th, 1581, as appears from the inquifition taken after his deceafe (Efc. 24 Eliz., i. 46). The date of the month, as given in the title of the ballad, is therefore erroneous. By his will, he directs his body to be interred in the Chapel of Tichfield Church, bequeathing fufficient money to his executors to renovate the faid chapel, which was to be divided by iron grating from the reft of the church. He alfo bequeaths the fum of £200 to the poor. Warton's account of Tichfield is interefting and curious,—" I vifited Tichfield-houfe, Aug. 19, 1786, and made the following obfervations on what is now remaining there. The abbey of Tichfield being granted to the firft Earl, Thomas, in 1538, he converted it into a family manfion, yet with many additions and alterations: we enter, to the fouth, through a fuperb tower, or Gothic portico, of ftone, having four large angular turrets. Of the monaftic chapel only two or three low arches remain, with the moor-ftone pilafters. The greater part of what may properly be called the houfe, forming a quadrangle, was pulled down about forty years ago. But the refectory, or hall of the abbey, ftill remains complete, with its original raftered roof of good workmanfhip: it is embattelled; and has three Gothic

windows on each fide, with an oreille or oriel window.
It is entered by a portico which feems to have been
added by the new proprietor at the diffolution; by
whom alfo the royal arms *painted*, with the portcullis
and H. R. (Henricus Rex), were undoubtedly placed
over the high-table. At the other end is a mufic-
gallery. Underneath is the cellar of the monaftery,
a well-wrought crypt of chalk-built arches; the ribs
and interfections in a good ftyle. In a long cove-ceiled
room, with fmall parallel femicircular arches, are the
arms of King Charles the Firft on tapeftry; he was
protected here in his flight from Hampton-court.
Two or three Gothic-fhaped windows, perhaps of the
abbey, in a part of the houfe now inhabited by a fteward
and other fervants. In thefe and other windows fome
beautiful fhields of painted glafs are preferved; parti-
cularly one of Henry the Eighth impaling Lady Jane
Seymour, who were married at Maxwell, twenty miles
off, and who feem from thence to have paid a vifit at
this place to Lord Southampton. Here are fome fine
old wreathed chimneys in brick. In an angle of the
dilapidated buildings, to the weft of the grand entrance
or tower, is an elegant fhaft of a pilafter of polifhed
ftone, with the fpringing of an arch which muft have
taken a bold and lofty fweep: thefe are fymptoms of
fome confiderable room or office of the monaftery."

Page 263, line 4. *Ne.* That is, not.

Page 266, line 6. *Moue.* "More" in the original.

Page 267, line 19. *The Bibles they did rent and teare.*
"Rent," that is, rend. "While with his fingers he
his haire doth rent," Legend of Orpheus and Eury-
dice, 1597.

"Chriftians I can not terme you that haue defaced
the Communion of Chriftians, and in deftroying the
booke of Chryftes moft holy Teftament, renounced
your parts by his Teftament bequethed unto you."—
*Norton, To the Queene's Maiefties poore deceiued Subiects
of the Northe Contrey,* 1569.

"The earles have beene at Durefme, with ther force
in armor, to perfwade the people to take ther partes,

and fome of ther company have throwen downe the comunion table, and torne the Holy Bible in pieces, fo as it appereth directly they intende to make religion ther grownd."—*Letter from the Council of the North to the Queen,* November 15th, 1569.

FINIS.